The E

The Ethics of Global Poverty offers a thorough introduction to the ethical issues surrounding global poverty. It addresses important questions such as:

- What is poverty and how is it measured?
- What are the causes of poverty?
- Do wealthy individuals have a moral duty to reduce global poverty?
- Should aid go to those who are most in need, or to those who are easiest to help?
- Is it morally wrong to buy from sweatshops?
- Is it morally good to provide micro-finance?

Featuring case studies throughout, this textbook is essential reading for students studying global ethics or global poverty who want an understanding of the moral issues that arise from vast inequalities of wealth and power in a highly interconnected world.

Scott Wisor is Assistant Professor of Arts and Humanities at the Minerva Schools at KGI, USA.

The Ethics of...

When is it right to go to war? What are the causes of poverty? Are human intelligence and machine intelligence the same? What is cyber-terrorism? Do races exist? What makes a person a refugee?

Each engaging textbook from *The Ethics of...* series focuses on a significant ethical issue and provides a clear and stimulating explanation of the surrounding philosophical discussions. Focusing on moral debates at the forefront of contemporary society they have been designed for use by students studying philosophy, applied ethics, global ethics, and related subjects such as politics, international relations, and sociology. Features to aid study include chapter summaries, study questions, annotated further reading, and glossaries.

Published titles:
The Ethics of War and Peace: An Introduction
Second Edition
Helen Frowe
978-0-415-72481-4

Forthcoming titles:
The Ethics of Cyber Conflicts: An Introduction
Mariarosaria Taddeo
978-1-138-82726-4

The Ethics of Surveillance: An Introduction
Kevin Macnish
978-1-138-64379-6

The Ethics of Immigration: An Introduction
Adam Hosein
978-1-138-65952-0

The Ethics of Development: An Introduction
David Ingram and Thomas J. Derdak
978-1-138-20344-0

The Ethics of Sex: An Introduction
Neil McArthur
978-1-138-21320-3

The Ethics of Global Poverty

An Introduction

Scott Wisor

Routledge
Taylor & Francis Group

LONDON AND NEW YORK

First published 2017
by Routledge
2 Park Square, Milton Park, Abingdon, Oxon OX14 4RN

and by Routledge
711 Third Avenue, New York, NY 10017

Routledge is an imprint of the Taylor & Francis Group, an informa business

British Library Cataloguing in Publication Data
A catalogue record for this book is available from the British Library

Library of Congress Cataloging in Publication Data
Names: Wisor, Scott, 1981–author.
Title: The ethics of global poverty: an introduction/Scott Wisor.
Description: Second edition. | Abingdon, Oxon; New York, NY: Routledge
is an imprint of the Taylor & Francis Group, an Informa Business, [2017] |
Includes bibliographical references and index.
Identifiers: LCCN 2016027258 | ISBN 9781138827059 (hbk) |
ISBN 9781138827066 (pbk) | ISBN 9781315738765 (ebk)
Subjects: LCSH: Poverty–Moral and ethical aspects. | Social justice.
Classification: LCC HC79.P6 W567 2017 | DDC 174/.4–dc23
LC record available at https://lccn.loc.gov/2016027258

ISBN: 978-1-138-82705-9 (hbk)
ISBN: 978-1-138-82706-6 (pbk)
ISBN: 978-1-315-73876-5 (ebk)

Typeset in Times New Roman
by Deanta Global Publishing Services, Chennai, India

Printed and bound by CPI Group (UK) Ltd, Croydon, CR0 4YY

For Kathryn

Contents

Acknowledgements

Many thanks to Eamon Aloyo, Alejandra Mancilla, Rosa Terlazzo, Holly Lawford-Smith, and several anonymous reviewers for excellent written comments on early versions of the manuscript and book proposal. More generally, I am grateful for many conversations over the years with scholars and practitioners working in ethics and international affairs that have shaped my thinking on many of the topics in this book. While my interlocutors are too numerous to thank here, their work is visible throughout the text. I am grateful to colleagues in the Centre for the Study of Global Ethics and the Department of Philosophy at the University of Birmingham, which provided a fertile environment for thinking through the ideas in the following pages. At Routledge, I am grateful to Rebecca Shillabeer, Lucy Vallance, and Sarah Gore for their support of this project. Though I have received tremendous assistance, all mistakes remain my own.

Acknowledgements

think the point of warfare is not to be ethical but to win, given that defeat can be so devastating for the vanquished. Therefore, ethics has no place in warfare. But of course this is not true—it is precisely because so much that is morally valuable is at stake in deciding to go to war and deciding how it should be fought that we must carefully study just war theory. So too for the ethics of global poverty. It is because so much moral harm is committed against poor people, including by people who claim to be acting in the name of poverty alleviation, that we must make the ethics of global poverty central to efforts to eradicate global poverty.

Before examining ethical questions in depth, we will spend the first part of the book getting clear on what global poverty is, what it is caused by, and how we can learn about it. Chapter 2 investigates the nature of global poverty. How should we think about what poverty is, and how should it be measured? Do people born into poverty stay in poverty, or do the people who live in poverty change over time? What is life like for people who live below the poverty line?

Chapter 3 investigates the causes of global poverty. There are a number of theories that both academics and public commentators claim explain the persistence of global poverty. Some are not very good: that people are poor because of their behavior, or because of their culture, or because of the bad decisions they make. Others have some truth to them, but don't explain the bulk of the story: for example, that poverty is a result of bad geography, which gives people diseases and offers them few productive opportunities. The best explanation is that some people are poor because they live under extractive and exploitative institutional arrangements, which prevent them from making further progress in their lives.

Chapter 4 explores the epistemology of global poverty. How do people study poverty and poverty alleviation? Is there a science to understanding poverty eradication? Can learning more about poverty translate into more effective anti-poverty programs?

With this introductory understanding of global poverty in hand, Part II turns squarely to questions of our ethical duties. Given that poverty exists, what are people morally required to do about it? This part focuses exclusively on the duties of well-off individuals. While there are interesting questions about what poor people owe to themselves and other similarly situated individuals, and what they may do in the name of combatting their deprivation, this will not be our focus here.[3]

Chapter 5 focuses on one approach to understanding the duties of wealthy individuals to people who are deprived—what we will call the duty of humanity. On this view, the mere fact that one group lives comfortable lives with excess income to spare while another group suffers a great deal due to material shortfalls is thought to ground duties of assistance. Possessing the capacity to help and the knowledge of suffering, the wealthy are required to assist the poor.

Chapter 6 considers an alternative account of the duties of wealthy individuals to poor people abroad—the duty of justice. It is not merely by virtue of a common humanity that anti-poverty assistance is owed. Rather, it is because individuals in wealthy countries have been (historically and in the present day) complicit in harming individuals in poor countries and they are therefore bound by duties of justice to prevent and rectify these harms.

Chapter 7 considers associative duties—duties that arise out of the relationships we have. In the case of global poverty, such duties might derive from a shared history or culture, an enduring relationship of mutual aid and support, a common colonial history, or enduring diplomatic and commercial relations.

Finally, in Chapter 8, we consider arguments against moral duties to alleviate poverty. Why might someone deny that morality requires wealthy individuals to work to reduce global poverty? Though I do not have much sympathy for this approach, we will give a fair hearing to both philosophical and practical arguments in favor of this view.

Part III explores one way duties to eradicate global poverty might be discharged—through the provision of foreign aid. Chapter 9 considers arguments in favor of and against foreign aid, as provided through both private and public channels. It also considers how recent innovations in the provision of foreign aid aim to accelerate global poverty reduction.

Chapter 10 considers the difficult question of aid allocation. Given that the number of people in need far exceeds the resources that have been made available to combat poverty, how should limited funds be allocated? Should aid go to those who are most in need, or to those who are easiest to help? Is it wrong to spend money on HIV treatments, which are comparatively expensive, when malaria and other diseases are much easier to treat?

Part IV moves beyond the aid debate to look at a series of proposed global institutional reforms that might accelerate progress in poverty reduction. Chapter 11 considers immigration policy, and the impressive ability of international migration to reduce global poverty. It also explores reasons offered against a more permissive international migration regime.

Chapter 12 considers arguments for and against humanitarian intervention, and the role external militaries might play in reducing the conflicts that cause many states to remain mired in poverty.

Chapter 13 examines the role that international trade plays in promoting poverty reduction, and considers how certain provisions of international trade agreements impede the ability of countries to make development progress.

Part V concludes the book, focusing on some of the specific practical moral problems that arise in anti-poverty programs. Chapter 14 examines the problem of speaking for others, especially with regard to activist groups who are involved in anti-poverty campaigning. It explores western activist campaigns, the visual depiction of poor people, and other issues arising from efforts to give a platform to those whose voice is not typically heard.

Chapter 15 examines consumerism, and morally evaluates ethically conscious consumer efforts, such as the RED campaign and Fairtrade, to reduce global poverty. It also discusses the question of whether consumers are required to consider the impact of their other consumptive activities on global poverty.

Chapter 16 examines the micro-finance industry. It considers whether some commercial transactions that offer small loans to poor people are unethical, and whether it is morally permissible to profit from poverty. It examines what moral constraints, if any, should be placed on the provision of micro-finance.

For students who are using this as a textbook in a formal educational setting, the book is structured so that it can be used over the course of a single term, but it is equally accessible for readers pursuing the topic outside the classroom. Covering one to two chapters per week, the book can be completed in 2 or 3 months' time. Of course, readers are welcome to read more quickly than that! Most of the book's chapters can be read independently of the book's other material and do not necessarily need to be read in order.

While this textbook aims to be comprehensive in its coverage, it is not exhaustive. The ambitious reader will gain a great deal by supplementing the book with a consistent engagement with the latest news, debates, and scholarship on global poverty. While there is a lot of nonsense written about global poverty, there is more good information and analysis available today than at any point in history. Online platforms, including blogs, social media, the websites of traditional media outlets, and podcasts all give the reader access to high-level analysis and discussion of global development and global poverty. Engaging with these sources of information while working through the book will allow the reader to learn more about the struggles against global poverty, and the ethical issues that arise from these efforts. A list of suggestions for further reading can also be found at the end of each chapter.

One final note. This book is introductory, and aims to give a fair treatment to the various ethical issues surrounding global poverty. But it is not strictly neutral. It will be clear where I think certain arguments succeed or fail, and why I think certain positions on global poverty are better or worse than others. All the more reason to consult additional sources in order to develop your own arguments and positions.

Notes

1   In the next chapter we will learn more about the concepts and measures used in generating some of these statistics.
2   These statistics are drawn from the World Bank's World Development Indicators, available at http://data.worldbank.org/data-catalog/world-development-indicators (accessed December 3, 2015).
3   On this question, see the forthcoming book from Alejandra Mancilla, *The Right of Necessity: Moral Cosmopolitanism and Global Poverty*. London: Rowman and Littlefield International, 2016.

References

Chetty R., Stepner M., Abraham S., Shelby L., Scuderi, B., Turner, N., Bergeron, A., and Cutler, D. 'The association between income and life expectancy in the United States, 2001–2014', *JAMA* (April 10, 2016).

Krishna, A. *One Illness Away: Why people become poor and how they escape poverty*, Oxford: Oxford University Press, 2008.

Part I

Understanding Poverty

The first part of this book gives the reader an introduction to global poverty. At the end of this part, the reader should understand various conceptions and measures of global poverty, what living standards are like for the world's poorest people, how we can come to gain knowledge about the causes of material and social deprivation, and what the best explanations are for the persistence of global poverty.

This book follows a recent trend in moral and political philosophy that is sometimes known as non-ideal theory. The precise nature of non-ideal theory is contested, and we won't sort out the many issues involved here. But a brief comment on the methodological approach is in order before we dive into empirical details of global poverty.

Ideal theory develops moral and political principles by making idealizing assumptions about the subjects of inquiry, the way in which they interact, and the way in which they will decide upon principles to govern social cooperation and contestation. John Rawls, the most important political philosopher of the 20th century, developed principles of justice by constructing a hypothetical thought experiment known as the original position (Rawls 1999). Individuals in the original position are stripped of any knowledge of who they are or what talents they will have in the world. They are asked to develop principles of justice to govern the basic structure of society, with knowledge of some basic information about how the world works but no details about their own place in that world. This powerful thought experiment is intended to prevent reasoning about justice in a way that favors narrow self-interest. Rather, the original position is intended to help develop impartial principles of justice that are justifiable on contractualist grounds to all members of society. In both his method and substantive recommendations, Rawls is thought to be doing ideal theory.

At least for the purposes of examining moral questions arising from global poverty, I believe this approach is mistaken. Ideal theorists may overlook various features of the moral problems that they are analyzing if they are inattentive to how the real world works. In contrast to ideal theorists, non-ideal theorists do not start from idealized assumptions about moral agents or the interactions they will have. Rather, they tend to start their theorizing by reflecting on the pressing moral problems that actual people encounter in the real world, and develop principles that can deliver moral and political progress given the contexts they currently inhabit and might hope to inhabit in the future. For our purposes, an important component of non-ideal theorizing is to engage with actual social practices and the injustices that individuals suffer, to reflect upon the lived experiences of people who have been oppressed, and to give consideration to their voices. Rather than base our theorizing on hypothetical thought experiments or idealized assumptions about how the world is, it is better to engage in philosophical argumentation that relies on information about actual economic, social, and political life. To successfully reason in this way, one must engage with other disciplines (in our case this will often be the social sciences) and with the views and perspectives of individuals who live in poverty or work to combat it. Importantly, non-ideal theorists also take seriously feasibility constraints that exist in the real world, and develop moral and political principles for these circumstances of injustice, rather than developing principles for some distant utopian society.

Elizabeth Anderson argues that there are three major reasons to engage in non-ideal philosophy. First, we need to develop moral and political principles that are workable given the actual motivational and cognitive makeup of people as they are. Second, we need to develop principles for the world we have rather than thinking we can simply close the gap between an ideal world and the one we live in. Difficult moral and political terrain lies between here and there, and morality may require different actions given current injustice and the moral constraints on what we may do to improve the world. Third, if we begin from idealized assumptions about how the world ought to be, we may overlook important features of injustice of the world we actually inhabit (Anderson 2010, p. 3). Iris Marion Young, one of the greatest political theorists of the 20th century, also endorsed non-ideal theorizing. On her view, it was not simply that non-ideal theorizing would develop better normative principles, but that it would create greater opportunities for transforming oppressive social relations (Young 2000, pp. 8–9).

Consider a different example. If one is interested in the moral question of whether prostitution should be made illegal, decriminalized, or fully legalized, at least part of the answer to this question will depend on how different social and legal arrangements affect sex workers and other relevant stakeholders. Does prostitution increase if sex work is legalized? Are sex workers more likely to be harmed and exploited if prostitution is criminalized? How will the rates of sexually transmitted infections differ between competing regulatory arrangements? The answers to these questions will influence, though not fully determine, what the normatively optimal institutional arrangement is for regulating (or not) prostitution. In other words, a proper diagnosis of the moral problem must engage with sex work as it is actually practiced, in order to develop optimal moral and political principles.

In the non-ideal tradition, we will spend the entire first part of the book exploring the nature of global poverty, its causes, and the methods for studying it. We will embrace the view that moral and political theorizing which is entirely disconnected from social realities can have at best limited impact upon the world, and at worst have highly pernicious effects by misdiagnosing social problems. In contrast to many philosophers who believe we can adequately analyze the nature of duties to alleviate global poverty purely through philosophical thought experiments, readers of this book will directly engage with the best available social science in order to answer important ethical questions related to global poverty.

This extensive empirical introduction leaves many important ethical questions to the later chapters. Critics of non-ideal theory might object that all of these details may be important for politicians or international aid agencies, but have no place in a book on the ethics of global poverty. A philosopher should be able to figure out the ethics of global poverty without knowing anything about the nature of the problem. She can simply theorize from her armchair to determine whether poverty is morally problematic, if so, what duties moral agents have to combat it, and what they are permitted to do in order to discharge their duties. Indeed, very many philosophical papers have been written on the ethics of global poverty without engaging in any analysis of the actual causes or consequences of poverty in the real world. While I do not endorse this approach, each chapter of the book can be easily comprehended without having to read the preceding chapters. Readers so inclined may choose to skip the more empirically oriented chapters of the book.

Suggested Reading

Valentini, L. 'Ideal vs. non-ideal theory: a conceptual map', *Philosophy Compass* 7 (2012): 654–664.

Wiens, D. 'Prescribing institutions without ideal theory', *Journal of Political Philosophy* 20 (2012): 45–70.

References

Anderson, E. *The Imperative of Integration*, Princeton: Princeton University Press, 2010.

Rawls, J. *A Theory of Justice: Revised edition,* Cambridge: Harvard University Press, 1999.

Young, I. M. *Inclusion and Democracy*, Oxford: Oxford University Press, 2002.

2 What Is Poverty?

Before exploring the ethics of global poverty, we need to get clear on the subject of our inquiry. To do so, we will examine the concept of poverty. An adequate conception of global poverty should be able to identify who is poor, identify what their poverty consists of, and identify what characteristics or features of their life would need to change to make it such that they are no longer poor. With this conceptual understanding in hand, adequate measures of global poverty should be able to provide information on the levels, trends, distributions, and dynamics of material and social deprivation. In this chapter we will explore five competing conceptions of global poverty, some of the ways in which it is measured, and how poverty is thought to be distributed across the globe.

Conceptions of Global Poverty

Why do we need to do conceptual analysis of poverty? Isn't it immediately obvious who is poor and who is not? Aren't people with big houses and nice cars free from poverty, and people struggling to put food on the table poor? Unfortunately, it is not that simple. There are heated debates about who is poor and who is entitled to anti-poverty assistance. The identification of individuals or households as living in poverty plays an important role in guiding public action. Once these individuals have been identified, data gathered regularly over time can tell us whether poverty is increasing or decreasing, where poverty is concentrated, and which social groups are disproportionately deprived. Analysts also use poverty data to evaluate policies, projects, and institutional designs that aim to reduce global poverty.

How poverty is conceived of and measured appears at first to be a mundane topic of little philosophical or practical interest. But upon further investigation poverty measurement raises profound philosophical and practical questions that are of deep importance for efforts to reduce global poverty. Philosophically, the analysis of the concept of poverty requires delving into core areas of the discipline—we have to do epistemology to defend a way of approaching how to think about poverty, we have to do metaphysics to examine ontological issues related to the identification of social groups, and we have to do moral and political philosophy to examine the values that should inform our conception of poverty.

Practically, the measurement of poverty is used to advocate for scarce resources, to allocate those resources, to evaluate the effectiveness of various programs, policies, and institutional designs, and to ground claims regarding the justice of competing distributive arrangements. Depending on which measure of poverty one picks, the world can look like it is making rapid progress in the fight against poverty, or it can appear to be failing to reduce deprivation.

There are at least five competing conceptions of poverty, each of which has a different definition, each of which picks out different individuals as poor.

Monetary conceptions of poverty define the poor as those who don't have enough resources to reach some minimal standard of living. Monetary poverty can be measured by either income or consumption-expenditure. Because most poor people do not have formal jobs that pay regular incomes, often finding work in the informal sector or in agriculture, it is difficult to measure the full basket of what they have 'earned' by measuring income alone. Consumption-expenditure attempts to estimate a price for the goods that people consume for which they have not made monetary payments. For example, if a farmer uses some of the food she grows to feed her own family, this counts as consumption-expenditure, but not income.

There are two common methods for determining the level of monetary consumption or income a person should have to be classified as no longer poor. The first sets a monetary poverty line at the cost of meeting basic food needs. This obviously sets an extremely low bar, as everyone needs goods other than food to survive, such as shelter, health care, clothing, transportation, water, and sanitation. The second method sets the monetary poverty line at the cost of food plus some of these other basic necessities. A third approach, much less common, sets the monetary poverty line at a level at which individuals in the real world who have that much money generally are able to avoid severe deprivations. Analysts can look at the income distribution in a given society, and determine the monetary level at which individuals are able to reliably avoid serious deprivations (Woodward 2010).

A second conception of poverty defines the poor as those individuals who are unable to meet their basic needs. Basic needs theorists, who came to prominence in the 1980s, reacted against many of the flaws in purely monetary conceptions of poverty. Whereas monetary conceptions merely examine the current flow of resources, the basic needs conception focuses squarely on whether one is in fact able to satisfy important needs given the resources available to them (Stewart 2006).

A third conception of poverty defines people who lack basic capabilities as poor. The capabilities approach to poverty (and human development) has been hugely influential, shaping the practice of international development and leading to a huge body of academic work. First proposed by Nobel prize winning economist and philosopher Amartya Sen (1999), and later developed by philosopher Martha Nussbaum (2000) (and subsequently many others), the capabilities approach, among other things, seeks to identify the 'space' or 'currency' of distributive justice. That is, capabilities theorists seek to offer an account of the metric by which individual shares in society are to be measured so as to be able to evaluate the justice or injustice of the overall distribution of these shares across the population.

Capabilities are broadly defined as the genuine opportunities to be and do the things that you value or have reason to value (Sen 1999). Poverty is defined more narrowly as a deprivation of *basic* capabilities. The capabilities approach focuses squarely on individual freedoms to achieve functionings. Functionings are things like being well nourished, being literate, being healthy, and so on. Capabilities are the genuine opportunity to be well nourished, to learn to read, to have good health, and so on. A person who is poor lacks the genuine opportunity to achieve adequate functioning in various dimensions including health, education, shelter, and nutrition.

These assessments of genuine opportunity are meant to be sensitive to both the context in which an individual lives—such as her physical environment, her local economy, the prevailing social norms in her community—as well as her personal heterogeneities—that is, her specific needs and capacities. For example, in determining whether a person has the capability to be well nourished, we might simply evaluate whether the person has access to the requisite number (say, 1,800) of calories per day. But taking account of social context and personal heteroge-neities, we would need to determine whether the person in question needs more calories because she works in a demanding job, such as working the fields or pull-ing a rickshaw, and whether her personal biological and physical characteristics, such as being tall, having a higher metabolic rate, or facing disease vectors that require greater nourishment, result in her needing many more calories to be able to achieve the functioning of being well nourished.

A fourth conception of poverty defines people as poor who are socially excluded from normal functioning in society. This conception of poverty was first developed by the French philosopher René Lenoir. Social exclusion is also prominent in an early conception of poverty proposed by Adam Smith (better known today as the father of contemporary economics, but also a very important philosopher). He wrote,

> A linen shirt is, strictly speaking, not a necessary of life. The Greeks and Romans lived, I suppose, very comfortably, though they had no linen. But in present times, a creditable day labourer would be ashamed to appear in public without a linen shirt, the want of which would be supposed to denote that disgraceful degree of poverty which, it is presumed, no one can fall into without extreme bad conduct.
>
> (Smith 1776, Book 5, Ch 2)

This introduces an important distinction. Some conceptions of poverty are absolute: they specify a standard of living below which a person is deemed to be poor without reference to the living standards of her peers. When measured against an absolute standard of poverty, an individual's poverty status is insensitive to the achieve-ments or deprivations of others in her society. Relative poverty, by contrast, deems a person to be poor by evaluating her position against other people in her society. Relative conceptions of poverty are prevalent in modern day Europe—for example, the United Kingdom sets the poverty line at 60 percent of the median British income. In 2013, 16.8 percent of the population was deemed poor on this relative poverty line. In contrast, the US government uses an absolute poverty line. This is intended to be three times the cost of food for a family, currently set at $23,800 per year for a family of four, or $11,670 for a single adult.[1] One motivation for including social exclusion in a conception of poverty, and taking account of the costs of being excluded from normal functioning, is that a person's relative status in society generates absolute and objective deprivations for the individual. If she does not have the resources available to function as a normal member of society, she may thereby experience absolute deprivation from her relative exclusion.

Finally, there is a recent conception of poverty that is based on individual human rights (Woodward 2010). Specifically, this conception of poverty defines a person as poor if she is not able to secure her basic economic and social rights. Economic and social rights have long been recognized in international law and in some domestic law. For example, the Universal Declaration of Human Rights recognizes that a person has a right to education, to health care, to an adequate standard of living, and so on. The rights-based conception of poverty may specify very similar dimensions of deprivation that constitute poverty. The important innovation with this conception is not new dimensions for determining whether people are poor, but to frame material and social deprivation as human rights issues. The language of rights strengthens the claim that rights holders have against duty bearers to ensure that their anti-poverty rights are secured.

Measures of Global Poverty

The measurement of poverty is an important and often overlooked activity in the study of global development. Competing measures of deprivation portray different levels, trends, and distributions of deprivation. These competing profiles of global deprivation can influence the distribution of scarce anti-poverty resources, and the design of anti-poverty policies.

The most commonly used measure of global poverty is the World Bank's International Poverty Line. The International Poverty Line is currently set at 1.25 USD, in 2005 prices.[2] Difficult calculations are involved in converting consumption in other currencies into US dollars as valued in 2005. Two adjustments are needed— the currency must be converted from the local currency to US dollars, and from the year of consumption to the base year of 2005. In addition to the International Poverty Line, the World Bank also maintains data for alternative poverty lines: 1.00 USD, 2.00 USD, and 2.50 USD, all in 2005 prices. Each of these different poverty lines depicts different levels, trends, and distributions of global poverty.

Critique

The World Bank's International Poverty Line has been widely criticized for failing to adequately reveal the true extent, trend, and depth of global poverty

(Reddy and Minoiu 2007, Woodward 2010). The purchasing power conversion of prices to a base currency and year is sensitive to the prices of all goods in an economy, but only a small subset of those goods are consumed by poor people. So if the price of basic foodstuffs goes up and the price of consumer electronics goes down, aggregate purchasing power conversions may not change, even though life will have gotten much harder for the worst off. Another problem is the method by which the line is set. The World Bank averages the poverty lines for a small subset of the world's poorest countries to set the International Poverty Line. Yet it is not clear that these very low income, and often undemocratic, countries should establish the global standard of living. Furthermore, by focusing exclusively on monetary poverty, the International Poverty Line is insensitive to two important considerations. First, two individuals with the same level of monetary consumption may have very different outcomes, based on their differential ability to convert income or consumption into achievements. Second, the IPL is insensitive to deprivations that are not easily captured by monetary measurement, such as whether a person is free from violence, whether she is able to be well educated, or whether she receives high-quality health care and is able to avoid disproportionate disease burden.

At the time of writing, the chief economist of the World Bank, Kaushik Basu, had convened a new Commission on Global Poverty to make recommendations on possible technical changes that might be made to the measurement of international monetary poverty, as well as to consider what other development measures might be included in the official World Bank statistics. This is welcome news for critics who have long argued that the World Bank's measurement of global poverty provides a misleading picture of global progress.

Multidimensional Poverty

A second approach to measuring poverty is multidimensional. Responding to the limitations of monetary measures of poverty mentioned above, multidimensional measures of poverty track individual or household achievements in a range of non-monetary dimensions. Rather than tracking income or expenditure, multidimensional measures of poverty measure a person's access to or achievement in health, education, shelter, sanitation, and other dimensions.

The shift away from monetary poverty measurement began with composite indices measuring human development, many created and maintained by the United Nations Development Program. These composite indices measure achievements across a whole population. The most famous of these indices is the Human Development Index, which tracks income (per capita Gross National Income), health (life expectancy at birth), and education (mean years of schooling and expected years of schooling) across a population. Other prominent development indices include the Gender Gap Index, the Social Institutions and Gender Index, the Basic Capabilities Index, and the Better Life Index.

While composite indices have usefully shifted the focus away from narrow monetary assessments of development progress, they are not useful for directing anti-poverty resources. In order to determine the poverty status of individual members of society, it is necessary to move beyond indicators that are measured across a whole population (such as life expectancy) and to examine deprivations and achievements at the household or individual level (such as individual access to health care).

To measure multidimensional poverty (rather than human development), the Oxford Poverty and Human Development Initiative developed the Multidimensional Poverty Index (MPI), which is now in use at the United Nations Development Program. The MPI measures household deprivations in education (years of schooling and school enrollment), health (nutrition and child mortality), and standard of living (cooking fuel, sanitation, water, electricity, floor type, and asset ownership). The MPI identifies households as multidimensionally poor if they are deprived in more than one-third of the indicators.

According to the MPI, 1.7 billion people worldwide are multidimensionally poor. Importantly, multidimensional and monetary assessments of deprivation often diverge dramatically. The MPI is an impressive achievement and has done a great deal to show how monetary and multidimensional assessments can diverge in their assessments of progress in poverty alleviation, and to help governments and NGOs target a wider range of dimensions in which deprivation can occur.

Poverty Dynamics

At this point we are beginning to have a sense of what poverty is and how it is measured. One important feature of poverty merits discussion at this point. In popular conceptions of poverty, people are permanently stuck at low levels of income and employment opportunity, and constantly struggle, and usually fail, to improve their lot. But this is misleading in at least one sense. While it is true that over the course of a person's life, there is a low probability that they will permanently move out of poverty into living standards associated with the middle or upper classes, it is not true that they are constantly stuck at one given level of achievement.

Andiruh Krishna (2008) uses a unique method of interviewing to understand the life course of individuals living in poverty. In his stages-of-progress method, he asks individuals to recount the major events in their lives, and assesses how well their lives were going at that time. He finds that the population living in poverty is not fixed. Instead, it is constantly churning: some people move out of poverty while others descend into poverty. Some people are born into middle class families, but often get knocked into poverty by shocks. A natural disaster sweeps away their home and livelihood. An illness strikes, and assets are depleted in purchasing (largely ineffective) health care. Conflict breaks out, forcing people to flee. Alternatively, a person might make progress, by diversifying their income sources, having a bountiful harvest, or gaining access to secure employment. Surprisingly, this is also true in high-income countries. While our common conceptions often imagine that people are born into lower, middle, or upper classes and more or less stay there, much upward and downward movement occurs over the course of people's lives. In the United States, which is the only OECD country without universal health coverage, three in five bankruptcies are caused by medical bills (LaMontagne 2014). People are knocked back into poverty by these unforeseen health events.

Feminization of Poverty

Commentators on global poverty often claim that poverty is feminized. The feminization of poverty thesis involves several different claims: that women are disproportionately represented among the poor compared to men, that the proportion of women in poverty is increasing, that women's poverty is worse or more severe than men's, that female-headed households are worse off than male-headed households, or that poverty is feminized in some important respects (Chant 2007, p. 1).

Determining which of these theses is true would be very important for the design of anti-poverty policies. Unfortunately, it simply cannot be known at the present time whether women are poorer than men and if that trend is increasing, because poverty is measured globally at the household level for both monetary and multidimensional poverty. This means it is not possible to know within the household whether men are poorer than women and, therefore, not possible to know this information for all women and men.

It is also important to note that much of the gender inequality that exists between men and women is not clearly captured in the narrower category of poverty. Men are disproportionately represented in political office, have greater mobility and control over decision making, are less likely to be subject to domestic violence, and dominate high-paying jobs. Whether or not these broader gender inequalities manifest themselves in disproportionate poverty for women depends on the specific social context. More research is needed, based on individual level measurements, to know more about whether and how poverty is unevenly distributed among men and women.

Getting Better?

Is the world getting better? Is it getting less poor? There is considerable dispute about the trends of poverty reduction. A reasonable estimate is that some monetary poverty reduction has occurred over the last 20 years, almost entirely driven by progress in China, and to a lesser extent a few other emerging economies (Jayadev, Lahoti, and Reddy 2015). It is a bit clearer that there has been progress in education (especially in primary and secondary enrollment) in health (especially in reduced child mortality and increased life expectancy) and other areas (including improved access to adequate drinking water and reduced fertility rates) (Kenny 2011). Figures 2.1 and 2.2 show general progress in extending lives and reducing early death, though the progress is unevenly distributed.

But is this rate of progress morally commendable? Or should we think that progress has been far too slow, and people have been complacent in the face of massive material and social deprivations? There are at least three ways to morally assess trends in social progress. The first method merely makes diachronic

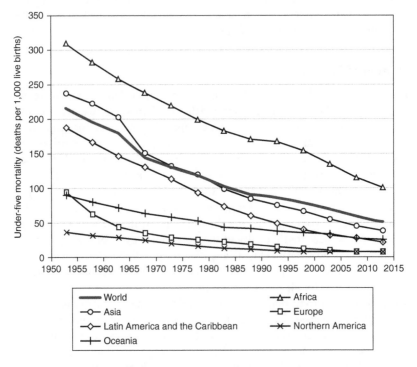

Figure 2.1 Probability of Dying before Age 5 (or Under-5 Mortality Rate), for the World and Major Areas, 1970–2015.

Source: United Nations Economic and Social Council, 2014.

assessments of past and current deprivation levels. That is, we compare contemporary levels of poverty to past levels of poverty. Any progress in the right direction should be morally commended. Using this standard, there is good reason for thinking moral progress has been made. Fewer children are dying from preventable diseases, lives are longer, and there is more material prosperity than there has been in the past.

The second method of morally evaluating social progress is to compare current trends against what is feasible given current capacity for poverty reduction. On this perspective, the international community deserves moral condemnation for what is unacceptably slow progress against very severe and easily preventable deprivation. While there have been reductions in child mortality rates, and declines in monetary and multidimensional poverty, this progress has been much slower than it could have been if there was a more serious and sustained effort to make progress against global poverty. This is especially true because there are unprecedented levels of wealth, knowledge, and technology which make our capacity for global poverty reduction greater than ever before.

A third method of morally evaluating rates of progress in poverty reduction takes account of not only what could be feasibly achieved, but what risks and

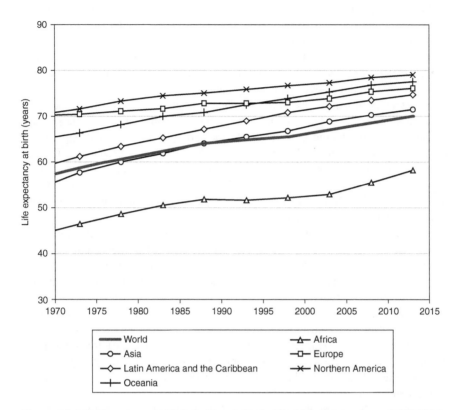

Figure 2.2 Life Expectancy at Birth (in Years), for the World and Major Areas, 1970–2015.

Source: United Nations Economic and Social Council, 2014.

vulnerabilities might threaten future efforts at global poverty eradication. When one adds to the overall moral assessment a consideration of future risks and vulnerabilities, this too raises reasons to morally criticize those who are responsible for introducing future threats to progress on poverty eradication. Most prominently, climate change and biodiversity loss pose significant threats to future progress, and may erase recent gains that have been made in poverty reduction. Stronger storms, greater droughts, rising sea levels, and attendant economic and social disruption may cause future descents into poverty. This gives further reason to be morally critical of any progress against poverty to date.

Categorizing Countries

At this point we have examined how poverty is conceived, how it is measured, and how we might judge progress in poverty reduction over time. In addition to assessing individual deprivation, the analysis of poverty often involves the categorization of entire countries in terms of their level of development. A number of sometimes competing terms are often used. Countries are often deemed to belong to 'the third world', 'the developing countries', 'the Global South', 'the least developed countries' and so on. These terms can all be problematic in various ways, and are sometimes misleading, in that the referent set of countries usually do not all share the common features that are picked out by the identifying term. For example, many 'developing' countries are in fact not making any development progress, and may even be losing ground.

Nonetheless, it can be useful to talk about categories of countries to be able to discuss and analyze patterns in international development, and to determine whether a country should be a candidate for particular international opportunities or benefits. Sometimes this categorization has material consequences for the residents of those countries. For example, access to concessionary international finance (either in the form of debt relief, below market loans, or direct grants or investment) and preferential trade arrangements is often allocated to countries based on their country categorization.

The World Bank classifies countries according to whether they are low-, lower-middle-, middle-, or high-income countries based on per capita income (using Gross National Income). Countries below 1,000 USD are low-income, below 4,000 USD are lower-middle-income, below 12,000 USD are upper-middle-income, and above 12,000 USD are high-income countries.

The United Nations uses a different classificatory system, and maintains a list of Least Developed Countries (LDCs) which are granted special treatment in trade and foreign assistance. This categorization takes account of 13 different indicators meant to track a country's per capita income, its availability of human capital, and its economic vulnerability. There are currently 48 countries categorized as Least Developed Countries.

Perhaps the best available method of classifying countries (not yet adopted by any international institutions) takes a multidimensional approach and considers both the welfare status of individuals in a country and the nature of the political and economic relations in the country. Vasquez and Sumner (2012) suggest that there are five clusters of developing countries. The first cluster has very high poverty rates and features largely 'traditional', that is agrarian and informal, economies. Most poor people live in these populous countries, including Pakistan, India, and Nigeria. The second cluster have high poverty rates and are primarily resource exporting, such as Chad and Tajikstan. The third cluster have relatively democratic governments but are highly unequal and reliant on foreign assistance, including Kenya, Guatemala, and Peru. The fourth cluster are emerging economies that have low inequality but extensive environmental degradation and high restrictions on civil and political liberties, most notably China, but also others including Egypt, Iran, and Belarus. The fifth and final cluster includes countries with unequal emerging economies that have low dependence on external finance, such as Mexico, Turkey, and South Africa. This five-fold classification is useful in so far as it helps to distinguish the different constraints countries face in achieving material prosperity. The low-income levels for many people in India have a different source, and different potential remedies, than the low-income levels in Kenya. It is therefore useful to distinguish countries based on their key characteristics, and to think about how anti-poverty policy might vary depending on these different characteristics.

Chapter Summary

At this point the reader should have an initial grasp of the competing ways in which poverty can be conceived of and measured. While philosophical texts often refer to poverty without defining it, we can get clearer on the meaning of various arguments about the ethics of poverty if we have a handle on what the term means. Assessing global progress against poverty reduction involves both empirical investigation of living standards and moral evaluation of what is possible given current levels of wealth, knowledge, and technology.

Questions for Discussion

1. Read the Universal Declaration of Human Rights and the International Covenant on Economic and Social Rights. Which of the rights included in these documents count as anti-poverty rights? Do you think the list of anti-poverty rights is too expansive or too limited?
2. The World Bank's International Poverty Line is (at the time of writing) meant to be the value of 1.25 USD 2005 PPP. Could you live on $1.25 per day? What do you think a reasonable income poverty line would be where you live? If this is higher than $1.25 per day, why is that?
3. What are the advantages and disadvantages of multidimensional poverty measurement versus strictly focusing on monetary deprivation?
4. Visit the website of the United Nations Development Program's Human Development Report office, and explore some of the composite indices on human development and gender equity. How do countries in your region fare? Do you agree or disagree with any of the rankings?
5. Should the definition of poverty be relative to prevailing living standards in a specific society, or should there be an absolute measure of poverty that applies in all places?

Notes

1. The United States poverty line and associated guidelines are available at: http://aspe.hhs.gov/2015-poverty-guidelines (accessed December 3, 2015).
2. At the time of writing, the World Bank was updating its poverty line based on new price information. The World Bank will now use a global poverty line of 1.90 USD (using 2011 PPPs).

Further Reading

Alkire, Sabina, and Santos, Maria Emma. 'Poverty and inequality measurement', *An introduction to the human development and capability approach* (2009), edited by S. Deneulin and L. Shahani. London: Earthscan, 120–161.

Banerjee, Abhijit V. and Duflo, Esther. 'The economic lives of the poor', *The Journal of Economic Perspectives: A Journal of the American Economic Association* 21.1 (2007), 141–167.

Deepa, Narayan, Patel, Raj, Schafft, Kai, Rademacher, Anne, and Koch-Schulte, Sarah. 'Voices of the poor: Can anyone hear us'. *World Bank, Washington DC* (2000).

Wisor, Scott. *Measuring Global Poverty: Toward a pro-poor approach*, Basingstoke: Palgrave MacMillan, 2012.

References

Chant, S. *Gender, Generation, and Poverty: Exploring the 'Feminisation of Poverty' in Africa, Asia, and Latin America*, Cheltenham: Edward Elgar, 2007.

Kenny, C. *Getting Better: Why global development is succeeding and how we can improve the world even more*, New York: Basic Books, 2011.

Krishna, A. *One Illness Away: Why people become poor and how they escape poverty*, Oxford: Oxford University Press, 2008.

Jayadev, A., Lahoti, R., and Reddy, S. 'Who got what, then and now? A fifty year overview of the global consumption and income project', Working Paper, available at http://papers.ssrn.com/sol3/papers.cfm?abstract_id=2602268 (accessed December 3, 2015).

LaMontagne, C. 'NerdWallet health finds medical bankruptcy accounts for majority of personal bankruptcy', March 26, 2014, available at www.nerdwallet.com/blog/health/personal-health-finance/medical-bankruptcy

Nussbaum, M. *Women and Human Development*, Cambridge: Cambridge University Press, 2000.

Reddy, S. and Minoiu, C. 'Has world poverty really fallen?' *Review of Income and Wealth* 53.3 (2007), 484–502.

Sen, A. *Development as Freedom*, New York: Anchor Books, 1999.

Stewart, F. 'The Basic Needs Approach', in D. A. Clark, *The Elgar Companion to Development Studies*, Cheltenham: Edward Elgar, 2006.

United Nations Economic and Social Council. 'World demographic trends: Report of the secretary general', 2014, available at www.un.org/en/development/desa/population/pdf/commission/2014/documents/ECN920143_EN.pdf

Vazquez, S. T. and Sumner, A. 'Beyond low and middle income countries: What if there were five clusters of developing countries?' IDS Working Paper 404, Brighton: Institute of Development Studies, 2012.

Woodward, David. 'How poor is poor: Towards a rights-based poverty line', *New Economics Foundation*, 2010.

3   The Causes of Poverty

In Part II of the book, we will examine debates over whether there are moral obligations to reduce or ameliorate global poverty. Participants in these debates nearly always make arguments that rely upon empirical premises. Some of these empirical premises are claims about the causes of poverty. In public discourse, critics of programs to reduce poverty often claim that poverty is caused by a lack of personal responsibility, or a weak work ethic, or bad decision making on the part of poor people. Defenders of programs to reduce poverty commonly claim that poverty is caused by inequalities of opportunity, or failing schools, or bad macro-economic policy. In this chapter, we explore the causal mechanisms that explain why some people, and some societies, stay or become poor while others prosper. Though this remains a contested debate among social scientists, we will give pride of place to institutional explanations of global poverty.

It is useful to distinguish two questions about the causes of poverty. The first question is about why some countries are so much poorer than other countries. This question is arguably the more important of the two. Because the number of people suffering absolute deprivation in poor countries is so much higher than in rich countries, the economic growth of those countries can have a profound effect on the pace of global poverty reduction (assuming that the benefits of growth are shared within the growing country).

Branko Milanovic, one of the world's leading experts on income inequality, has calculated the degree to which an individual's current income level is attributable to their economic class at birth and their country at birth (Milanovic 2011). Milanovic finds that more than 50 percent of a person's income is determined by the country in which the person lives or was born (http://elibrary.worldbank.org/doi/pdf/10.1596/1813-9450-6259). Because country of national origin is the most important determinant of whether or not a person lives in poverty, figuring out why some societies prosper and others do not is fundamental to reducing global poverty. In other words, the best predictor of whether any given person on the planet lives with severe material deprivation is the per capita income of her country of residence. The World Development Report from 2009 nicely captures the huge importance that a person's place has on their life chances.

> Place is the most important correlate of a person's welfare. In the next few decades, a person born in the United States will earn a hundred times more

than a Zambian, and live three decades longer. Behind these national averages are numbers even more unsettling. Unless things change radically, a child born in a village far from Zambia's capital, Lusaka, will live less than half as long as a child born in New York City—and during that short life, will earn just $0.01 for every $2 the New Yorker earns. The New Yorker will enjoy a lifetime income of about $4.5 million, the rural Zambian less than $10,000. A Bolivian man with nine years of schooling earns an average of about $460 per month, in dollars that reflect purchasing power at U.S. prices. But the same person would earn about three times as much in the United States. A Nigerian with nine years of education would earn eight times as much in the United States than in Nigeria. This 'place premium' is large throughout the developing world. The best predictor of income in the world today is not what or whom you know, but where you work.

Unless people are allowed to freely move from their country of birth (to be discussed in Chapter 11), increasing the prosperity of badly off countries will be the best method of reducing global poverty. Clearly, national progress matters in making progress against global poverty.

But the second question in not unimportant. Why do some individuals within a given society live in poverty while others do not? And why is it that countries with similar levels of per capita income have such wide variation in the degree to which people are able to be healthy, nourished, educated, and free from other severe deprivations. Social scientific analysis that reveals the determinants of individual rather than national progress can help to improve the design of anti-poverty policies and programs.

One reason that it is important to focus on the causes of individual poverty is that it is very difficult for progress to occur in countries that are currently plagued by conflict, authoritarian governance, and persistently bad economic performance. It may be a very long time before some countries move from very low incomes to income levels and political stability that are characteristic of many medium- to high-income countries. But in the meantime, even without rapid gains in per capita incomes, societies can learn to make rapid progress in reducing deprivations in health, education, sanitation, access to clean water, and other important areas of life.

Why Nations Fail

The subtitle for this section takes its heading from a recent book by Daron Acemoglu and James Robinson (2013). These authors argue that political institutions are the primary reason that countries either succeed or fail in providing prosperity for their residents. It is a thesis I broadly endorse. But before exploring the importance of political institutions for poverty reduction and broader human development, we shall explore other competing explanations for why some societies prosper and others do not.

Culture

During a visit to Israel in the 2012 US presidential campaign, Mitt Romney caused a minor controversy when he proclaimed that the reason Israel is able to sustain high economic growth and maintain high living standards, while Palestine does not, is that 'culture makes all the difference'.[1] On this view, which he attributed to David Landes, an economic historian at Harvard, the key factor that determines whether countries are poor or rich is the shared cultural institutions they adopt. Many people claim, for example, that the 'Protestant work ethic' explains the material prosperity of the United States. After a public backlash, Romney was forced to attempt to clarify his position and subsequently emphasized the role of liberty, rather than culture. Indeed, differential political and economic freedom does offer a better explanation of the widely divergent economic status of Palestinians and Israelis.

The culture of poverty thesis is often one that is asserted not just for nations as a whole but for sub-groups within them. Oscar Lewis, an American anthropologist, famously defended this view beginning in the middle of the 20th century, most notably in his 1959 book *Five Families: Mexican case studies in the culture of poverty* (1975). He argued that people raised in poverty would come to adopt values and habits that would, over time, perpetuate poverty. There are not many scholars of global poverty that take this thesis seriously today, but it remains a prominent view in public political discourse. In the United States, Congressman Paul Ryan recently claimed that domestic poverty within the United States was caused by 'this tailspin of culture, in our inner cities in particular, of men not working and just generations of men not even thinking about working or learning to value the culture of work, so there is a real culture problem here'.[2] Again, this created political controversy, as many opponents of this view pointed out that good jobs are often not available in the communities Ryan seemed to be charging with an inadequate work ethic, nor are good schools which would help to develop the skills that would make people employable.

The cultural thesis is not just endorsed by politicians: Landes and others have argued that some shared cultural beliefs or the values that are held by societies explain why it is that they prosper. Indeed, even Bill Easterly, an important development economist and a perennial critic of foreign assistance programs, who we will meet elsewhere in the book, argues that the values societies hold helps to explain whether or not they prosper (Easterly 2013).

The claim that poverty is primarily caused by culture is not persuasive, although cultural factors may play a minor role in determining the rate of progress against poverty. There are several reasons this thesis should be rejected. First, it is often simply false that poor people somehow lack an adequate work ethic, or do not believe in making progress, or do not desire better lives for themselves and their families. When large portions of a population are not working, this is because they have been excluded from opportunities that would make them suitable candidates for jobs, or there are simply not enough jobs available to them. But in most countries, the poor work harder, longer, in much more dangerous and degrading conditions than the better off. This is usually in the informal sector as well-paid, formal sector employment is limited in most low-income countries. Second, in so far as lowered aspirations or detrimental behaviors are present among certain populations, it is more likely that this is a response to circumstances of limited opportunity and severe material and social deprivation, rather than being a cause of those circumstances.

Another major problem for the culture of poverty thesis is that many countries which have very similar cultural traits have very divergent standards of living. There is much cultural similarity between, say, communities near the border of northern Mexico and communities on the southern border of the United States, but they have widely divergent incomes. And many countries that have had great economic success, such as Germany, Japan, South Korea, and Australia, have widely divergent cultural traditions. Furthermore, one variant of this thesis, that cultures that value hard work are those that create prosperity, ignores the many high-performing economies which are often also accompanied by very generous time off from work. Germans, often popularly characterized as extremely hard working, receive a generous 34 days of paid leave per year, much more than poor people in low-income countries could afford to take. It is the people struggling to get by, and living in severe deprivation, who work the hardest—every day is a work day for people in the informal sector, and in low-paid manufacturing employment it is common for people to work 7 days a week.

Analysis of global poverty that focuses on the role of culture tends to mistake the direction of causality between cultural and behavioral traits, on the one hand, and oppression and deprivation on the other. Theorists who allege that culture or behavior causes poverty see culture and behavioral traits as prior to material and social deprivation. But a much more plausible explanation is that any perceived behavioral or cultural causes of poverty are largely themselves a result of oppression, injustice, and deprivation. People may make what appear to be unwise choices, dropping out of school, or engaging in illegal work. But these may be rational choices in the face of low-quality schools, few employment opportunities, and limited chances for social mobility.

Although the cultural thesis is not a good explanation of global poverty, it does not follow from this that anti-poverty programs may not address behavioral or cultural constraints on social and economic progress. But these constraints must be seen as minor constraints as compared to the larger structural factors at play.

Population

Overpopulation is another common explanation for the persistence of global poverty. The view is roughly as follows. Countries with high fertility rates, and therefore rapidly growing populations, see any economic gains they might be making lost to the newly added members of society. Per capita income falls because of the increasing size of the population (Eswaran 2006). These bulging, young populations, often out of work, are prone to criminality, conflict, and can also be easily mobilized for war. As a result, as long as women in poor countries continue to have large numbers of children, these countries will remain badly off. While the population thesis may be a minor variable in explaining the lack of prosperity in some countries, it is not a primary cause of global poverty.

Globally, as seen in Figure 3.1, the total fertility rate is inching toward the replacement rate—that is, the rate at which the population only replaces itself, but does not grow, over time (roughly 2.1 children per woman). Most population growth today is a result of decreased mortality and increased life expectancies, and presumably nobody recommends decreasing life expectancy to reduce global poverty. On the low end, high-income countries like Italy, Japan, and Germany have a birth rate of about 1.4 births per woman. Without immigration, the population in these countries will decrease over time. Indeed, every geographic region except for sub-Saharan Africa is now below three births per woman, and these fertility rates are expected to continue to decline. On the high end, some low-income countries, often with high levels of gender inequality, have birth rates of upward of five children per woman, though this is still down from six or seven births per woman in the mid-20th century. In other words, a few countries will see their populations continue to expand as a result of higher fertility rates, but the population of many other countries will be stagnant or decline, especially absent immigration. Global increases in overall population are not driven by high fertility rates, but by increases in life expectancy.[3]

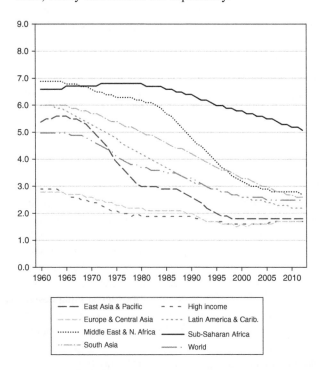

Figure 3.1 Fertility Rate, Total (Births per Woman) (TFR). http://blogs.worldbank.org/opendata/ between-1960-and-2012-world-average-fertility-rate-halved-25-births-woman

Note: Regional aggregations are for all income levels.

And even for those countries where the population will continue to grow, it is far from clear that a growing population is always a deterrent to national development. In countries that have previously experienced rapid growth, periods of sustained economic growth were often accompanied by population growth, caused by a mix of immigration, increased life expectancy, and high fertility.

Excess population growth is often also criticized as a primary cause of environmental degradation. Again, population growth is at best a secondary cause of the growth in greenhouse gas emissions and environmental degradation. Industrialization, and subsequent high levels of consumption, combined with the extensive burning of fossil fuels, is the primary cause of increasing rates of greenhouse gas emissions. Indeed, it is the low fertility populations of high-income, highly industrialized countries that have the highest global emissions, and the high fertility populations of low-income countries that contribute the least to climate change (and will be greatest harmed by it). Decoupling economic activity from environmental harm is the best way to protect the environment, not reducing population size in countries with small environmental footprints.

Nonetheless, reducing fertility rates is a worthy development objective. High fertility rates are above all a large burden on women, and a constraint in combatting gender inequality. Carrying and raising large numbers of children is physically taxing, often restricts the set of opportunities available to mothers, and can present significant health risks. Furthermore, it may be true that some countries will see growing populations as a threat to raising per capita incomes (Schultz 2006). It turns out, however, that we need not focus exclusively on restricting population growth to change the fertility rate. The status of women in society is the best predictor of whether fertility rates will drop. The best thing that can be done to address high fertility rates is to promote gender equality. While this will be good for women, it will not be the sole or primary determinant of whether a country escapes poverty.

Geography

Many scholars blame bad geography for the lack of material progress in many countries. On this view, there are two important geographic considerations that explain why some societies prosper and others do not. One is the geographic opportunities that a given territory provides: access to productive natural resources, adequate rainfall, a port, or some other geographic advantages are thought to explain why some nations were able to raise productivity and industrialize, while others do not. A second consideration is the geographic risks a given territory presents: high disease burden, unfavorable heat or rainfall patterns, mountainous terrain that easily protects rebel groups and impedes transportation networks, or the presence of non-renewable resources like oil and mining that can fuel autocratic governments or conflict.[4]

The importance of geography in explaining the success or failure of societies is associated with two of the world's most widely read and influential scholars, the anthropologist Jared Diamond and the economist Jeffrey Sachs. Diamond argues, contra the cultural thesis, that geographic and biological features of certain environments explain why industrialization and subsequent economic growth took hold in Europe before it did elsewhere (Diamond 1999). For Diamond, the emergence of industrialization in European societies, and later European colonial societies in Australasia and North America, was a product of the unique geographical features present in Europe.

Sachs argues that today's biggest development challenges are in countries that are small, landlocked, tropical, and without access to ports. For Sachs, these countries can become stuck in the poverty traps of conflict, poor governance, and stagnant economic performance (Sachs 2006). Sachs also wrote a series of influential articles on the detrimental role that non-renewable natural resources can play in economic development (to be discussed in Chapter 13). Given what he sees as the geographic trap that some societies find themselves in, Sachs recommends a 'big push' of targeted foreign aid and investment to help countries overcome their geographic disadvantages (see Chapter 9).

While geography certainly plays some role in shaping the economic opportunities available to a given country, and to the economic and political risks they face (especially the resource curse and the problem of bad neighbors), it is not a primary explanation of why some countries have such high living standards while others do not. As we will see below, countries that are able to establish inclusive institutions, which foster peaceful, democratic, and productive growth, can exist in a wide range of geographic environments. The difference between the material prosperity of South Korea and the severe deprivation of North Korea is not explained by differential geographic endowments. Differential progress is explained by the different histories of institutional development that have resulted in inclusive political institutions that pursue growth-promoting policies in South Korea while North Korea has what is arguably the world's most oppressive government.

Leadership and Policies

A fourth explanation for why some countries succeed and others do not is that prosperous countries just have better leaders who choose better policies. On this view, the difference between living standards in Singapore and Uganda comes from the relevant leadership skills and policies of Lee Kuan Yew and Yoweri Museveni. Singapore, under Yew's leadership, selected wise policies that promoted export-led growth, while Uganda, under Museveni's leadership, mismanaged the economy and failed to grow.

The idea of pro-development leaders implementing pro-poor policies has considerable traction in some development circles today. Many donor governments and international institutions place great faith in the leadership abilities and policy selections of some dictatorial (if nominally democratic) regimes. Rwanda's Paul Kagame and Ethiopia's recently deceased Meles Zenawi happily engaged in extended conversations with donors about making progress on the Millennium Development Goals, reducing child mortality, or raising agricultural yields. And it is true that, for at least a time, these leaders oversaw development progress in their countries. But they have also overseen brutal, dictatorial repression of political opponents. The government of Rwanda is widely suspected in complicity in the murder of opposition politicians who had fallen out of favor with the government, including the extraterritorial killing of Patrick Karegeya, the former head of intelligence for the Rwandan government, who was assassinated in a hotel in South Africa (HRW 2014). The government of Ethiopia under Zenawi's leadership jailed influential bloggers critical of the government, and redirected development resources away from communities that were seen to be opposed to the regime (HRW 2010). Perhaps China is the best known example of an authoritarian government that has overseen sustained periods of growth. (In China's case, the Communist Party has overseen the most rapid progress against poverty in the history of the world.) This state-led industrialization is the poster child for rapid poverty alleviation under autocracy.

Although some states do grow under autocratic governance, there are two major flaws with the view that it is specific leaders and their policies that determine whether countries prosper. First, endorsing this explanation requires a highly selective reading of the evidence. For every Kagame or Zenawi that oversees some development progress, there are many more authoritarian leaders who dictate policies that deter growth and allow poverty to persist, as did the ruling junta in Burma or President Obiang in Equatorial Guinea. Indeed, China's authoritarian-led growth of the past several decades was preceded by tens of millions of deaths under Mao's reign. In a recent study, Daron Acemoglu, Suresh Nadu, Pascal Restrepo, and James Robinson find that, controlling for other variables, democracies grow faster than non-democracies, with a democratic transition adding 20 percent to GDP over the next 25 years. The best explanation is that inclusive political institutions help to resolve political conflict which can stifle growth, encourage economic investment, institute pro-growth economic policies, and foster investment in public goods like infrastructure, education, and health.

The second flaw in the 'good leaders plus good policies' explanation of growth is that although leaders inclined toward poverty reduction may support policies that improve growth and reduce poverty for a time, eventually they will face a choice between relinquishing power and allowing growth to continue apace through accountable institutions. That is, at some point the policies that foster growth will create constituencies whose interests come into conflict with the ruling party. The ruling party then faces a choice of ceding power and continuing to grow or preserving power and adopting policies that are harmful to continued growth and poverty reduction. Facing this choice, autocrats choose personal power and wealth over the public good. Democracies, though far from perfect, are much more likely to favor the public good.

Institutions

As the reader has already seen, my preferred explanation of why some countries succeed and others fail is that they develop strong, inclusive, accountable institutions that create the environment in which innovation and productivity gains are rewarded, and democratic demands for investments in health care and education allow further development and poverty reduction to occur.

Acemoglu defines inclusive institutions as follows:

> Technological progress takes place and spreads most naturally under a specific type of economic institution, which we have called inclusive: institutions that provide incentives and opportunities for innovation and economic activity for a broad cross-section of society. These incentives are based on secure property rights for innovators, businesses, and workers, while opportunities are undergirded by a level playing field, in the form of a lack of entry barriers into businesses and occupations, and basic public services and infrastructure that enable a large portion of the population to participate in economic activity. Inclusive economic institutions are supported by inclusive political institutions, which are defined by two characteristics: first, a pluralistic, broad-based distribution of political power, so that no single individual or group can exercise power and rule without constraints and in an arbitrary fashion; and second, sufficient state centralization, so that there is a sort of monopoly of violence in the hands of the state—rather than warlords, strongmen, or bandits—upon which order and security over the territories making up a nation can be grounded.
>
> Standing in direct contrast to inclusive institutions are extractive institutions. Extractive economic institutions are characterized by insecure property rights for the majority, coercion, and lack of freedom directed at extracting resources from the majority for the benefit of a narrow elite; a playing field tilted to favor the elite often thanks to entry barriers into businesses and occupations; and a general lack of opportunities and public services for most. These economic institutions are kept in place by extractive political institutions, concentrating power in the hands of narrow interests or groups without any meaningful checks or constraints on the exercise of this power. In some cases, extractive political institutions emerge from a lack of state centralization; the lawlessness and insecurity endemic in places such as Somalia allow extractive practices to exist even in the absence of a well-defined national elite.
>
> (Acemoglu 2012, p. 14)

But how do good institutions get established? If the key to success is having open, strong, accountable institutions, why don't all countries put them in place? The reason, discussed earlier, is that the sorts of inclusive political institutions which allow societies to flourish often restrict the opportunities for some elite groups to maintain their power and protect their material interests. Why can't bad governments ensure growth? Even if they institute policies that will be favorable to raising productivity initially, this will raise the productivity of different sectors, creating newly powerful groups in society. Those groups will want to pursue policies and institutional arrangements that favor their interests. And at some point this will come into conflict with the dictator's own interests. The dictator will be forced to choose between repression, to protect his interests, and openness, which allows growth to occur but sacrifices the interests of autocratic rules. The self-interested autocrat and his supporters will always in the end pursue the policy that favors their interests over the public good.

So how is it that some societies overcome extractive institutions and transition to inclusive institutions? This is a difficult question to answer, and is highly dependent upon the specific society in question. The short answer is that certain changes, sometimes known as critical junctures, can and do occur when either exogenous or endogenous shocks to the system take place, creating the opportunity for political reform. These critical junctures are disruptions to the status quo, such as an external military invasion or a financial crisis, that allow reformers to change the political equilibrium and change the rules of the game so that they are better structured to promote the public good. It is hard to predict when these junctures may occur and even to know if they have happened, but in hindsight one can see institutional arrangements turn on crucial events that disrupt existing power arrangements.

It is important to note that while the institutional thesis is favored by a number of prominent contemporary economists and political scientists, there are important disputes regarding both the nature and causes of institutions that promote prosperity. For example, Francis Fukuyama emphasizes the importance of state capacity, especially bureaucratic autonomy and a monopoly on the use of force, whereas Douglas North and co-authors (2009) emphasize the openness of economic institutions that protect property rights (what they call open-access orders), while Acemoglu and Robinson emphasize the inclusiveness of political institutions. Future academic research into the institutional thesis can hopefully further illuminate how endogenous or exogenous forces can further promote institutional development, and how, absent critical junctures, institutional reform can proceed (see Andrews 2013), while also focusing on preventing institutional decay (Fukuyama 2014).

What lessons should we draw from the institutional explanation of development for the ethics of global poverty? First, one should always attend to the effect that any proposed policy or development program will have on domestic institutional quality. In particular, will the policy or program increase accountability to citizens, or will it contribute to the maintenance of extractive political institutions? Second, when critical junctures do appear to be occurring (such as a coup, an outbreak of civil resistance, or an economic crisis) both internal and external actors should be conscious and recognize the opportunities for moving toward a path of progressive institutional development, and support those changes in so far as possible. Third, the design of international institutions can either inhibit or promote the development of inclusive domestic institutions. The prevailing international institutional environment ought to be reformed so as to encourage the development of inclusive domestic institutions. Fourth, the development of strong, inclusive institutions is an extremely long game, and outsiders who seek quick, silver bullet institutional changes (through the violent overthrow of ruling governments, for example) that would quickly turn countries from development disasters to development successes fundamentally misunderstand the nature of poverty and the determinants of progress.

Why Are Some People Poor?

The primary focus of this chapter is on explanations for national progress, because a person's country of residence is a primary determinant of whether he or she is able to meet her basic needs. But the second question, why within countries some people are poor and others are not, deserves brief comment here. As with explanations of the poverty of countries, the causes of material and social deprivation facing specific individuals within a given country is often a point of contention in public debate. Unfortunately, public debate is rarely grounded in a plausible social scientific explanation.

An important starting point is to recognize that individual life chances vary across a number of axes, including race and ethnicity, gender, geographic location, and disability status. One must then determine whether these variations reflect some inherent pre-disposition to poverty within those groups, or rather that the disadvantage and discrimination the group faces creates disproportionate levels of poverty.

One argument that is rarely taken seriously in academic circles but pops up from time to time in public commentary is that people live in poverty because of some failure for which they are responsible. These arguments attempt to identify some personal failure on the part of an individual living in poverty, or note some inherent inferiority, to argue that the person is responsible for their deprivation, and thus others are not responsible for helping to lift her out of poverty.

One simple way to refute these views is to examine measures of social mobility within a given society. There are competing ways of measuring social mobility. One common method is to determine the likelihood that an individual who is born to one social class is able in her lifetime to move to another. For example, if a person is born to parents who are in the bottom 20 percent of income distribution, what is the likelihood that she will end up in that income quintile or another? In the United States, a child born in the poorest quintile has a 9 percent chance of making it to the top quintile—this is in contrast to Denmark, where the figure is twice as high (*The Economist* 2014). The proponent of the view that some personal failing causes individual poverty must then concoct a story as to why this failing is less prevalent in Danish rather than American children. In other words, what is it that is wrong with American kids such that they remain stuck in poverty while Danish kids can escape it?

But, one might think that the distribution of the characteristics that allows individuals to succeed is not randomly distributed among the population. They might think it is genetically inherited. On this view, intelligence or productivity are determined by one's biology, and this explains social and economic differences among social groups. Historically, this argument has often been given to justify formal discrimination against women and racial minorities. This form of biological determinism has been refuted by scholars (Gould 1996) who show that social environment, rather than biology, plays a much stronger role in determining economic outcomes.

Another related thesis suggests that poor people somehow lack motivation, or do not have the grit or fortitude to succeed, or undertake counter-productive behaviors. As with other explanations that place the responsibility on the person who is living in poverty, rather than the circumstances and opportunities that are available to her, this explanation does not have much evidential support.

However, there is important new research showing the psychological impact of living with scarce resources. While it is not true that people living in poverty are somehow less rational or mentally capable at birth than their peers who do not live in poverty, it is true that living with limited material and social resources places enormous burdens on cognitive systems that can result in lower performance on a range of cognitive tests. Anadi Mani, Denshil Mullainathan, Eldar Shafir, and Jiaying Zhao argue that lower than average cognitive performance and decision making is explained by the burden of poverty.

> The poor must manage sporadic income, juggle expenses, and make difficult tradeoffs. Even when not actually making a financial decision, these preoccupations can be present and distracting. The human cognitive system has limited capacity. Preoccupations with pressing budgetary concerns leave fewer cognitive resources available to guide choice and action. Just as an air traffic controller focusing on a potential collision course is prone to neglect other planes in the air, the poor, when attending to monetary concerns, lose their capacity to give other problems their full consideration. This suggests a causal, not merely correlational, relationship between poverty and mental function.
>
> (Mani et al., p. 976)

For example, these scholars show that when poor people are prompted to imagine financial distress, and then asked to solve a math problem, they perform worse on that problem than when not prompted to think about financial distress. Similarly, poor farmers perform worse on cognitive tests just before the harvest, when assets are low, then just after the harvest, when assets are high.

The implication of these findings is quite different from what people usually suggest when they identify suboptimal decision making among poor people as a cause of poverty. Rather than being a reason to deny anti-poverty assistance to deprived people, it is a reason to redesign that assistance. If it is the case that the circumstances of scarcity are the cause of suboptimal decision making, this does not show that people ought to be held responsible for their poverty. Rather, the implication is that (a) in so far as possible, policies which reduce conditions of scarcity will reduce constraints on better decision making and (b) anti-poverty programs should take account of the excess cognitive burdens of living in poverty, for example by reducing the administrative burden in accessing public benefits.

Chapter Summary

This chapter does not aim to settle the important social scientific questions surrounding the determinants of poverty for countries or individuals. But it does aim to make clear the views that will lie in the background for the remainder of this book. The quality of political institutions is the primary determinant of whether or not countries succeed or fail. In the contemporary world, many countries which have high levels of poverty inherited extractive political institutions from the colonial period. Those countries that have developed inclusive political institutions which are able to foster productive economic opportunity have largely escaped severe material deprivation. Within countries, some people are worse off than others, largely as a result of inequalities of opportunity, and high vulnerability of people on low incomes to exogenous shocks that can reverse any sustained progress in poverty reduction. These inequalities often track social groups including gender, race, ethnicity, caste, and religion.

Questions for Discussion

1   Identify two countries in the same region that have differing levels of income. Of the possible factors discussed in this chapter, which do you think best explains the differences between the two countries today? For example, why is Chile much better off than Peru, or Japan much better off than China?

2   What are some popularly offered explanations for why some individuals are poor in the community in which you live? Do you think these explanations are correct? Do any of the explanations listed above apply to those individuals?

3   Both countries and individuals are subject to poverty dynamics—they make some progress but then are often knocked off the path of progress. What, if any, significance should the existence of poverty dynamics have for the design of anti-poverty policies?

4   Find a recent story about poverty in the local media. What explanation does the author give for why some people are poor? Is it a plausible explanation? Is there a competing explanation that might better explain the current deprivation people face?

Notes

1   This quote was widely reported at the time. For one citation, see http://www.business-insider.com/mitt-romney-israel-economy-culture-racism-2012-7

2   Widely reported at the time, this quote can be found at: www.msnbc.com/politicsnation/ryan-generations-men-not-working (accessed December 3, 2015).

3   More information available at http://www.economist.com/node/14743589 (accessed December 3, 2015).

4   More on the resource curse in Chapter 13.

Suggested Reading

Mullainathan, S. and Shafir, E. *Scarcity: The true cost of not having enough*, New York: Penguin, 2013.

Beinhocker, Eric D. *The Origin of Wealth: Evolution, complexity, and the radical remaking of economics*, Boston: Harvard Business Press, 2006.

References

Acemoglu, D. 'The World Our Grandchildren Will Inherit: The Rights Revolution and Beyond', 2012. Available at www.nber.org/papers/w17994.

Acemoglu, D. and Robinson, J. *Why Nations Fail: The origins of power, prosperity, and poverty*, New York: Crown Business, 2012.

Andrews, M. *The Limits of Institutional Reform in Development: Changing rules for realistic solutions*, Cambridge: Cambridge University Press, 2013.

Diamond, J. *Guns, Germs, and Steel: The fates of human societies*, New York: W.W. Norton, 1999.

Easterly, W. *The Tyranny of Experts: Economists, Dictators, and the Forgotten Rights of the Poor*, Basic Books: New York, 2013.

The Economist 2014. 'Mobility, measured', February 1, available at www.economist.com/news/united-states/21595437-america-no-less-socially-mobile-it-was-generation-ago-mobility-measured

Eswaran, M. 'Fertility in Developing Countries', in *Understanding Poverty*, eds. A. Banerjee, R. Bénabou, and D. Mookherjee, Oxford: Oxford University Press, 2006.

Fukuyama, F. *Political Order and Political Decay*, New York: Farrar, Strauss, and Giroux, 2014.

Gould, S. *The Mismeasure of Man*, New York: W.W. Norton, 1996.

HWR, Human Rights Watch. 'Development without freedom: How aid underwrites repression in Ethiopia', 2010, available at www.hrw.org/sites/default/files/reports/ethiopia1010webwcover.pdf

HWR, Human Rights Watch. 'Rwanda: Repression across borders', 2014, available at www.hrw.org/news/2014/01/28/rwanda-repression-across-borders

Lewis, O. *Five Families: Mexican case studies in the culture of poverty*, New York: Basic Books, 1975.

Milanovic, B. *The Haves and the Have Nots: A brief idiosyncratic history of global inequality*, New York: Persus Books, 2011.

North, D., Wallis, J., Weingast, B. *Violence and Social Orders: a conceptual framework for interpreting recorded history*, Cambridge: Cambridge University Press, 2009.

Sachs, J. *The End of Poverty: Economic possibilities for our time*, New York: Penguin, 2006.

Schultz., T. 'Fertility and income', in *Understanding Poverty*, eds. A. Banerjee, R. Bénabou, and D. Mookherjee, Oxford: Oxford University Press, 2006.

World Development Report. 'Reshaping economic geography', Washington, DC: World Bank, 2009.

4   The Study of Poverty

In the preceding two chapters, we have examined how poverty is conceived, measured, and distributed across the globe, and explored some of the most prominent explanations for the persistence of poverty in some places and its reduction elsewhere. But how can we have real knowledge of what causes poverty and how it can be alleviated?

William Easterly is arguably the world's most prominent aid critic. In his bestselling book *The White Man's Burden: Why the West's efforts to aid the rest have done so much ill and so little good*, he provided a compelling argument against the free distribution of anti-malarial bed nets. The idea behind free distribution was clear enough: mosquitoes spread malaria, and malaria is responsible for high levels of mortality and morbidity in many countries. But Easterly claimed that the free distribution of bed nets resulted in the misuse of those nets. Because people had not purchased the nets, they did not have an incentive to see that they were wisely used for better health outcomes. Easterly claimed that 'planners' who sought to distribute free bed-nets were failing to secure better health outcomes, while 'searchers', who eventually learned the best way to promote the use of bed nets was through market mechanisms, discovered a solution to the problem not by setting out with prescriptions of how to solve poverty, but with an open mind to learn from, and test, how to reduce poverty. This argument against the free provision of material resources has been influential in many development circles. But was his theory correct?

Pascaline Dupas and Jessica Cohen (2008) set up an experiment to test whether the free distribution of bed nets does in fact cause the nets to be misused, and whether selling nets, even at subsidized prices, was a better method of fighting malaria. They offered nets at varying prices, from free to 0.75 USD, at prenatal clinics in Kenya. By randomizing the prices at which the nets were available, they were able to determine how sensitive demand for the nets was to price. It turns out that demand for nets dropped significantly with the introduction of even very small prices. Furthermore, researchers went to people's homes and found that people who had purchased nets were no more likely to be using them effectively, nor more likely to be free from malaria. It turns out that Easterly's theory was wrong, and distributing anti-malarial bed nets for free is a more effective health intervention than selling subsidized nets.

Similarly, for many years, competing explanations had been provided for the high absenteeism rates of rural children in school. Some thought that children did not go to school because the rewards were not sufficiently high—that is, parents did not believe that good jobs awaited children who completed their schooling. It was, all things considered, better to have them home to help around the house. Others suggested that high rates of teacher violence and abuse, as well as abuse from other students, was to blame. Still others suggested that it was a lack of good materials and books, poor teacher quality, or high teacher absenteeism. Still others blamed cultural causes—that children and their parents did not value education and so chose to skip class. But people who were seriously inquiring into the subject were not sure how to parse these competing, and sometimes contradictory, claims about why many young students do not attend school.

Beginning in 1998, an international NGO, the International Child Support, launched the Primary School Deworming Initiative in Busia District in Western Kenya. Because the NGO did not have sufficient resources to fund all areas initially, the program was rolled out in phases at different schools in the district. The design of this roll-out allowed for a careful evaluation of the effects of deworming on child health, education, and productivity later in life. Researchers found that deworming a single child produced on average 28 days more education, and for the youngest children affected by the deworming project, cognitive improvements equivalent to an additional 0.5 to 0.8 years of schooling. Because the deworming interventions are relatively inexpensive, the deworming project appears to be extremely cost effective—researchers suggest that for each 3.50 USD spent, an additional year of schooling is completed (Miguel and Kremer 2004). But does this explanation for low enrollment rates in a specific region in Kenya apply elsewhere? And would the initial enrollment gains from deworming programs have persistence over time?

These are two examples of crucial questions about the causes of and solutions to the persistence of global poverty. To listen to politicians or development officials describing poverty, you would think that what causes poverty and how it can be combatted is widely known. But the truth is that the study of poverty, like other problems in the social sciences, is wrought with intellectual dispute and controversy. And since most academic investigation into social problems focuses on high-income countries, the state of the art research on global poverty may be characterized by even deeper disagreement and uncertainty than the study of domestic poverty. In this chapter, we will focus on some of the methods for studying global poverty, and the strengths and weaknesses involved in those methods. We will give considerable attention to randomized control trials, a currently popular method of testing the effectiveness of development interventions that has provoked considerable debate among scholars of international development.

Qualitative Methods

As the international development project got underway beginning in the 1950s and gaining speed through the 1970s (for a thorough analysis and critique, see

Easterly 2013), the most prominent academic position in shaping development policy was the development economist. This person was tasked with prescribing the right policies to national governments and international agencies, who would then administer new programs and policies that were to advance national growth. The development economist often arrived with models of economic activity that were highly idealized, perhaps derived from experiences in much more advanced economies, and made confident predictions on what policies should be implemented to create economic growth. But many researchers argued that these policy prescriptions were often ignorant of the actual lives of the people they were meant to be helping. This ignorance resulted in badly misguided recommendations for the making of public policy. Unsurprisingly, the expert advice of development economists during these decades did not result in large economic and social progress.

One way that researchers, many from outside the discipline of economics, argued that you could get better information about the lives of people living with deprivation, and the ways in which they might be improved, was through qualitative research. Carvalho and White (1997) define the qualitative approach as research

> that typically uses purposive sampling and semi-structured or interactive interviews to collect data—mainly, data relating to people's judgments, attitudes, preferences, priorities, and/or perceptions about a subject—and analyses it through sociological or anthropological research techniques.

Qualitative research methods are characterized by less formal, less structured, and more in-depth research with smaller numbers of research participants and more direct interaction between the researcher and the people she is interested in learning about. Rather than analyzing national level economic indicators or developing formal models of economic interaction to derive policy prescriptions, qualitative researchers focus on extended, in-depth studies of the lives of people living in poverty, giving privilege to the perspectives and voices of people who live with deprivation on a daily basis.

Qualitative research methods are particularly valued by researchers who aim to identify and represent neglected and marginalized viewpoints and perspectives. Feminist theorists and anti-colonial researchers, for example, have privileged the ways in which qualitative research methods can be used to dissent from received wisdom regarding various social problems. Qualitative research methods are also well suited to studying the problems that affect highly marginalized groups who may be difficult to reach or identify through standard research survey methods, such as sexual minorities, political dissidents, victims of abuse, criminals, international migrants, and other marginalized communities.

Participatory Poverty Assessments

One prominent form of qualitative research is the participatory poverty assessment. Participatory poverty assessments encourage people living in poor communities to use focus group discussions to develop their own metrics for identifying how well or badly people are faring in their community, ideally as a mechanism for thinking about how programs and policies might best assist those people who are badly off, and increasing the accountability of institutions responsible for anti-poverty interventions (Norton 2001).

The largest and most famous participatory poverty assessment was conducted by the World Bank for its famous *Voices of the Poor* report.[1] The report reviewed participatory studies in 50 countries with 40,000 participants, and undertook a further 23 country studies with 20,000 men and women to understand (a) how they conceive of a good and bad life, (b) what their most important priorities are, (c) how they interact with public institutions, and (d) how they view gender and other social relations. This work fed into the World Development Report for 2000/2001, and informed policy-making at national and regional levels. The report was influential in shifting much development thinking: it emphasized the importance of powerlessness in characterizing poverty; it emphasized the multidimensional nature of poverty, it highlighted the vulnerability of the poor, it showed that poor people are subject to serious exploitation and abuse by private and public institutions; and it emphasized the importance of changing gender relations for understanding household dynamics. Many of these key findings could only be established through participatory research.

Life Histories

Andiruh Krishna is a leading scholar of public health (who we have met previously) who uses the method of life histories to learn about change over time in the poverty of individuals, and to explain the causes of those changes. He has developed the *Stages-of-Progress* method of researching poverty. This method develops an understanding of poverty that is relevant to the local context in which the research is taking place, and tracks the changes in a household's poverty status over time. By working with participants to learn their life histories, Krishna is able to identify the determinants of success or failure over the long term as perceived by the participant.

Consider the case of Heera, in Rajasthan. Krishna relates his life history as follows:

> My father fell ill about 18 years ago. We must have spent close to 25,000 rupees on his treatment, but to no avail. When my father died, we performed the customary death feast, spending another 10,000 rupees. We sold our cattle, and we also had to take out some loans. We worked harder in order to repay these debts. Then, about ten years ago, my wife fell seriously ill, and she has still not recovered. We borrowed more money to pay for her medical treatments. More than 20,000 rupees were spent for this purpose. It became hard to keep up with our debts. Somehow we could make do for another two or three years. Then the rains failed for three years in a row, and that was the end of the road for us. We sold our land. Now my sons and I work as casual labor, earning whatever we can from one day to the next.
>
> (Krishna 2008, p. 13)

The life history method helps to highlight first that not all people are born poor but rather poverty is dynamic—some people rise and others fall over time. Second, it shows how intersecting shocks can cause descent over time. Third, it guides public policy in important ways: by showing that preventive policy, especially the expansion of effective health care, can prevent poverty descents. This careful analysis of the full course of a person's life is rarely possible through quantitative research methods.

Key Informant Interview

The key informant interview is a staple of qualitative research. Whereas many qualitative research exercises might randomly select participants, or choose participants based on certain characteristics (such as their employment status, or age, or gender), the key informant is a person who may have a unique understanding of a particular problem under consideration. A study that seeks to understand the use of fertilizer among farmers may choose to speak in extensive detail with the local shopkeeper who sells fertilizer, and several farmers who have different habits regarding the use of fertilizer. Or a study that seeks to understand the use of contraception among sex workers may identify a senior sex worker who can speak to the practices and trends of sex workers, a local NGO representative that works with at risk populations, or a public health official who has experience in harm reduction strategies.

Sustained Engagement

Some of the best qualitative research involves sustained engagement with a single community over time, and uses repeated qualitative interviews to generate quantitative measurements. For example, Caroline Moser (2009) has worked and studied in the city of Guayaquil, Ecuador, for over 40 years. She has a long working relationship with many of the families there, and engages in both deep qualitative research and quantitative assessment of the determinants of progress over time. Moser's book, based on 40 years of researching Guayaquil, shows that in-depth qualitative information need not be completely devoid of quantitative information. Qualitative researchers may develop quantitative scales with their participants, or find other numerical information that emerges from their fieldwork.

While qualitative research methods offer many strengths, they face several limitations. Most qualitative research (though not all) involves small sample sizes. A large number of data points is usually needed to measure change over time or identify the causal mechanisms that alter socio-economic performance. Qualitative research can also be deeply shaped by the perceptions of both participants and researchers. Both groups, as with everyone else, come to the research with their views having been formed by their life experiences, their training, their ideological and political commitments, and more. This can influence, and arguably bias, the results of participatory research. Furthermore, qualitative research methods simply are not suitable to answer many important policy questions. If a country seeks to, for example, determine the optimal tax rate on consumer goods and services, qualitative research can at best provide one input to answering this question. For example, qualitative researchers might learn about how and when individuals evade consumption taxes, or how consumers react to price changes brought about by changes in tax structure. But they will not be able to answer the broad macro-economic questions regarding changes in consumption, investment, and public spending that result from the tax change.

As with any research method, there are limitations and constraints on the usefulness of qualitative research methods. But they are an absolutely indispensable tool for the study of global poverty and have played a very important role in improving the understanding of what it is like to be poor, what causes poverty, and how poverty can be avoided. They provide a richness and depth not often accessible via quantitative research methods.

Quantitative Methods

Quantitative research is generally defined as research 'that typically uses random sample surveys and structured interviews to collect data—mainly, quantifiable data—and analyses it using statistical techniques' (Carvalho and White 1997). A thorough review of all quantitative research methods is beyond the scope of this chapter, but a few important methods that are important for the study of poverty deserve thorough discussion.

A vast amount of the information needed to measure progress in monetary and multidimensional poverty reduction and to evaluate the determinants of progress in poverty reduction comes from household surveys in developing countries. Over time the construction and coverage of these surveys have increased considerably, though there is still a long way to go in improving the quality, coverage, and use of multi-topic surveys. The World Bank's Living Standards Measurement Survey, USAID funded Demographic and Health Surveys, the Core Welfare Indicator Questionnaire, and other regular surveys provide much of the information on global progress. When you read a statistic on life expectancy in Zambia or educational enrollment in South Asia, it is likely derived from one or more of these multi-topic surveys.

But quantitative researchers are not just interested in the way things are; they are interested in learning about how they came to be and how they might change. With data in hand provided by a range of data collection methods, most commonly multi-topic surveys, researchers aim to figure out what causes or determines progress or failure. How can these lessons be used to inform the design of policies and institutions?

Analyzing Correlation

A first step in much quantitative analysis is to analyze correlation. The analysis of correlation determines whether or not two or more variables are statistically related to each other. For example, when one receives the data from a multi-topic survey, they may be interested in whether there is a strong correlation between literacy levels and income. Do people with higher literacy levels earn more money? If the two variables are highly correlated, this indicates two things. First, that one variable may be predictive of the other. That is, if you learn that a person has high literacy levels, it will be likely that they have a high income. Second, that the two variables have some kind of association. They are related in some way, although the nature of that relationship requires some further investigation.

With large datasets in hand providing a range of information on health status, housing, sanitation, drinking water, income, consumption, familial relationships, and employment and work status, researchers are able to begin investigating the relationship between different variables. One common approach is known as regression analysis. Regression analysis uses a variety of statistical methods to determine more about the nature of the relationship between different variables, and in particular how changes to independent variables are likely to affect dependent variables. Neither simple correlation analysis nor regression analysis can determine whether two variables are causally related. This is the key question in much contemporary development economics. Suppose, taking the case above, that you learn in some society that income and literacy are highly positively correlated. So, as a public official, you begin directing resources to raising literacy rates. But, upon doing so, you find that incomes do not rise for people with now higher literacy rates. It turns out that while literacy and income were correlated, higher literacy does not cause higher incomes. There is some other unobserved variable that must have explained the past correlation between literacy rates and income.

Randomized Control Trials

While non-experimental methods are often used to study issues in development economics, including causal relationships, experimental methods are sometimes preferable to evaluate specific development projects because the ability to assign participants to control and treatment groups ensures that some latent variable cannot explain differences in outcomes.

Randomized control trials (RCTs) are increasingly used in the evaluation of development projects and are one of the most popular, and contested, methods of studying poverty. We started this chapter discussing whether the distribution of free anti-malarial bed nets was better or worse for preventing malaria than the sale of anti-malarial bed nets, and saw how an experimental design can provide an opportunity to give a conclusive answer to this important policy question. Just as a new drug for treating cancer will be given to some patients and not others, and the differential health outcomes between treatment and control groups will determine whether the drug is effective in treating cancer, so too can you randomize whether people are given bed nets for free, or given the opportunity to purchase them, and then evaluate the difference between the control and treatment groups.

In various forms of non-experimental analysis, it is difficult to be sure whether one has truly isolated the important variable that explains differential outcomes from other variables. There is always the risk that some latent, unmeasured variable is what causes the movement in both variables. In the example above, perhaps incomes are higher in urban areas, as are literacy rates. Raising literacy rates in rural areas may do nothing to change incomes in those areas if the labor market does not reward literacy and gains in literacy cannot translate into higher incomes in those areas.

Proponents of randomized control trials like to say that unlike those who claim to know what works in fighting poverty, they do not know what works—but they aim to find out. RCTs have produced extremely useful findings in evaluating development efforts. They have discovered that a year after the free distribution of clean cookstoves, households were not likely to have the stoves in use and were not likely to have improved respiratory health (Hanna et al. 2012). They have shown micro-finance (Chapter 16) to be ineffective at reducing material deprivation, but have shown savings programs to be very effective. They have shown that deworming programs deliver not just health benefits, but educational benefits by keeping children healthy enough to stay in school (Miguel and Kremer 2004).

There are, however, several critiques of RCTs. The first is a concern about what economists call external validity. External validity refers to the applicability of the findings in one location or among one group of subjects to other locations or groups of subjects. While deworming had a large initial effect on enrollment in schools in Busia District in Kenya, would a deworming program have the same effect in Nairobi? We certainly wouldn't expect a deworming program to impact dropout rates in Chicago. So how do we know when the results of an anti-poverty RCT are applicable elsewhere? And do we know if they would be applicable again in the same place at a different time?

Another concern relates to internal validity. Even if we grant that a given experiment undertaken in one setting may not be evidence of similar causal relationships in other settings, there is a further question about whether even in the same setting the experiment is accurately reflecting the social phenomenon under investigation. In other words, are the causal findings real or illusory? It may be that something in the design of the experiment itself makes it such that the results suggest a causal relationship that is not really there. For example, participants in randomized control trials often know that they are part of an experiment. In an experiment in Tanzania designed to determine whether this matters, Bulte et al. (2014) conducted both a standard RCT and a double-blind experiment to determine whether access to new agricultural technologies (modern seeds) or increased effort explained improved agricultural outcomes. It turns out that (difficult to observe) differences in effort among those who knew themselves to be part of the randomized trial explain all of the differences in outcomes. In other words, access to different seeds, which in a standard RCT would have appeared to explain differential outcomes, actually had no explanatory power. The mere fact that people knew they were in a study made the real difference.

A third concern is that randomized control trials are simply not capable of evaluating large-scale, systemic changes that are responsible for most poverty reduction. Large political changes, for example, are believed to have far-reaching consequences for the welfare of citizens. Following the end of apartheid and the removal of policies restricting the housing, transportation, ownership, and employment opportunities for black South Africans, their incomes rose (Leibbrant and Levinson 2011). But it would neither be feasible nor ethical to conduct an experiment on ending apartheid regimes. Similarly, many humanitarian interventions are justified on grounds that the well-being of residents in the intervened state will improve considerably if military intervention against a given government or armed group occurs. But no one could seriously entertain the idea of randomizing candidate humanitarian interventions, with external militaries simply flipping a coin to determine whether the country should face intervention or not. Similarly, there is much debate about the role that reducing trade barriers plays in improving human welfare. While it has been suggested that experiments could be run on international trade regimes (Hassoun 2011), no state would ever cede control over its trade policy to academic researchers. Furthermore, even if states would participate in a limited experiment, it is not clear that these findings would prove meaningful in the real world of international trade, where aggregate trade benefits should be greatest when more countries are liberalizing trade policy. For those who believe that deep structural and political change is the key to large-scale poverty reduction, RCTs do not appear to generate the right kind of evidence needed to guide policy makers.

Given the ethical, political, and practical constraints that restrict the set of possible interventions that may be tested through randomized control trials, it is best to think of RCTs as one important building block in the evaluation of small-scale development programs. Like other tools, RCTs have limitations and constraints, but they are a welcome addition to the overall toolbox for studying global poverty.

Natural Experiments

As noted above, it is sometimes not feasible, or ethical, to conduct an experiment to determine the impact of a particular change on poverty reduction. But events in the world do not respect such constraints, and sometimes the world presents a natural randomization of people into treatment and control groups that permits of a quantitative evaluation of the impact of the 'intervention'. These natural experiments provide a method of understanding the impact of a certain exogenous change without requiring that the change be brought about through experiment.

For example, it would be unethical to restrict the calorie consumption of pregnant women, given the health risks that this would present to the mother and the child. But many women fast during Ramadan, some doing so before they have confirmed that they are pregnant. This allows for an evaluation of the variation of outcomes for children whose gestation overlapped with Ramadan. Almond et al. (2015) find that having the early gestation period overlap with Ramadan results in 0.5–0.8 standard deviation lower performance in mathematics tests at age 7 than children who did not overlap with Ramadan. They also performed worse in reading and writing than similar children who did not gestate during

Ramadan. This study suggests that supporting the nutrition of mothers in early pregnancy may be a wise investment from the perspective of both health and education. This natural experiment provides useful policy guidance in the design of anti-poverty policy, even though it is not an experiment that would be ethical or feasible to conduct.

Another type of regression analysis exploits the difference in achievements of people just above and just below some naturally occurring cut-off, allowing for inferences about causation. Regression discontinuity analysis offers another promising method in non-experimental settings in which naturally occurring social processes can be treated as methods of impact evaluation that reveal causal relationships. For example, if school children must pass an entrance exam at a certain score to enter secondary school, analysts can examine achievements just above and just below this cut-off (assuming students just above and below are very similar) to examine the effect entrance to secondary school has on life achievements.

Q-Squared

Both quantitative and qualitative research methods have their strengths and limitations. The most promising approach to research into social problems today therefore involves a mix of these approaches. Many research projects now include both quantitative and qualitative research components. The so called Q-squared approach (Kanbur 2003) aims to combine the strength of both rigorous quantitative evaluation and rich qualitative description. In fact, most randomized control trials are complemented by accompanying in-depth investigation with key informants. It is quite common for experimental research design that seeks statistical evidence of causation to be complemented by qualitative research. This is in part because quantitative analysis that attempts to reveal causal relationships often still cannot give an account of why people or social processes act or behave in the way that they do.

For example, a wide range of quantitative evidence shows that many people living in poor countries are likely to seek health care from traditional healers rather than medical professionals. They spend money on these treatments and often do not improve their health status, which has a negative impact on their productivity and thus poverty status. Quantitative analysis can reveal a great deal about health care expenditure and health outcomes. But the answer to why it is that many poor people prefer the apparently less effective health care provider is better answered through qualitative methods. Jacob Appel (Karlan and Appel 2011) was living in Ghana working on quantitative experiments measuring the effectiveness of poverty programs when an employee of his (his housekeeper) reported that she had injured her leg. Appel inquired about the course of treatment she sought. She reported that she had been to a traditional healer who had prescribed herbal treatments, treatments costing up to half of her weekly salary. Appel was disappointed, in that this care was unlikely to help her heal. So at his encouragement they went to the hospital together. There, Appel saw a health care system that repeatedly disrespected the patient, was poorly staffed, and was unresponsive to her needs. He could see that she was pushed, by disrespectful treatment and long wait times, away from medical providers to traditional healers, because the latter group was far more accommodating and respectful than the former. The combination of qualitative and quantitative research methods, in health and other areas, offer the most promising approach to the proper understanding of multidimensional poverty, its causes, and its possible remedies.

Chapter Summary

When you read philosophical arguments relating to ethical issues arising from the persistence of global poverty, they nearly always will involve empirical premises. The truth of the conclusion depends in part on whether the empirical premises are true. As we have seen, it is no simple task to determine how much poverty there is, or what causes it. Understanding the methods by which researchers attempt to learn about poverty is important for students who seek to be able to critically evaluate arguments about the ethics of global poverty. Beware the ethical argument that makes the empirical study of poverty sound easy or obvious! This chapter has only glanced at some of the important arguments regarding the study of poverty—students are encouraged to consult the recommended readings for further information.

Questions for Discussion

1   Are there any recent government initiatives in your area that are aimed at tackling poverty? How are these initiatives to be evaluated? Do you think the system of evaluation currently in place will allow for a rigorous assessment of the poverty-reducing effects of the policy?

2   Jeffrey Sachs faced criticism for not conducting randomized control trials in his much touted Millennium Villages program. He argued against such trials, stating that he didn't want to send researchers around to villages that were not receiving benefits from the programs. Do you think there are ethical reasons to not conduct RCTs? Do you think these reasons override the potential benefits of learning from these experiments?

3   Many studies have attempted to determine whether, on the whole, foreign aid improves growth in developing countries. What problems can you imagine might arise in attempting to draw firm conclusions from these comparative studies?

4   For many aspects of anti-poverty work, there is not adequate research to guide development policy. What should be done in cases where there is not clear evidence on what works? Is it morally wrong to undertake an anti-poverty program before conducting extensive research to determine whether the proposed program will reduce deprivation?

Note

1   For the full suite of reports on this project, visit the World Bank's Voices of the Poor
    website, available at http://web.worldbank.org/WBSITE/EXTERNAL/TOPICS/EXTPO
    VERTY/0,,contentMDK:20622514~menuPK:336998~pagePK:148956~piPK:216618~t
    heSitePK:336992,00.html

Suggested Reading

Angrist, Joshua D. and Pischke, Jörn-Steffen. *Mostly Harmless Econometrics: An empiricist's companion*, Princeton: Princeton University Press, 2008.

Cartwright, N. and Hardie, J. *Evidence-Based Policy: A practical guide to doing it better*, Oxford: Oxford University Press, 2012.

Chambers, Robert. *Whose Reality Counts? Putting the first last*, Intermediate Technology Publications Ltd (ITP), 1997.

Khandker, Shahidur R., Koolwal, Gayatri B., and Samad, Hussain A. *Handbook on Impact Evaluation: Quantitative methods and practices*, World Bank Publications, 2010.

References

Almond, D., Mazumder, B., and van Ewijk, R. '*In Utero* Ramadan exposure and children's academic performance'. *The Economic Journal* 125 (2015): 1501–1533.

Bulte, E., Beekman, G., Di Falco, S., Hella, J., and Lei, P., 'Behavioral responses and the impact of new agricultural technologies: Evidence from a double-blind field experiment in Tanzania', *Am. J. Agr. Econ.* 96.3 (2014): 813–830. doi:10.1093/ajae/aau015

Carvalho S. and White, H. 'Combining the Quantitative and Qualitative Approaches to Poverty Measurement and Analysis', World Bank Technical Paper 366, Washington, DC: World Bank Publications.

Cohen, J. and Dupas, P. 'Free distribution or cost-sharing? Evidence from a malaria prevention experiment'. No. w14406. National Bureau of Economic Research, 2008.

Easterly, W. *The White Man's Burden: Why the West's efforts to aid the rest have done so much ill and so little good.* New York: Penguin Press, 2006.

Easterly, W. *The Tyranny of Experts: Economists, dictators, and the forgotten rights of the poor*, New York: Basic Books, 2013.

Hanna, R., Duflo, E., and Greenstone, M. 'Up in smoke: The influence of household behavior on the long-run impact of improved cooking stoves', MIT Department of Economics Working Paper No. 12–10, April 16, 2012, available at http://ssrn.com/abstract=2039004 or http://dx.doi.org/10.2139/ssrn.2039004

Hassoun, Nicole. 'Free trade, poverty, and inequality'. *Journal of Moral Philosophy* 8.1 (2011): 5–44.

Kanbur, R. *Q-squared, Combining Qualitative and Quantitative Methods in Poverty Appraisal*, Delhi: Orient Blackswan, 2003.

Krishna, A., *One Illness Away: Why people become poor and how they escape poverty*, Oxford: Oxford University Press, 2008.

Leibbrandt, M. and Levinsohn, J. 'Fifteen years on: Household incomes in South Africa'. No. w16661. National Bureau of Economic Research, 2011.

Miguel, E. and Kremer, M. 'Worms: Identifying impacts on education and health in the presence of treatment externalities'. *Econometrica* 72.1 (2004): 159–217.

Moser, C. *Ordinary Families: Extraordinary lives—assets and poverty reduction in Guayaquil, 1978–2004*, Washington, DC: Brookings Press, 2009.

Norton, A. 'A rough guide to the PPAs', Overseas Development Institute, 2001.

Part II

Duties to Eradicate Global Poverty

Ethics, broadly construed, covers a wide range of topics. Meta-ethics concerns the ultimate nature and justification of morality. Meta-ethicists focus on whether there is right and wrong, good and bad, and how, if at all, these concepts can be known, should be understood, and are best justified. Ethical theories provide substantive accounts of what right and good action are, identifying principles or rules for how agents are morally required or permitted to act. Practical or applied ethics concerns itself with the specific topics of ethical concern, such as abortion, capital punishment, affirmative action, and promise-breaking. In this section, we are going to focus on how different ethical theories provide different answers to the question of what ought to be done regarding global poverty.

A central component of ethics is the study of the nature of the duties that individuals and groups hold to each other, and to non-human animals, the environment, and future generations. Ethical duties can be both general and specific. We have a general duty to make the world a better place or to avoid unnecessary deception, and specific duties, to keep the promise we just made, to obey the stop light we are approaching, or to refrain from stealing the wallet of the person next to us on the bus.

To fully understand any particular ethical duty, it is necessary to address several distinct but interrelated questions. The first is justification—why is it that certain ethical duties exist, and create demands on the conduct of moral agents? The second is scope—to whom do these duties apply, and in which spheres of activity, and whom may be lodged justifiable complaint if they are not discharged? The third is stringency—are these duties strict (or perfect), and therefore must be followed, or are they weaker (or imperfect), and need only be discharged some of the time to some degree or other? A related final consideration is the weight of ethical duties—how important are they as compared to the other competing concerns that enter into our moral thinking and our lives more generally?

In this second part of the book we will consider four views about duties regarding global poverty. The first argues that duties regarding global poverty are best thought of as deriving from a common humanity—the mere fact that some people are suffering and other people are capable of providing assistance is sufficient to justify strong duties of the wealthy to assist those in need. The second view holds that duties of justice generate obligations from the wealthy to poor people, on account of the fact that wealthy individuals and their institutions have committed significant harms, both today and in the past, against poor people. The third view holds that duties to eradicate poverty are grounded in associative relationships—that is, certain enduring and morally significant relations hold between wealthy and poor individuals such that they ground the obligation to combat severe deprivation. And the final view denies that wealthy individuals bear anti-poverty moral duties.

In each chapter, we will examine the main arguments for and against the existence of duties to people living in extreme poverty. Each philosophical view has different implications for the nature, scope, justification, and weight of ethical duties regarding global poverty. And each view is loosely associated with a prominent tradition of thinking in the history of western philosophy. By the end of this part of the book, the reader will understand the main lines of argument for and against the existence of duties of affluent individuals to eradicate or alleviate global poverty, and why one might object to the existence of these duties.

5   Duties of Humanity

On January 12, 2010, an earthquake hit the small Caribbean island of Hispaniola, home to the Dominican Republic and Haiti. Before the earthquake, Haiti was by almost all indicators one of the poorest countries in the world. From child and infant mortality to malnutrition, life expectancy, and income, Haiti was the worst-off country in the Western Hemisphere. At 4:53 p.m., the already precarious livelihoods of many Haitians were shattered by a 7.0 magnitude earthquake whose epicenter was just outside the capital of Port-au-Prince.

The immense suffering caused by the earthquake lasted long after the buildings collapsed. The first phase of suffering was a result of the direct devastation from the earthquake itself. Because most physical structures in Haiti were constructed out of rudimentary materials without the reinforcements that would be able to withstand a major earthquake, somewhere between 100,000 and 200,000 victims were killed in the earthquake. Without adequate infrastructure, or equipment to guide the rescue, people who were injured but not yet deceased had little chance of immediate rescue. In a second phase, which in many ways continues today, widespread suffering befell Haitians because of the after-effects of the earthquake—lacking adequate shelter, employment opportunities, a public health system, and public security, Haitians lived in insecure housing, faced bleak economic prospects, went hungry, and suffered from the spread of disease (including an outbreak of cholera brought by UN troops who were supposed to bring stability to the country) and were at risk of physical and sexual violence. The Haitian government was a paradigmatic extractive institution, lacking capacity to deliver public goods and systems of accountability to ensure genuine responsiveness to democratic demands in rebuilding.[1]

As news of the devastation spread across the world, the call for help went out to individuals, governments, development agencies, and international institutions. Haitians were in dire need. Now was the time to lend a helping hand. Celebrities, politicians, and average citizens held benefit concerts, rallies, and undertook unprecedented fundraising efforts. Phone companies set up systems that allowed people to give quickly and directly to humanitarian relief organizations. The shared sentiment among the international community was clear—we all must chip in to help Haitians in need. In the months and years following the earthquake, upwards of 9 billion USD was raised to help

Haiti 'build back better'. The Red Cross alone received half a billion dollars in donations.

The Case for Duties of Humanity

What moral reasons might justify this call to action? In 1972, Peter Singer published one of the most famous articles in contemporary philosophy. In it, he considered a catastrophe occurring at the time, a famine in what is today Bangladesh. In 'Famine, Affluence, and Morality', Singer provided the following thought experiment. Suppose that you are on your way to work, perhaps to teach a class or attend an important meeting or start the assembly line. On your way, you come across a child drowning in shallow pond. As an adult, you could easily enter the pond and save the child from drowning. You may incur minor costs for doing so: you may need to pay dry cleaning for the clothes you have soiled, or suffer minor repercussions at your workplace for arriving late. What should you do?

Singer, like most of us, believes that you are obviously morally required to save the drowning child. No minimally adequate morality would allow us to blithely oversee the death of an innocent child simply because we did not want to pay a small dry cleaning bill or be a bit late for work. Singer thinks a single moral principle explains our intuition in this case—namely, that if we can prevent something very bad at minimal cost, we are morally required to do it.

Relying on the intuition generated by the shallow pond case, Singer constructs a simple three-premise argument that, if correct, overturns widely shared beliefs about our duties to reduce global poverty.

> First premise: Suffering and death from lack of food, shelter, and medical care are bad.
>
> Second premise: If it is in your power to prevent something bad from happening, without sacrificing anything nearly as important, it is wrong not to do so.
>
> Third premise: By donating to aid agencies, you can prevent suffering and death from lack of food, shelter, and medical care, without sacrificing anything nearly as important.
>
> Conclusion: Therefore, if you do not donate to aid agencies, you are doing something wrong.
>
> (Singer 2009, p. 15)

Singer's argument, in its initial formulation, involves a strong (or very demanding) version and a weak (or less demanding) version. The strong version states that it is morally wrong to fail to save a life up until the point at which you are giving up something of morally comparable value to that which would be saved. To consider how stringent our duties of beneficence would be on this formulation, think about the things that may exist in your life that you could consider giving up in order to relieve global poverty. At what point would something that you have to give up be morally equivalent to saving a person's life? Upon reflection, something of equivalent moral weight will be very significant indeed. In fact, it may require giving away all of your money up until the point at which you are at the point of minimal subsistence, perhaps just at the basic consumption level at which you can continue to earn income to give away to charity.

A weaker version of Singer's position would only require that you donate financial resources to aid agencies up until the point at which you would be giving away something of moral significance. In Singer's most recent work on the topic, he seems to concede that most people will not give up most of their salary for anti-poverty work. So he recommends a sliding scale by which high-income earners can decide what a minimally adequate scheme of donations would require. Singer suggests that individuals earning over 100,000 USD give 5 percent of their income to charity, with incremental increases the higher the annual wages go, up to the point where individuals making over 10,000,000 USD give one-third of their annual income to charity (Singer 2009).

Singer is a proponent of utilitarianism. Utilitarians are committed to the view that moral agents ought to select that action which will, in aggregate, maximize the good. The good is defined as individual utility, which for Singer is measured as either the degree to which someone satisfies their preferences or the degree to which they experience pleasure and avoid pain.[2] Utilitarianism certainly supports the view that we ought to give much of our money to anti-poverty work. There is much greater marginal utility to be gained by the recipient of a given portion of foreign aid than there is marginal utility to be lost by the person who forgoes an expensive meal out or a fancy new shirt to provide that foreign aid. However, while Singer is a utilitarian, he believes that the argument he has provided does not rely on the endorsement of utilitarianism. The duties of humanity (also commonly known as duties of beneficence or duties of assistance) he proposes are meant to be ecumenical, in the sense that they could be (and on his view ought to be) endorsed by non-utilitarians.

Despite the initial simplicity and plausibility of Singer's argument for humanitarian duties to alleviate global poverty, Singer's argument faces a range of objections that threaten his conclusion that wealthy individuals have very demanding obligations to reduce global poverty.

Competing Intuitions and Competing Principles

Singer's argument relies on the intuition that it is morally wrong to fail to save the drowning child. This intuition is quite strong in the case he presents us. But it conflicts with other intuitions we have. When asked, most people do not think they have an obligation, let alone one as stringent as Singer suggests, to give away all of their wealth and a significant portion of their income to poverty alleviation. (Even if they did think this, their behavior indicates otherwise, whereas, with other moral duties, such as the duty to not kill innocent people, most people both think this is a strict moral duty and act in a way that respects the duty.) Of course, Singer believes that the intuition in the case of the drowning child is the one we should trust ... not our views on charitable giving. But why is that? Perhaps our selfishness, or our embrace of consumerism, or our misguided desire to match the living standards of our peers have convinced us that most of the money we earn should remain ours. Yet if we are able to set aside these confounding factors, Singer thinks we should realize that we really do have strict duties of beneficence to prevent suffering around the world.

However, when considering cases that appear similar in all relevant respects to the drowning child, most people generate different intuitions about whether we have a duty to rescue those in need. Gerhard Øverland and Christian Barry ask us to consider a similar example:

> Bob is sitting in his house doing some Internet banking. Unbeknownst to his neighbours (the Smiths) he can see and hear them through an open door in the veranda. He notices that they are discussing the state of their terminally sick child, Jimmy. They need new and expensive treatment to save Jimmy … Clicking over the money would save Jimmy, but most of Bob's savings for retirement would be gone. Bob decides not to click the mouse.
>
> (Barry and Øverland 2009, p. 241)

In this case, most people do not think that Bob acts wrongly if he does not transfer over the money. And this case seems to have all of the same features as Singer's drowning child. So then it appears that there is a clash of intuitions, each apparently widely held and reliably produced.[3] Given these competing and strongly held intuitions, it becomes unclear whether we should endorse the general principle that 'whenever one can prevent suffering from happening without giving up something of comparable moral cost, one should do so'. If the principle cannot account for our conflicting intuitions in competing cases, we may have reason to weaken or modify the principle in a way that still explains our views in the drowning child case but also issues the correct judgments in other cases.

For example, a competing principle might state, 'When one can prevent something bad from happening, one's relationship to the bad activity is clear; others are not well position to provide assistance. If one is guaranteed success in preventing the harm, at minimal cost to oneself, one ought to do it.' This alternative principle requires that a person be clearly related (such as being physically proximate or directly able to provide assistance) to the morally problematic situation, that they be assured of success in preventing the harm, that they be the only agent capable of providing assistance, and that the action be minimally costly to them. This principle still generates a requirement that the child be saved from drowning, but does not require extensive donations to relieve global poverty.[4]

Demandingness and Fair Shares

A different way to reject Singer's argument is to claim that his conclusion is overly demanding. On this view, our moral principles must make only modest demands on us as moral agents. They cannot require that we be moral saints (Wolf 1982), or that we act beyond a standard of what a reasonable person could be expected to do. The demandingness objection is certainly what a lot of people have in mind when they try to reject Singer's argument. Surely it cannot be wrong for me to own a car, or to pay to send my children to a good university, or to occasionally enjoy a nice dinner and a movie with my partner.

Yet it is not clear that over-demandingness is in itself a reason to reject a moral theory or moral principle. Morality requires what morality requires, and in some cases the requirement might be for very great sacrifices indeed. Some individuals, for example, might be morally obligated to give their lives to protect their children from an impending threat. The mere fact that this is an exceedingly demanding moral obligation does not prove that it is not a moral obligation. If it turns out that basic facts about the world or basic features of morality require a great deal of sacrifice from moral agents, then that is what morality requires (Goodin 2009).

One way to respond to apparently overly demanding accounts of morality is to argue that morality must take account of the sorts of agents that human beings are and could be. Even if morality sometimes demands great sacrifices, a general morality that constantly requires extremely demanding duties of beneficence is not one that can reasonably be adopted by normal human beings.

A second objection to Singer's strict duties of beneficence holds that duties of beneficence are imperfect. Imperfect duties are those duties that we are required to discharge some of the time to some extent. But unlike strict duties, which we may never violate, imperfect duties may be overridden by even self-interested, non-moral reasons on at least some occasions. On this view, people are required to assist in the eradication of poverty, but only to a point. Proponents of this weaker view must then specify some threshold at which a moral agent has discharged her moral duties to eradicate poverty.

A third and related approach, argued most prominently by Liam Murphy (2000), defends the idea that in circumstances in which not all individuals discharge their duties of assistance, individuals are only morally required to do as much as they would need to do if everyone did their share. If my neighborhood street is strewn with garbage after a festival, my fair share duty is to help to pick up that amount which, if we all do some garbage collecting, would leave the street clean. I am not morally required to clean the whole street.[5]

An attraction of the fair share view is that it retains a sense of fairness about how much of a sacrifice people should make to solve a problem, given that other people may not comply with what morality requires of them. That is, I am obligated to do my part to solve the problem, but I don't have to take up the slack indefinitely while others fail to discharge their moral obligations.

This requires establishing the threshold at which one has done their fair share. One way to identify this threshold is to figure out what it would take for the problem under consideration to be solved under conditions of full compliance. Suppose, for example, that you determine the amount of financial resources it would take to lift everyone out of global poverty.[6] Then divide this figure by the number of people who are currently in a position to provide assistance. This is how much you are morally required to give.

This response is attractive because it retains a sense of humanitarian obligations to others while defusing worries about over-demandingness. But it presents new problems as well. Given that it is foreseeable that some people will not comply with their duties, why should the moral demands on complying agents be weakened, since doing so will result in avoidable suffering for the potential recipients of their efforts?

Consider the Global Fund to Fight AIDS, Tuberculosis, and Malaria. This fund currently receives donations from a number of countries. It is foreseeable that many other countries will not donate their fair share to the fund to combat these diseases. But morally reflective governments might take this foreseeable non-compliance by the uncharitable as a reason to *increase* their donations. When a collection of agents seeks to achieve some goal, and some of those agents don't hold up their end of the bargain, the moral importance of achieving the goal is unchanged. It may be, therefore, that it is precisely in circumstances of non-compliance with moral duties that we are morally required to do more than our fair share.

Idealization and Reductionism

A different set of objections focus more squarely on Singer's way of framing the problem of global poverty rather than focusing on his conclusions regarding duties of assistance. Singer's argument makes idealizing assumptions about the nature of global poverty that problematically masks some of its most important features.

Prominent among these oversights is the mistaken view that poor people are simply moral patients rather than being moral agents. The child drowning in the pond is helpless, and presumably incapable of exercising agency. But poor people's lives are nothing like this. They struggle daily to put food on the table and to make their lives better. Just like you and I, they make mistakes and poor decisions, but on average they are working hard, coming up with creative solutions to improve the lives of themselves and their families despite the bad misfortune of being born into environments in which material and social deprivation persist.

The history of international development work, as we will discuss in Part III, is littered with projects that have failed because they did not have the consent, or support, of their intended beneficiaries, or were insensitive to the unique social and political context in which deprivation persists. The architects of these failed projects were very much in a Singer-style mindset: 'These people are poor, this project will lift them out of poverty, we must save them!' By failing to take seriously the agency of individuals living in poverty, and being insensitive to the underlying political mechanisms that produce deprivation, Singer mistakenly treats poverty reduction as a mere matter of wealthy saviors assisting people in poverty (Wisor 2011).

People are poor because they are deprived of the individual and collective power to secure their basic rights and unleash their creative potential. A diagnosis of the problem of poverty that is insensitive to the power dynamics and institutional arrangements that produce deprivation is likely to fail to produce an adequate solution. Moreover, it is morally objectionable to talk about and treat people living in poverty as if they are not moral agents in their own right, capable of adapting to and struggling against highly unjust circumstances. Such disrespect itself deserves moral condemnation, even if the disrespect is not intended and is part of broader efforts to provide assistance.

Poverty Is No Pond

Following the earthquake in Haiti with which we started this chapter, there were unanimous pledges to help the Haitian people rebuild. The motto was to build back better, with Haitians at the center of the rebuilding effort. Four years on (at the time of writing), we are able to assess how this aid effort was undertaken. Unfortunately, providing anti-poverty assistance in Haiti is much more difficult than saving a drowning child.

While some of the donations to rebuild Haiti have done some good, it is extremely difficult to say that the aid effort was successful in its pledge to 'build back better'. The government of Haiti received less than 1 percent of immediate humanitarian relief and somewhere between 15 percent and 20 percent of longer term relief funds. While the government is extractive and corrupt, it is extremely difficult to see how institutional improvement can occur, and a government can function at all, if an aid program is run almost entirely outside of its control.

The Red Cross raised over a half a billion dollars to provide assistance in Haiti, more than any other charity. In one project investigated by ProPublica, they claimed to have built 130,000 homes in a neighbourhood outside Port-au-Prince, but the number of permanent homes that had been constructed was six (Elliot and Sullivan 2015). The Red Cross has saved millions lives throughout its history. Why did it struggle in Haiti? The reasons for their failures are familiar to critics of foreign assistance: they relied heavily on employees who did not speak the local language, understand the domestic context, or respect the intended beneficiaries of their projects. Constraints to development prior to the earthquake, such as an inadequate system protecting and regulating property rights in land, made it difficult to proceed with housing projects. And they lacked local partnerships and political buy-in that would allow for successful operations on the ground.

As Leif Wenar (2011) argues, poverty is no pond. International development efforts face a range of challenges that make it difficult to successfully promote poverty reduction. It is difficult to coordinate the many different actors, often with conflicting and overlapping agendas, involved in aid provision; it is difficult to enlist local participation in support of projects while often aiming to change local practices; it is difficult to prevent resources from being diverted; aid may have deleterious economic effects, including freeing up government resources for more harmful activities like arms purchases while also undermining local economies; aid projects may overlap, thereby undermining the effectiveness of each individual project; aid may weaken demand for accountable governance; and aid may wrongly impose certain external values to the detriment of locally valued customs.

Thus, it is no surprise that, according to one of the most careful analysts of relief efforts in Haiti, today,

> Several thousand people still live in tents that were supposed to be temporary housing for families displaced in January 2010. Haiti remains the 'Republic of NGOs.' Five years and $9 billion later, Port-au-Prince does not have decent roads, clean water, or a reliable supply of electricity.
>
> (Ramachandran 2015)

A Better Way for Duties of Humanity?

This chapter has focused prominently on Peter Singer's duties of humanity, and sounded a decidedly pessimistic note about his approach. But an alternative vision of duties of humanity is available that might offer a more promising way of thinking about duties of assistance to reduce global poverty.

People living in poverty, by virtue of being human beings, having the capacity to suffer and sharing a fundamental interest in living a full, dignified life, deserve support from their fellow human beings. They are moral agents that are able to choose the life they want to lead among a set of acceptable options, and we all have duties to each other which cross national boundaries. One of those duties is to provide assistance when we can. Whether or not one has any association with one's fellow humans who are living in poverty, we should help them to secure their basic human needs. This duty may not necessarily be discharged through donations to charity (though it may be) and it need not be insensitive to the social and political contexts in which poverty is produced. Based on a common humanity and nothing more, affluent people have duties to reduce the suffering associated with material deprivation, but these duties may involve derivative duties that ensure such efforts do not disrespect or harm their intended beneficiaries, and take seriously the agency of people living in poverty. This view may not convince people who deny such duties exist, but it is a more attractive formulation of the view that humanity has duties, while guarding against the worst abuses of the 'savior' mentality that can come to influence charitable giving.

Chapter Summary

Duties of humanity emphasize a basic fact of our world: some people have massive needs and others have the capacity to help. This brute fact certainly seems to justify some moral duties to provide assistance. Whether these moral demands require maximizing one's beneficence is more controversial. Importantly, even if one has the capacity to help, they must understand poor people as active agents who are constantly struggling to improve their own lives, and not passive recipients of charity. And they must recognize, as we will explore in future chapters, that charitable giving is difficult and can lead to harm if not done with great care.

Questions for Discussion

1   Several years ago, two community police officers were criminally charged for failing to save a child drowning in a pond. Is there any reason that we are not morally required to save the drowning child?

2   How much sacrifice is morally required of an innocent bystander to assist someone else in need? Is this related to the question of how much financial support one should provide to anti-poverty organizations?

3 If people are not psychologically inclined to endorse moral principles that are very strict or demanding, does this provide any reason to weaken those principles for wider public acceptance?
4 There are many problems that are international in nature. If you choose to devote your time and money to addressing these problems, are you required to select that international problem where you could prevent the most harm from happening?

Notes

1 As we will see later in the chapter, the origins of the extractive nature of the Haitian government had historical and international roots. For a good review of Haiti and the earthquake, see Farmer (2011).
2 Singer appears to have changed his views over the years, shifting from being a preference-satisfaction utilitarian to having more sympathy for hedonic utilitarianism.
3 Barry and Øverland offer a competing principle that aims to take account of our intuitions in both cases. Namely, that in general individuals do not need to take on large costs to prevent bad things from happening, but that they may have such duties in special circumstances, and in those circumstances may reasonably demand subsequent compensation for the costs they take on (Barry and Øverland 2009, p. 242).
4 I do not claim that this is the right principle to endorse. I simply note here that many alternative principles may justify the conclusion that one ought to save the drowning child, while not requiring that one give away their money to global poverty.
5 There are, of course, different ways of formulating fair shares. On one formulation, everyone should give an equal amount. On another formulation, they should give different amounts based on differential capacity to give.
6 Economists sometimes undertake related exercises. See, for example, Segal 2011.

Suggested Reading

Cullity, G. *The Moral Demands of Affluence*, Oxford: Oxford University Press, 2004.
Lichtenberg, J. *Distant Strangers: Ethics, psychology, and global poverty*, Cambridge: Cambridge University Press, 2014.
MacFarquhar, L. *Strangers Drowning: Grappling with impossible idealism, drastic choices, and the overpowering urge to help*, New York: Penguin, 2015.

References

Barry, C. and Øverland, G. 'Responding to global poverty', *Journal of Bioethical Inquiry* 6.2 (2009): 239–247.
Elliot, J. and Sullivan, L. 'How the Red Cross raised half a billion dollars for Haiti and built six homes', *ProPublica*, June 3, 2015, available at www.propublica.org/article/how-the-red-cross-raised-half-a-billion-dollars-for-haiti-and-built-6-homes
Farmer, P. *Haiti After the Earthquake*, New York: Public Affairs, 2011.

Goodin, R. 'Demandingness as a virtue', *The Journal of Ethics* 13.1 (2009): 1–13.

Murphy, L. *Moral Demands in Nonideal Theory*, Oxford: Oxford University Press, 2000.

Ramachandran, V. 'Haiti: five years after the quake, the band plays on', Center for Global Development Blog, January 1, 2015, available at www.cgdev.org/blog/haiti-five-years-after-quake-band-plays

Segal, P. 'Resource rents, redistribution, and halving global poverty: The resource dividend', *World Development* 39.4 (2011): 475–489.

Singer, P. 'Famine, affluence, and morality', *Philosophy and Public Affairs* 1.3 (1972): 229–243.

Singer, P. *The Life You Can Save*, New York: Random House, 2009.

Wenar, L. 'Poverty is no pond: Challenges for the affluent', in *Giving Well: The ethics of philanthropy*, Oxford: Oxford University Press, 2011.

Wisor, S. 'Against shallow ponds: An argument against Singer's approach to global poverty', *Journal of Global Ethics* 7.1 (2011): 19–32.

Wolf, S. 'Moral saints', *The Journal of Philosophy* (1982): 419–439.

6 Duties of Justice

Equatorial Guinea is at once one of the wealthiest and poorest countries in the world. It is one of the wealthiest, in that it has a per capita GDP that can rival countries like Norway and Sweden, depending on the price of oil. It is one of the poorest, in that three-quarters of the population lives below the national poverty line. Equatorial Guinea has been ruled by Teodoro Obiang since 1979. Obiang is as ruthless and oppressive as dictators come. It is a testament to his successful political oppression that he is the longest ruling head of state in Africa.

His power comes from his wealth, and his wealth is generated from oil revenues. He controls the oil reserves in Equatorial Guinea, which are developed by western oil companies including Exxon and Marathon Oil, freely traded on international markets, and exported for consumption across the globe. The vast wealth of Obiang and his family is stored in overseas bank accounts and invested in international property. And he is treated as a diplomatic equal in international circles, has access to a full range of international privileges, including international financial institutions, and the ability to sell natural resources on the open market. Equatorial Guineans remain poor because Equatorial Guinea is ruled by a ruthless dictator. But that ruthless dictator is supported by an international system that permits powerful elites to take and hold power, and to use that power to profit from natural resources that belong to the people.

Uruguay is a middle-income country in South America, with a respectable per capita income of 16,000 USD, with 11 percent of the country living below the poverty line of about 9 USD per day, and life expectancy of 77 years.[1] It has living standards far better than Equatorial Guinea, but still has further to go in extending the length and improving the quality of life for its residents. One wise step that any government can take to extend life expectancy is to implement public policies that reduce the use of tobacco. These measures have dramatically reduced tobacco consumption when implemented in high-income countries.

In 2006, under President Tabaré Vázquez, a former oncologist, Uruguay sought to pursue anti-smoking legislation, including prohibiting smoking in enclosed public places, raising taxes, restricting advertising and marketing, and more, steps taken by many high-income countries. Philip Morris, a tobacco company whose annual revenues exceed the GDP of Uruguay, is suing Uruguay at the World Bank's International Centre for the Settlement of Investment Disputes.

They are suing on the grounds that health warnings on tobacco products limit their ability to brand these products, interfering with the rights of investors under a bilateral trade agreement with Switzerland. Should this case succeed, a number of developing countries that are aiming to reduce tobacco consumption may see their anti-tobacco policies under external pressure (NPR 2014).

These are but two of a wide range of cases in which the structure of international institutions and international relations shape the prospects for development and poverty eradication in low- and middle-income countries. International institutions regulate (or fail to regulate) the globalization of trade, finance, intellectual property regimes, arms sales, pollution, migration, and more. International institutions can play an important role in improving the prospects of the worse off, but too often they undermine the best efforts of people living in poverty to live better, longer, more prosperous lives.

These features of the international system have led to the second big wave in thinking about the ethics of global poverty. A number of scholars of ethics and international affairs have turned their attention away from seemingly endless debates surrounding the individual duty to alleviate global poverty through charitable donations, and toward the political, economic, and social structures that shape individual life chances, and play a large role in determining the degree to which poverty continues to persist today. In particular, they have been concerned with the degree to which powerful and wealthy countries and corporations shape national policies and international institutions, and how those institutional arrangements can sometimes harm people living in poverty.

The Case for Duties of Justice

For Thomas Pogge, the most important feature of current economic and social relations that grounds transnational duties to alleviate global poverty is the existence of a global institutional order which negatively impacts the prospects for poverty alleviation. In his view, there are two ways in which the global institutional order harms individuals (Pogge 2010, p. 20). Indirectly, it shapes national institutions in a way that it permits and protects autocratic and oppressive governments, and incentivizes civil conflict and coups by allowing those who take power to exploit resources and borrow money on international markets while selling them arms and allowing them to sign treaties. Directly, the global institutional order affects people living in poverty by setting rules which affect their access to needed medicines, the volatility of food prices, their ability to sell their produce on lucrative international markets, and more.

But what do global institutional arrangements have to do with individual moral duties? On the institutionalist view, wealthy people do not bear duties of assistance to people living in poverty only out of some basic charitable duties of humanity. Rather, it is because well-off individuals support and uphold institutional arrangements and participate in social practices that impede the prospects of poverty eradication that well-off individuals bear duties of justice to those who are significantly deprived.[2]

Institutionalists note that wealthy individuals are, unlike the person who happens to be walking by the pond in which the child is at risk, deeply embedded in economic, political, and social institutions that are collectively shaped by coordinated joint action, and these institutions foreseeably and avoidably produce human rights deficits and human poverty. For these thinkers, individual obligations to relieve global poverty are not best grounded in duties of humanity, but are better thought of as duties of justice.

Because Pogge sees citizens of high-income countries as imposing harmful institutional arrangements on poor people, he has a much harsher moral assessment of wealthy individuals than most of us currently hold. He argues that individuals in wealthy countries have stringent duties to eradicate global poverty, and are violating this stringent duty. He suggests that most people in wealthy countries are living a lie. They believe that they are morally innocent with regard to the harms that befall people in foreign countries, and that any steps that they take to support those people are purely supererogatory. But this view is mistaken. The truth is that wealthy individuals are collectively contributing to a wide range of harms that are committed against poor people. He writes,

> My account is not flattering: the global economic regime that our countries designed and impose kills more efficiently than the Nazi extermination camps; the daily suffering from poverty and disease greatly exceeds that caused by World War II in its darkest years. World poverty is actively perpetuated by our governments, and knowingly so. We citizens, too, have enough information to know what is going on, or at least to find out easily, if we care.
>
> (Pogge 2010, p. 2)

On his view, the existence of global poverty, and its causal connection to international institutions, is what generates demanding obligations for well-off individuals to people living in poverty.

The argument that we have duties of justice to reduce global poverty is more complex than Singer's argument for duties of humanity, but we can reduce it to a small number of premises. Individuals have a stringent duty to not seriously harm innocent individuals. The vast majority of people who are poor globally have not done anything sufficiently wrong to make them liable to serious harm. Existing institutions are arranged so that they produce foreseeable and avoidable shortfalls in basic human rights and a minimally decent standard of living. Alternative institutional arrangements could be established, at little cost, that would produce far less global poverty and far fewer human rights violations. Given that individuals in well-off societies contribute to, uphold, and often benefit from these institutional arrangements, those individuals have strict duties to avoid harming people living in poverty. This duty can be discharged either through working to change existing institutional arrangements, or by making compensatory contributions to anti-poverty organizations.

The argument that well-off individuals are violating strict duties of justice in upholding institutional arrangements relies on both empirical and normative premises. The argument must establish two major claims—that institutional arrangements harm people currently living in poverty, and that wealthy individuals bear responsibility for these institutionally mediated harms.

What must one show in order to establish that current institutional arrangements harm people living in poverty, and that these arrangements create anti-poverty obligations? Pogge places several constraints on his account of harm to attempt to show that such arrangements are harmful. First, it has to be the case that alternative arrangements are available which would be morally preferable to existing arrangements. Philosophers generally hold that ought implies can—if there is something we morally ought to do, it has to be the case that we actually could do that thing. If, for example, it simply would not be possible to establish better international institutions because it is politically impossible or there are not better alterative arrangements, then we would not have this duty. This is sometimes known as the 'Feasible Alternatives Thesis' (Barry and Øverland 2012). Second, it has to be the case that current institutional arrangements are not merely suboptimal, but that they seriously harm people and make them significantly worse off. In the law, it is common that *de minimis* harms do not count as not harmful at all. A similar principle might inform our assessment of global institutional arrangements. If they simply made a small difference at the margins, this would not be sufficient to ground duties of justice. But, on Pogge's account, the structure of international institutional arrangements produces massive deficits in human rights and living standards. Third, it has to be the case that these shortfalls are foreseeable. We only bear moral responsibility for them in so far as we can reasonably anticipate, or can be reasonably expected to anticipate, that they will result from our activities.

What must one show to establish that individuals bear responsibility for the harms their institutions commit? This is a more general philosophical problem regarding the relationship between individuals and collectives. In favor of the view that individuals bear responsibility for institutional harms, one can marshal several pieces of evidence that individuals provide support to these institutions, and could reform the institutions if they chose to. Pogge writes,

> As citizens with voting rights and the rights of freedom of speech, press and peaceful assembly, we bear ultimate political responsibility for what our country does in our name; and as workers and taxpayers we constitute and contribute the economic and military strength that enables our government to play an important role in the design and imposition of supranational rules and regimes. Given the great and avoidable harms these rules and regimes foreseeably inflict on the world's poor, we collaboratively violate their human rights on a massive scale. We can end our role in this injustice either by successfully pressuring our government to be supportive of an institutional realization of human rights or by continuously compensating for our share of the harm we collectively cause through private efforts such as donations to effective NGOs.
>
> (Pogge 2014, p. 79)

For proponents of duties of justice, there is no denying that individuals bear responsibility for the institutions that represent them. If this were not true, we would face an apparent paradox, where large collectives can do a great deal of harm, but no specific moral agents bear responsibility for these harms.

Objections to Duties of Justice

Like the argument for duties of humanity, the argument for anti-poverty duties of justice is meant to rely on ecumenical premises—the conclusion is meant to be reachable from a diverse range of moral belief systems and ethical theories. The argument relies on the widely held view that it is wrong to unnecessarily inflict harm upon individuals who have not done anything to make themselves liable to harm. Nonetheless, many scholars object to this view, some preferring to focus on duties of humanity, and others simply denying stringent anti-poverty duties of justice.

Deny Harmful Relationships

One way to object to the view that wealthy individuals have duties of justice to reduce global poverty is to deny that the harming relationship exists between wealthy individuals and people living in poverty. In Pogge's formulation, wealthy countries have harmed poor people because they have structured global institutional arrangements in ways that produce foreseeable and avoidable human rights deficits and material poverty. But some commentators argue that even if better, feasible alternatives are available, the present global institutional order does not harm poor people in the relevant sense of that word. While they may be less than perfect, these critics deny that global institutions are sufficiently harmful to ground anti-poverty duties of justice.

Furthermore, one can argue that the notion of harm used in arguing for duties of justice may be different than the ordinary meaning of that term. For example, the spread of international trade is generally believed to have been responsible for improving welfare and reducing global poverty. It may also indirectly contribute to improved protection of civil and political rights. While it is almost unanimously agreed among economists of international trade that the existing trade regime is suboptimal (for example, by permitting wealthy countries to maintain harmful subsidies and trade barriers, and for providing excessive protection to patents over needed medicines), the current regime of international trade is arguably the most beneficial the world has ever known. Never has the exchange of goods, services, and ideas been easier than in present day, and never before has international trade been so thoroughly regulated by an international rule of law (in contrast to centuries past, where international trade was regulated through the use of military force). How, then, can it be said that current institutional arrangements governing international trade are harmful?

The proponent of the view that citizens in high-income countries are violating duties of justice may respond that the morally relevant counterfactual is not how bad institutional arrangements could be or have been in the past, but rather how well they could be designed so as to avoid foreseeable material deprivation and human rights abuses. The sub-optimality of current international arrangements is not insignificant from the perspective of the billions of people who could greatly benefit from easily imposed alternative institutional arrangements that would allow them to more easily meet basic needs for food, shelter, water, and health care. This suboptimality does not involve a simple failure to maximize well-being for humanity. It involves many millions of deaths every year, deaths that could be prevented without imposing anything close to equivalent costs on the developed world.

Assert Historical or Local Harm

Another objection argues that many of the problems afflicting low-income countries are internal to those countries, and not primarily explained by external actors or the global institutional order (Cohen 2010). For example, Sudan has been beset by civil wars since independence, and the newly created South Sudan (which seceded from Sudan after suffering for decades at the hands of the government of Sudan) itself descended into civil war within 3 years of independence. These wars are not waged by the countries who Pogge and others argue bear duties of justice to people living in poverty. Critics see local corruption, harmful traditional social practices, ethnic strife, and other impediments to social progress as primary deterrents to poverty reduction that are not a result of global institutional rules (Sonderholm 2012). In so far as external actors were primarily responsible for these harms, those actions lay in the distant past, during the period of colonization. The colonizers most responsible for historical harm may no longer be in existence, or poorly positioned to provide rectification. (The Dutch, Belgians, and Spanish may have been global powers in their day, but today have much less influence over international affairs.)

There are at least two ways for the defender of duties of justice to respond to these criticisms. First, it may be that a common colonial history does create contemporary moral obligations. As we saw in Chapter 2, institutional development plays a large role in determining whether or not a country is able to prosper. A country can be inhibited from developing high-quality, inclusive institutions through the colonization of its institutions or from violent interference in domestic affairs. Colonization nearly always involves the establishment of extractive institutions. Colonialism was specifically intended to ensure that the colonized population did not exercise effective control over domestic resources, especially labor and natural resources. In rare cases, former colonizers have even conceded a legal right to reparations for populations harmed by colonization. For example, the British government agreed to make reparative payments to 5,000 Kenyans tortured during the British response to the anti-colonial Mau Mau uprising. The moral debt from these past harms may accrue to contemporary citizens in the former colonial powers to the citizens in the former colonies.[3]

Second, even if many causes of contemporary poverty are local (such as corruption, or poor natural endowments, or being landlocked, or having bad neighbors), the proponent of duties of justice need not show that global institutional arrangements are the primary cause of global poverty. They merely need to show that these arrangements make a significant contribution to global poverty. It may be that local social practices or petty corruption exacerbate global poverty. But this does not change the fact that people would be healthier if they had access to needed medicines (access which is prevented by international trade rules) or wealthier if they were not disadvantaged by trade tariffs. Global institutional arrangements simply need to make a contribution to slowing poverty reduction in order to ground anti-poverty duties of justice.

Deny Individual Responsibility

A second class of objections to anti-poverty duties of justice affirms that governments and corporations have committed harms internationally, but denies that individual citizens who are represented by these institutions bear moral responsibility for those harms (Steinhoff 2012).

Consider several of the standard examples that are used to demonstrate that the existing international order harms people living in poverty. The current intellectual property regime sometimes allows drug companies to prevent the sale of generic versions of their lifesaving drugs in poor countries. This makes it such that both (a) lifesaving drugs which currently are in production are sold at prices which make it unaffordable for people who need them to save their lives, and (b) that new drugs which could treat currently neglected diseases are not developed because it would not be profitable to do so. Similarly, the current international market in natural resources allows corrupt, autocratic, and war-making governments to sell natural resources to benefit themselves rather than their citizens, often depriving those citizens of much needed revenue that could pay for education programs, public health initiatives, and social protection.

But well-meaning, wealthy individuals might reasonably object that they have very little influence over the international trade negotiations that protect the intellectual property of pharmaceutical companies or regulate the trade in natural resources. When many people learn that they are alleged to be complicit in harming poor people abroad, they retort, 'I have never done any such thing! Sure, governments may create harmful trade rules, or oil companies may despoil local environments or fund local militias, but that is them, not me. I didn't vote for those trade rules or choose to buy oil from that country'.

The objection is strengthened when the individual points out that even if they stopped using fossil fuels altogether, or somehow managed to avoid buying it from human rights violating countries, this would have no impact whatsoever on autocratic rulers or international trade rules. This view, which concedes that global institutional arrangements are harmful but denies individual duties that arise from those arrangements, would have the following implication, which appears to be a sort of paradox: states, corporations, and international institutions that have committed harm do have duties of rectification to those who have been harmed, but no individual members of those institutions have any such duties.

Proponents of duties of justice view this response as unpersuasive. As Pogge argues,

> citizens may be implicated when institutions they uphold foreseeably pro-
> duce an avoidable human-rights deficit on a regular basis. For example,
> through their uncompensated support of the grievously unjust Nazi regime,
> many German officials and citizens facilitated the human-rights deficits this
> regime gave rise to—thereby participating in a collective crime and violat-
> ing the human rights of its victims, even if they never personally tortured or
> killed or harmed anyone directly.
>
> (Pogge 2010, p. 29)

So too, he argues, may citizens and officials in high-income societies today be held morally responsible for the policies of the governments and institutions they support. Even if one finds it very difficult to support political reform, there are other avenues through which they can either withdraw support from these institutions or provide compensation and rectification to those who are harmed by current injustice.

Emphasize the Benefits of Global Institutional Arrangements

Most global institutions both create some harm for some individuals and create significant benefits for other individuals. For example, the international trade regime, governed by bilateral and regional trade agreements and the World Trade Organization, confers both benefits and burdens on individuals living in poverty. Lower barriers to trade as a result of increased international cooperation have lowered the price of consumer goods, allowed consumption to rise, and promoted export-led growth. Furthermore, states which have joined the international trade regime appear to have increased their respect for human rights as a result (Hafner-Burton 2009). Similarly, while the burning of fossil fuels contributes to climate change and the resource curse, there are enormous benefits that have arisen from the ability to have access to reliable, cheap sources of energy. In particular, gaining access to energy has been essential for the growth necessary to reduce extreme poverty. Given the benefits of various global institutional arrangements that govern trade and energy, one could argue that these benefits are sufficient to outweigh problematic aspects of globalization. On this view, while current insti-tutional arrangements are far from perfect, they are better than any in the history of humanity, and confer many benefits on low-income individuals.

This defense of current institutions on the grounds that they create signifi-cant benefits in comparison to institutions of the past faces an obvious response. Suppose that a citizen of the Jim Crow American South wanted to argue in favor of institutions of segregated housing and education, denied civil and political rights to black Americans, and terrorist violence against black communities both by the police and by sanctioned groups like the Ku Klux Clan. That citizen might argue that while institutional arrangements in the Jim Crow South were far from perfect, they were far better than the preceding institutional arrangement. This is an absurd view. Recognizing the improvements in institutional arrangements does not serve as a defense of those aspects of prevailing institutions that continue to visit widespread human rights violations and material deprivation on people who have done nothing to be liable to such harm (see Pogge 2010). Unless the person who is defending the benefits of current global institutions can show that the shortfalls of those institutions are somehow necessary for the benefits to exist, or that the people harmed by the global institutional arrangements are somehow liable to that harm, this kind of objection is likely to fail.

Chapter Summary

Many philosophers hold that citizens of affluent states have responsibilities to people living in deprivation abroad, but not as a matter of kindness or generosity. Rather, they believe that duties of justice are owed to these individuals as a result of the harm wealthy individuals cause through their governments, corporations, and international institutions. As a matter of interpersonal morality, it is widely accepted that one has duties not to harm and to make rectification or compensation to those who have been harmed. Extending this principle to international, institutionally mediated relationships may justify the existence of anti-poverty duties. But establishing this claim requires showing that individuals can bear moral responsibility for the harms of the institutions that represent them, and that feasible alternative arrangements can be put in place that would be much better for people living in global poverty.

Questions for Discussion

1 Think of the country in which you live, and that country's colonial history. Do you think that you bear moral duties to present-day residents of former colonies (or, conversely, if you live in a formerly colonized country, do you think residents of former colonial powers owe you more stringent moral duties)? Or does the passage of time remove any responsibility for historical harm?

2 Governments to whom we pay taxes and corporations we support with our purchases sometimes harm people abroad. Does this harm create moral duties for you as a taxpayer or consumer?

3 If you learn that a corporation that you support harms people abroad, what do you think you ought to do?

Notes

1 This data is all from World Development Indicators, available at http://data.worldbank.org/country/uruguay (accessed December 9, 2015).

2 Proponents of the view that global responsibilities are best framed as duties of justice may concede that we also have duties of humanity. But they will tend to emphasize that our duties of justice take moral priority over our duties of humanity.

3   Such a claim requires quite a bit more philosophical support. First, it must be shown that collectives can bear moral responsibility. Second, it must be shown that collective moral responsibility can persist over time even as the makeup of that collective changes. Third, it must be shown that former colonies and the formerly colonized are the kinds of collectives that share such a moral relationship over time. Justifications for such duties may merely rest on the fact that one group inherits the moral debts of those who harmed others in that past, or they may rest on the fact that present levels of welfare are much lower than they would be had the historical harm not occurred, or they may rest on the fact that historical benefits from colonization continue to persist in the formerly colonizing countries. It is beyond the scope of this book to evaluate any of these claims in depth.

Suggested Reading

Barry, C. 'Applying the contribution principle', *Metaphilosophy* 36 (2005): 210–227.

Farmer, P. *The Uses of Haiti*, Monroe, ME: Common Courage Press, 1994.

Miller, R. *Globalizing Justice: The ethics of poverty and power*, Oxford: Oxford University Press, 2010.

Wrong, M. *I Didn't Do It for You: How the world used and abused a small African nation*, London: Harper Perennial, 2005.

References

Barry, Christian, and Øverland, Gerhard. 'The Feasible Alternatives Thesis kicking away the livelihoods of the global poor', *Politics, Philosophy & Economics* 11.1 (2012): 97–119.

Cohen, J. 'Philosophy, Social Science, Global Justice,' in *Thomas Pogge and His Critics*, ed. Alison Jaggar, Cambridge: Polity, 2010, 18–44.

Hafner-Burton, E. *Forced to Be Good: Why trade agreements boost human rights*, Ithaca, NY: Cornell University Press, 2009.

NPR, National Public Radio. 'Philip Morris sues Uruguay over graphic cigarette packaging', Morning Edition, September 15, 2014.

Pogge, T. *Politics as Usual: What lies behind the pro-poor approach*, Cambridge: Polity, 2010.

Pogge, T. 'Are we not violating the rights of the poor? A response to four critics', *Yale Human Rights and Development Journal* 17.3 (2014): 74–87.

Sonderholm, J. 'Thomas Pogge on global justice and world poverty: A review essay', *Analytic Philosophy* 53.4 (2012): 366–391.

Steinhoff, U. 'Why we are not harming the global poor', *Public Reason* 4.1–2 (2012): 119–138.

7 Associative Duties

The preceding chapters explored the two most prominent accounts of why affluent people have duties to eradicate poverty. In this chapter we consider a third. Associative duties are those duties that arise out of the relationships we inhabit. On the associative view, it is not the mere fact that some people are suffering and others have the capacity to assist them that grounds duties to eradicate global poverty, nor is it the fact that at least some poverty has been caused by wealthy individuals and institutions. Rather, moral duties to alleviate poverty arise from the persistent political and economic interactions which have enduring effects on the life chances of individuals at risk of living in poverty. In this chapter we will consider different kinds of associations that might ground duties to eradicate global poverty, and consider what practical impact taking such duties seriously might have on the actions of individuals and institutions that undertake to reduce global poverty.

Associative Duties

Associative duties are a class of moral duties that are special, rather than general. They do not apply to all people in all places. Rather they only arise when the right kind of relationship exists between the duty bearer and the claim bearer. That is, individual or institutional agents are only thought to have associative duties in unique circumstances. These duties are commonly understood to be agent-relative, meaning that the reasons which justify the duties involve reference to the specific moral agent involved, in contrast to the impartial duties which are owed to all persons irrespective of the particular circumstances or relations they inhabit.

Associative duties are a familiar part of ordinary morality. There are general duties of justice—for example, to not harm people who have not done anything to be liable to harm, or to tell the truth to people who one has no overriding reason to be dishonest with. There are general duties of beneficence—to provide aid, for example, to an accident victim if one is near to that accident, regardless of what relationship one has to the victim. And then there are the special duties that arise out of the relationships we have with other people. Parents have special duties toward their children, romantic partners to each other, employees to their employers, and promise makers to their promisees. These duties would not hold if the right kind of relation did not exist between both parties.

Associative duties can arise out of special, meaningful, and important relationships, but need not arise only out of positive relationships. Negative relationships too may generate associative duties. A criminal may bear special duties to his victim—for example, after he has been rehabilitated, he may have restorative duties to help the victim recover. Or a soldier who harms innocent civilians in battle may have special duties to see that those specific civilians are cared for, well beyond his general duty to protect civilians.

Associative Duties and Global Poverty

Some associative duties arise in circumstances in which institutions that shape cooperation and coercion are in place. Iris Marion Young argues for a 'social connection' model of responsibility, whereby

> individuals bear responsibility for structural injustice because they contribute by their actions to the processes that produce unjust outcomes. Our responsibility derives from belonging with others in a system of interdependent processes of cooperation and competition through which we seek benefits and aim to realize projects. Within these processes, each of us expects justice towards ourselves, and others can legitimately make claims of justice on us.
>
> (Young 2011, p. 105)[1]

Young identifies five virtues of the social connection model of global responsibility. First, it does not focus on the specific wrongdoing of individuals. It does not isolate individual guilty agents. Second, it requires judging background conditions that give rise to injustice, rather than specific actions. Third, it is more forward looking than backward looking. Rather than emphasizing causal mechanisms that have produced harms in the past, the social connection model aims to emphasize processes for social change in the future. Fourth, it emphasizes shared responsibility for injustices which are produced. And finally, the duties which arise from the social connection model of responsibility can only be discharged through collective action (Young 2011, pp. 104–112).

Here Young diverges from proponents of duties of justice, in that her focus is not on establishing clear lines of causal responsibility and liability for harms done, but rather on the fact that shared commercial and political relationships generate shared, if differential, responsibilities for addressing injustice. Ideally, for Young, associative duties will be discharged through joint political action to reform the structures that generate vulnerabilities to poverty and other injustices.

For those individuals who deny both that duties of humanity and that duties of justice ground obligations of the affluent to help to eradicate global poverty, associative duties offer a third, independent ground on which the existence of such duties may be justified. For those who are persuaded that such duties already exist, the presence of associative duties may nonetheless affect both the distribution of their efforts to alleviate deprivation and the way in which those duties should be discharged. In this chapter we will consider three different ways that associative duties are potentially relevant to global poverty. These different accounts each have implications for who bears associative duties and how they ought to be discharged.

Former Colonies and Their Former Colonizers

The United Kingdom maintains a heightened diplomatic presence and disproportionately large foreign aid programs in Kenya. Why should British taxpayers disproportionately direct resources to Kenya and its people? Arguably, the historical relationship between the former colonizer and the formerly colonized justifies stronger British anti-poverty duties to Kenyans.

The current level of human welfare in any given country and the quality of political institutions that country has are profoundly shaped by whether and how they were colonized. Consider the case of the colonization of Kenya. Kenya was viewed as a settler colony by the British. Unlike other colonies, in which the British mainly established a local presence to control the extraction of natural resources, Kenya was home to many British settlers who, through actual or threatened violence, displaced local populations and established agricultural communities in their stead. Under the direction of Winston Churchill, the British forced 150,000 people, predominantly from the Kikuyu tribe, into internment camps for their opposition to British policies which had displaced them from their lands. In the camps, torture was widely used (Elkins 2010). In the post-colonial period, the British government has continued to exert considerable influence in the country, though this has tended to be through diplomacy and foreign aid (Wrong 2009). Does the long history (generally very harmful though more beneficial in recent times) shared between these two countries create associative reasons for British support for anti-poverty programs in Kenya?

What might be said in favor of such a view? One appeal would rely on the inheritance of moral debts. This would not be an associative reason, but rather a duty of justice, discussed in the previous chapter. A second kind of reason might underlie associative duties based on formal colonization. It is not the inheritance of past debts, but the sharing of common languages, commercial structures, cultural traditions, and transnational familial relationships that justifies greater anti-poverty assistance from former colonizers to the formerly colonized. On this view, it is not the enduring harm from British colonialism which justifies stronger anti-poverty duties than would otherwise exist. It is the fact that many enduring relationships exist today between the two countries. Kenyan students often travel to study in British universities, (British) English is one of the official languages in the country, there are high levels of international trade between the two countries, Kenya is a member of the Commonwealth of Nations, and many British citizens continue to reside in Kenya. Perhaps this is why greater anti-poverty duties are held by Britons to Kenyans.[2]

But associative duties arising from the relationships of the former colonies and their former colonizers face several objections. For one thing, not all former colonizers remain powerful countries capable of supporting strong anti-poverty programming. Spanish and Portugese colonization had profound impacts on the way many states developed, but the Spanish and Portugese economies are not the titans they once were. They do not and feasibly cannot confer much in the way of foreign assistance, nor market access, that would be particularly beneficial to developing countries. Similarly, the Dutch colonized large parts of the world, but today are a smaller player in global affairs. To the countries that were colonized by once mighty but now fallen empires, using associative reasons to justify anti-poverty assistance seems to lead to a maldistribution of anti-poverty resources.

Furthermore, some of most invasive and enduring interventions abroad were undertaken by countries that are today illiberal regimes. The Soviet Union, now Russia, had a massive influence on a range of countries abroad (though none were formally colonized). But it is no surprise that low-income countries for the most part are not inviting Russian foreign assistance programs into their countries (though they often are willing to purchase Russian arms).[3]

Worse yet, in some cases former colonizers remain problematically involved, some would say unjustifiably so, in their former colonies. They are alleged to have national interests which at the very least are inconsistent with the national interests of the formerly colonized, and at worst seek to deliberately undermine domestic progress. In the strongest form of this critique, neo-colonialism has simply replaced colonialism, and commercial ties between domestic elites and international firms have simply replaced the old formal institutions that extracted resources from the colonies. While this is a stronger critique than I am inclined to endorse, one can understand the view of Rwandans who oppose aid from the French or Indians who oppose aid from the British.

An intuitive response is that this may be more of a practical than normative challenge. The view that associative duties might arise out of past colonial relationships might survive, in so far as those associative duties can be successfully discharged. If it is the case that the former colonizer cannot be trusted to discharge its associative anti-poverty duties with good intent and outcome, this does not show that such duties do not exist, but rather that they ought not be discharged until such time as the actor who bears the duties can be viewed as a good faith partner in anti-poverty efforts. Similarly, if a formerly colonized country rejects support from their former colonizer, this is a plausible reason to think that colonizer ought not discharge specific anti-poverty duties to the former colony.

It therefore might appear that the case is not particularly strong for anti-poverty duties to be viewed as stronger to foreign colonies in some political contexts. But it is not implausible that associative reasons do justify anti-poverty assistance in former colonies, and that in some cases contemporary relations between states do allow the discharging of those duties. When Belgians reflect, for example, on the current suffering in the Democratic Republic of Congo, and see its roots in King Leopold's savage exploitation of the resources and people of the DRC, it is plausible to see assistance to the Congolese today as an act of moral repair on the part of the Belgian state, however inadequate. And as citizens of the DRC reflect on the current role Belgians should play in their country, they may see the Belgians as a partner than can now be trusted to help advance the development of the country. They would not, arguably, deny that Belgian peacekeepers or Belgian humanitarian assistance can help to prevent conflict and to promote development.

Neighborly Relationships

A second kind of relationship that is often thought to justify special anti-poverty duties is that of geographic proximity. Just as an individual might have stronger duties to prevent or reduce the poverty of her neighbor than to a stranger she does not know, so too might states have stronger duties to those nearby than far away. Americans might provide greater poverty assistance to Mexicans, and the French to Algerians.

But why should being neighbors matter, morally? What kind of justification could one provide to justify greater anti-poverty assistance to the nearby rather than the distant? Geographic distance per se is a difficult ground upon which to rationalize stronger anti-poverty duties. As a number of philosophers have pointed out (most famously Singer 1972), distance as a variable may appear intuitively important, but this is only because it stands as a proxy for other morally significant variables, such as the cost or efficacy of providing assistance.

There are other reasons geographic proximity might generate some grounds for anti-poverty duties. With geographically proximate countries, we can be more likely to develop enduring relationships of cooperation, and sometimes conflict, that might generate stronger duties than exist with other states. Nearby states may use water from the same river, have strong bilateral trade relations enforced by specific trade agreements, share common security arrangements, address common environmental problems, and more generally share a common history, perhaps a common language, and have residents in each country who have a number of family members in the other country. These relationships may explain why, for example, the United States might provide more anti-poverty assistance to Mexico than would the United Kingdom.

Commercial Relationships

A third kind of associative reason might justify stronger or different anti-poverty duties than are generated by duties of justice or duties of humanity. As noted above, Iris Marion Young argues that responsibility for global justice can arise across borders in so far as structures that constrain and coerce individuals persist over those borders. International commercial relationships are an enduring feature of life in a globalized world that create structured vulnerabilities. Consumers regularly purchase goods and services that rely upon low-income labor in developing countries. Given that these strong commercial relationships exist, this might be yet another associative reason that should be given consideration in determining whether and how to discharge anti-poverty duties.

For example, following the Rana Plaza disaster in Bangladesh (to be discussed in Chapter 15), companies who could trace their supply chains to the collapsed factory might see the provision of assistance in securing labor rights in the country as warranted given their ongoing commercial relationships. Or after countries learned of their alleged complicity in the war in the Democratic Republic of Congo through the purchase of electronics using minerals sourced from the DRC, they might increase their assistance to these countries. They need not accept strict liability for these harms, but rather simply see that they are involved in an enduring way in the political and economic structures that produce these harms such that they have duties to reduce human vulnerability.

As with colonial and neighborly relationships, associative duties based on commercial ties face significant objections. Some of the world's very poorest countries, almost by definition, have minimal commercial ties with countries capable of providing anti-poverty assistance. Should there be fewer anti-poverty efforts directed at these people as a result? This seems implausible. If the Central African Republic, for example, applies for concessional loans from a development agency, it would be odd to reject this request on the grounds that the CAR is not involved in significant and enduring structured commercial relations with any of the potential lenders.

There is, however, something that can be said in defense of associative anti-poverty duties based on commerce or proximity. It is often thought that one's moral duties are distinct from one's self-interest, and that the presence of self-interest in the provision of foreign aid is pernicious, in that it leads to anti-poverty programming that is not in the interest of the world's worst off but in the interest of those doing the 'saving'. However, it can be advantageous to have one's moral duties align with their self-interest. If, for example, a humanitarian intervention that would save many lives is consistent with the self-interest of the intervening country, they may be more likely to stay the course in providing civilian protection when difficulties arise. So too, anti-poverty assistance may face greater support, including in the face of adversity, if providing that support is consistent with the national interest of the donor. In so far as reducing poverty is consistent with growing a base of consumers in a country with which a state has commercial ties, or is pursued because large numbers of poor people in a neighboring country threaten to create destabilizing flows of migrants or spread communicable diseases, this may, in the long run, result in more stable and effective anti-poverty programs. This line of reasoning doesn't come from the highest moral ground, but it attempts to understand states as inherently self-interested actors who will be unlikely to allocate anti-poverty assistance from a purely impartial perspective.

Private Donors and Associative Duties

Private donors are one group of moral agents who might have strong reasons to act from associative duties. One way in which associative duties might influence private donors is through the past actions of the donor. For example, the Rockefeller Foundation, the 15th largest foundation in the United States, received its funding through the profits generated through a wide range of industrial enterprises, most notably an oil fortune. Today, recognizing the role that greenhouse gas emissions play in contributing to various harms associated with catastrophic climate change, the Rockefellers have decided to invest considerably in environmental protection programs, and have decided to divest their endowment's assets from fossil fuel companies (Rockefeller 2014). While each of these decisions might be justified on other grounds, it is not implausible to think that associative reasons provide the strongest justification for the Rockefeller's decisions to promote sustainable development and environmental protection. Given that an oil fortune provided the opportunity for the fund to do good in the world, the case for integrating environmental concerns into the anti-poverty work of the Rockefellers is justifiable on associative grounds.

Associative duties can also arise out of relationships that are mutually beneficial or associations that do not create enduring moral debts. Consider two cases. George Soros was born and raised in a Jewish family in Hungary. He was a teenager when Nazi Germany occupied Hungary. He eventually left for England and pursued degrees in London, entering the world of finance and becoming one of the world's most successful fund managers. While living outside of Hungary, Soros was actively involved in the transition from communism to a more liberal, democratic, and capitalist society.[4] Given the unique personal and professional history of George Soros, we might find associative reasons that arise which justify his decision to prioritize some charitable efforts over others. His major philanthropic organization, the Open Society Foundation, has the stated aim to 'build open and tolerant societies whose governments are accountable to their citizens'. Given his personal experience as a persecuted religious minority who went on to oppose an autocratic government, it is plausible that Soros's foundation directs greater attention to societies that are politically repressive in transitioning to open forms of government, and protecting the civil and political rights of those who are at risk of persecution. So too might he focus on reform of global capitalism to prevent unnecessary financial crises, given his experience and expertise in finance. Similarly, Sudanese-born Mo Ibrahim, who made his fortune in telecommunications, focuses his charitable efforts on governance and leadership in African countries. He runs the Ibrahim Index of African Governance and awards the Ibrahim prize to the African leader who peacefully passes power to a successor. Given his position as an African-born philanthropist, whose home country has suffered under corrupt, dictatorial, and genocidal governments, he certainly might appeal to this as a reason to devote his wealth to addressing governance in Africa over other competing priorities.

Associative reasons can give justificatory force to the decisions of groups of individuals as well as private philanthropists. The American Jewish World Service, for example, prioritizes anti-genocide campaigning and programing. Given the historical relationship of Jewish people to mass atrocities, it is morally defensible that AJWS focus its international charitable work on threatened populations, even if those charitable efforts might be able to assist more people if allocated from a strictly impartial point of view.

As with associative duties justifying decisions regarding the provision of public resources, there are objections to the private provision of anti-poverty resources on associative grounds. Consider what justification might be given to the victim of, for example, child labor in India, who does not benefit from the programming at the Gates, Soros, or Ibrahim foundations. She might object, 'Why is it that their resources should go to problems that they have some special reason to attend to? Why does the source of their wealth, or their personal history, provide a reason to direct resources away from me and to some other priority? Why should I be deprived of their support merely because no associative reason connects us?' The fact that some people do not have strong associative ties to people who can provide assistance presents a challenge for the proponent of the view that there are associative duties to alleviate global poverty, and these should influence to whom these duties are discharged.

This demand for fully impartial reasoning regarding both the existence of anti-poverty duties, and where they should be directed, deserves a response. One plausible way to respond to this objection is to follow the lead of how people commonly think about associative duties. Most people, except for strict utilitarians and cosmopolitan egalitarians, accept that individuals are morally permitted to give some priority to the special relationships they inhabit. Furthermore, as mentioned above, it is advantageous to endorse an ethics of anti-poverty that allows individuals to align, to some extent, their personal motivations and interests with the activities that they undertake to reduce significant deprivation and human rights abuses. Aligning our moral duties with our natural sentiments, rather than acting against them, is likely to produce more overall action against poverty.

The defender of purely impartial anti-poverty duties may respond that while we are generally permitted to give priority to individuals and projects that we have a special association with, once we enter into the realm of anti-poverty programs, we must do the most good possible, regardless of our past or present associations. As a practical matter, it is unlikely that private donors will be persuaded to fully set aside their capacities, interests, and relationships in deciding whether and how to undertake efforts to reduce global poverty. As a moral matter, it is at least uncertain whether such pure impartiality is indeed required, although excessive partiality based on associative relationships can presumably be ruled out. If, for example, a wealthy donor who has long played the flute decides to discharge her anti-poverty duties by supporting aspiring flutists in low-income countries, this would presumably be a misunderstanding of the strength and nature of associative anti-poverty duties. But if a telecommunications magnate seeks to promote development through the provision of technical assistance in the development of communication technologies in her country of birth, and this assistance can be shown to have positive welfare benefits, this may be an appropriate way of both interpreting and discharging associative, anti-poverty duties.

Chapter Summary

This chapter highlights the way in which associative reasons provide an alternative moral perspective from which to understand and interpret anti-poverty duties. For the person who denies that either duties of justice or duties of humanity exist between affluent individuals and the materially deprived, associative reasons provide a third way through which anti-poverty duties may be justified. For the person who accepts that duties of justice or duties of humanity exist, associative reasons may alter their aggregate understanding of anti-poverty duties.

Questions for Discussion

1   In interpersonal morality, it is commonly thought that we have stronger duties to our friends, and family, and people to whom we have made promises. Do these associative reasons have a place in an overall ethics of global poverty?

2   If you are reading this book, it is likely you purchase products made by employees in low-income countries. Do you think your commercial habits create unique anti-poverty duties?

3   If associative reasons can give rise to anti-poverty duties, how should one compare the weight of their nearby associations (to family and friends) versus their distant associations (to people abroad)?

Notes

1   While Young uses the language of justice, I take this to be a claim of the strength of the duties involved in contrast to duties of beneficence. I treat Young as developing an account of associative anti-poverty duties because her emphasis is on shared connection rather than strict liability.

2   It is worth noting that on the associative view, if widespread absolute poverty were present in the United Kingdom, these associations might justify Kenyan anti-poverty duties to the British. But since widespread absolute poverty is not present in the United Kingdom, these duties do not exist.

3   Of course, it may still be the case that Russians do have duties to reduce global poverty, but given current political realities, it is counter-productive to encourage the Russian government to actively attempt to discharge these duties.

4   Controversially, he has made very large bets against national currencies, which critics argue have exacerbated financial crises, both against the British pound in 1992 and the Thai baht in 1997–98. While the ethics of currency trading are beyond the scope of this book, let's assume that short selling currency is one natural part of global capitalism and does not incur any moral obligation on the person who bets against a national currency to later compensate the citizens who may suffer an economic downturn when that currency collapses.

Suggested Reading

Rubenstein, J. 'Pluralism about global poverty', *British Journal of Political Science*, 43.4 (2013): 775–797.
Seglow, J. *Defending Associative Duties*, London: Routledge, 2013.

Seglow, J. 'Associative duties and global justice', *Journal of Moral Philosophy* 7 (2010): 54–73.
Ypi, L., Goodin, R., and Barry, C. 'Associative duties, global justice, and the colonies', *Philosophy and Public Affairs*, 37.2 (2009): 103–135.

References

Elkins, C. *Imperial Reckoning: The untold story of Britain's gulag in Kenya*, New York: Owl Books, 2010.
Rockefeller Brothers Fund. Divestment Statement, September 2014, available at www.rbf.org/about/divestment (accessed December 16, 2014).
Wrong, M. *It's Our Turn to Eat: The story of a Kenyan whistleblower*, New York: Harper, 2009.
Young, M. I. *Responsibility for Justice*, Oxford: Oxford University Press, 2011.

8 Denying Duties to the Most Deprived

U.S. senator and occasional presidential candidate Rand Paul is a self-proclaimed libertarian and one of the leaders of the new Tea Party movement in American politics, whose primary aim is to reduce taxes and government spending, thereby reducing the role of government programs in individual's lives. For many Tea Party activists, government programs represent a great threat to individual liberty. The first budget that Paul introduced in 2011 cut all foreign aid to all countries. Subsequent proposed budgets involved significant if not full reductions in foreign aid, from $37 billion annually to $5 billion. (He eventually preserved some foreign assistance after realizing that many people objected to cutting aid to US allies such as Israel, but maintained that over time it would be a good thing to eliminate all such assistance.) For Paul and his supporters, there is no moral duty to support poverty alleviation abroad. Indeed, providing foreign assistance is sometimes argued to be a violation of the moral rights of domestic taxpayers.

Thus far we have considered three kinds of reasons that are thought to justify the existence of moral duties for well-off individuals to contribute to the reduction of global poverty: that they have duties of beneficence to the deprived, that they have duties of justice to the deprived, or that they have associative duties to the deprived. Like Rand Paul, many people believe no such duties exist. Fewer philosophers hold that view, but there are notable exceptions. In this final chapter on moral duties and global poverty, we consider the ways in which people deny that individuals living in wealthy societies have moral duties to reduce global poverty. To my knowledge, no significant contemporary ethicists deny that it is a morally good thing to reduce global poverty. The world would be morally better if fewer people were poor. Some do deny, however, that wealthy people and societies are morally required to assist in this effort. As the author of a book on the ethics of global poverty, it will not surprise the reader that I do not find such views persuasive. But this chapter attempts to give those views a fair hearing, and considers reasons offered to deny the existence of duties to eradicate poverty.

Arguments denying duties of global poverty eradication should generally proceed in two steps. The first step is to reject the arguments offered in the preceding three chapters that aim to establish that there are moral duties to reduce global poverty. Because we have covered objections to these arguments in the preceding chapters, we will not rehearse them here. The second step is to offer positive arguments in favor of the view that wealthy individuals do not bear these duties. We will consider four such arguments in this chapter.

Libertarian Objections to Duties of Assistance

As a matter of political philosophy, libertarians argue that freedom, often narrowly interpreted as non-interference by government and by other individuals, is the primary value that should be upheld and protected by political institutions. Libertarians (with the exception of left libertarians)[1] often object to the welfare state, including its anti-poverty components, on the grounds that it violates the economic freedom of taxpayers and allegedly undermines the incentives to work for beneficiaries of publicly funded programs.[2] Given libertarian resistance to the idea that redistributive measures are owed to the economically disadvantaged within the domestic context, it is unsurprising that many libertarians also resist the idea that duties are owed to people suffering from material deprivation abroad.

As a matter of moral philosophy, libertarians often hold that, as long as they have not directly harmed others, they do not owe anything to people who face misfortune. The primary duty of most moral agents is to refrain from harmful interference in the affairs of others. As long as one does not violate someone else's rights, one has done all that morality requires. Moral agents, according to some versions of libertarianism, simply do not bear moral responsibility for assisting those who are in need.

In international affairs, libertarians often apply these commitments to global poverty and injustice. This usually involves two distinct claims. The first is a general resistance to a foreign policy that involves entanglements with foreign states. The primary objective of foreign policy should be simply to protect national security and national interest, but avoid international obligations in so far as possible. The second is a denial of individual moral duties that extend beyond state borders. As long as global poverty was not caused by a wealthy individual and she did not violate the rights of any people living in poverty, then she bears no moral duties to those people, regardless of how dire their circumstances are. As Jan Narveson writes about famine relief,

> Of course we have a right to feed them if we wish, and they have a negative right to be fed. But may we forcibly impose a duty on others to feed them? We may not. If the fact that others are starving is not our fault, then we do not need to provide for them as a duty of justice. To think otherwise is to suppose that we are, in effect, slaves to the badly off.
>
> (Narveson 1999, p. 156)

One initial response to the libertarian position recalls arguments from Chapter 6, which highlight the range of ways in which the activities of wealthy individuals and the institutions that they uphold are directly implicated in the persistence of global poverty. It might be precisely on libertarian grounds that, for example, compensation is owed to victims of colonialism who have been left with extractive political institutions, to people who live under autocrats backed by foreign military assistance, or to people who cannot afford needed medicines thanks to the structure of contemporary international trade agreements. That is, on grounds that the libertarian accepts, duties of rectification are owed to many people living in material and social deprivation. Contra Narveson, this objection holds, it *is* in some cases his fault that some people are starving.

Another response attempts to reject the limited morality of libertarianism by establishing that individuals have imperfect duties of assistance (see Chapter 5). Would the libertarian deny that there is a duty to save the drowning child in Singer's famous hypothetical thought experiment? Surrounded by massive amounts of suffering, does not any plausible morality require giving some consideration to the interests of the deprived? This need not be as demanding as strong formulations of Singer's duties of beneficence. But arguably some level of beneficence is required when so many fellow human beings are at risk of preventable hunger and premature death. However, if one is willing to commit to the view that morality never requires duties of beneficence, even when the costs to oneself are low and the benefits to potential victims are very high, then one can consistently apply this view to the problem of global poverty. The libertarian can consistently deny the existence of any duties of beneficence.

Parochial Objections to Duties of Assistance

An alternative approach suggests that duties of assistance are sometimes owed, but only to people who stand in the right kind of relationship with the potential duty bearer. The utilitarian philosopher William Godwin, in defending impartial duties of beneficence, famously asked,

> What magic is there in the pronoun 'my' to overturn the decisions of everlasting truth? My wife or my mother may be a fool or a prostitute, malicious, lying, or dishonest. If they be, of what consequences is it that they are mine?
> (Godwin (1793) 2013, p. 54)

Godwin argues that in thinking about cases of rescue, the paramount duty is to those who will contribute the most to overall utility in society. One ought not give consideration to the relationship they have with particular individuals, but rather reason from the impartial perspective of the universe.

Many contemporary philosophers disagree with Godwin, and argue that there are special duties based one one's relationship to others. Given the nature of these special relationships, to family, friends, and community members, which generate special moral ties, we have much stronger duties of assistance to those with whom we stand in the right kind of relationship. (Perhaps we only have duties of assistance to these people.) A neighbor or member of our community may be within our moral circle, but those with whom we have no prior relationship may be beyond the reach of our moral consideration.

For this denial of global duties of assistance to succeed, it must be the case that special relationships, of the kind that exist within the domestic sphere but not internationally, are the only thing that can ground duties of assistance. Many people suggest that there is a genuine tension between special duties owed as a matter of our unique relationships, and general duties owed as a matter of an impartial morality. But the person who wants to affirm the existence of global anti-poverty duties will simply argue that even though special duties may have a strong claim on a person's time and resources, they do not eliminate the existence of general moral duties. Consider a stranger who wanders into town, with whom no one has any prior relationship, and is in desperate need of assistance. The parochial conception of duties of assistance would deny that this person is owed any help, since they are not standing in the right kind of relationship to the community in which they have just arrived. Again, one could consistently hold this view, but it does not appear to be the kind of morality that most people will endorse.

Competing Priorities

A related argument holds that because domestic poverty exists (in some sense) in all wealthy societies, individuals have a duty to first eradicate poverty and injustice in their own society, before combatting poverty and injustice abroad. This is not an implausible thought. If one dedicates their time and resources to, for example, combatting racial disparities in educational achievement in their own country, they might claim, 'yes, global poverty is bad, but we must get our own house in order first. Racial inequality is a stain on the conscience of our nation, and this ought to be the top moral priority until racial justice has been achieved'. In other words, if there were no injustice or relative poverty in wealthy societies, wealthy individuals might have duties to people suffering abroad. But as long as unjust suffering exists nearby, domestic problems remain the moral priority. As contemporary slogans opposing foreign aid have it, charity begins at home.

But if we give this view a more precise formulation, it appears harder to defend. The claim is that all domestic poverty (or, perhaps, all domestic injustice) should be given a lexical priority over all global poverty (or, perhaps, all global injustice). In other words, there is no amount of global poverty reduction that could take moral priority over even a small amount of domestic poverty reduction.

There are three reasons to doubt that all domestic poverty reduction is more important than global poverty reduction. First, there is much more poverty abroad than in wealthy societies. On even a modest understanding of monetary or multidimensional poverty, several billion people abroad are very deprived. So what this claim amounts to is the view that the relative poverty of, say, 10,000 Swedes, is always more morally important, from the perspective of the wealthy Swede, than the poverty of billions of non-Swedes. Second, the deprived are much worse off abroad than they are in wealthy societies. Even a very poor person in Sweden will be far better off than a middle class person in a low-income country. The median income of a British citizen is in the top 3 percent of incomes globally. A person living at the poverty line in the United States would still be in the top

15 percent of incomes globally.[3] So the person who defends the lexical priority of domestic poverty over global poverty must maintain this position in the face of the fact that global poverty is vastly more extensive and more severe than domestic poverty. Third, it is arguably much more cost-effective to combat global poverty than domestic poverty. A few dollars per day can double the income of much of the world's population, but would be of little consequence for the relatively poor in most OECD countries. Consider a policy reform that might benefit a small number of people in domestic poverty at the expense of a larger number of people in global poverty. Suppose that a new trade tariff will protect the jobs of some working poor people in the United Kingdom, thereby displacing jobs from Bangladesh. In considering whether to support this policy or not, should domestic constituents give full weight to the impact on domestic poverty and no weight to the impact on global poverty? If they learned that the trade policy would cause a large number of people to lose employment and be severely impoverished in Bangladesh, should that be totally irrelevant to their determination over whether they should support the policy?

No Basic Structure

For many philosophers, citizens have duties of justice to each other just in so far as they exist in a political society that has a basic structure which exerts coercive power over individuals. On this view, justice is intimately related to the sovereign state, which exerts influence over the basic rights, opportunities, and outcomes for citizens subject to the state's powers. Thomas Nagel (2005), among others, has used this conception of justice to argue against the view that there can be anything resembling domestic justice in the global sphere, which implies that there can be no duties of global justice. For Nagel, social justice exists in the domestic sphere because the government claims legitimacy to coerce based on the interests of its citizens, and with an expectation that they agree to this coercion. Absent a unified world government, the idea of global justice, or a just global society, is a conceptual mistake. Given that there is no basic structure in the international arena, there can be no duties of justice that cross international boundaries. (This leaves open the possibility that humanitarian duties of beneficence cross international borders. To fully deny duties of poverty eradication, the anti-global justice argument must be conjoined with an argument against duties of humanity.)

There are two lines of response to this attempt to deny duties of global justice (which include duties to eradicate global poverty). First, it is not clear that the absence of a basic political structure implies no duties of justice can exist. Consider a failed state, such as South Sudan or Somalia. There is nothing at all like a modern state, with functioning institutions, widespread service provision, a monopoly on the use of force, a legitimate claim to rule, and so on. Does it therefore follow that no duties of justice are owed within these societies? This appears mistaken. One might think that, absent a basic structure but with other binding interrelations, the duty is to establish a basic structure that can secure minimal justice for all.

Second, one can assert that there is in fact a global basic structure. Proponents of this view can point to international trade law, made and adjudicated at the World Trade Organization, the United Nations, especially its management of international security, the international financial system, especially the World Bank, International Monetary Fund, and regional development banks, the management of international environmental issues, through the UN Framework Convention on Climate Change, and many other global governance institutions. Across a wide range of important spheres of public policy, international institutions do exert coercive influence over the livelihoods and prospects of the world's citizens. Given that such coercive institutions exist, duties of justice do indeed exist to ensure that these institutions are just.

Scholars who deny the possibility of global justice under existing institutional arrangements, as noted above, need not deny that it would be a good thing to reduce global poverty, or that people ought to contribute to this effort. But denying the possibility of global justice does appear to weaken the duties of wealthy individuals to people living in deprivation abroad.

Global Poverty Has Local Causes

In previous chapters we have seen many contemporary authors attempt to demonstrate that there are global forces that shape whether or not societies and individuals prosper. One way to deny the existence of poverty eradication duties is to argue that the causes of poverty are primarily local, not global, in nature (Cohen 2010). This empirical assertion must be joined with a normative assertion—namely, if the responsibility for deprivation lies with others, then one cannot bear moral responsibility for reducing deprivation.

Note that for a 'domestic poverty thesis' to succeed in denying duties to eradicate global poverty, one of two things has to be true. On one hand, the thesis would succeed if it is the case that poverty is exclusively, rather than only partially, caused by domestic forces. That is, it has to be the case that the deprivation in Haiti is fully caused by Haitians, and not in any way caused by people outside of Haiti. On the other hand, the thesis would succeed if the fact that poverty was only partially but not fully brought about by domestic causes provides sufficient reason to reject the idea that wealthy individuals have duties to reduce global poverty.

The empirical claim about the domestic causes of poverty faces a three-fold response. First, even if many of the proximate causes of deprivation in Haiti have to do with Haitian political institutions, the contemporary structure of Haitian political institutions is shaped by international forces. Second, the structure of international economic relations partially determines levels of deprivation in Haiti. Whether intellectual property regimes make available affordable drugs needed for good health, or whether international trade policy promotes or hinders the growth of the Haitian economy, has a deep influence on poverty levels in Haiti. And of course international migration policy has an enormous impact on the material well-being of Haitians, both through their earnings abroad and the remittances they send home. Third, if one looks a bit further back in history, it is very difficult to defend the thought that the contemporary poverty of Haitians and the prosperity of the societies who have forced a violent history upon the Haitian people are unrelated.

Suppose that the proponent of the domestic poverty thesis concedes that the actions of outsiders and the role of international institutions can play a role in slowing or accelerating progress against global poverty. They might still insist that since the primary causes of poverty are local, there can be no moral duties for the wealthy to reduce global poverty. But this claim fails to account for the ways in which international actions can interact with domestic progress against poverty. For some countries, they may be making genuine forward progress against poverty, but this progress is slowed by international institutional arrangements. As Thomas Pogge (2008, p. 20) notes, you can be sailing forward but still into a headwind. International institutional arrangements and the activities of wealthy states may sometimes be providing just such a headwind. For other countries, they may be stagnating or even backsliding in efforts to reduce poverty, with civil conflict, authoritarianism, or other problems of governance causing this stagnation. But these apparently domestic causes of poverty are often related to international rules that allow autocrats to use the international financial system, civil war combatants to have access to international markets in arms and sometimes formal military backing from outsiders, an international banking system which funnels stolen resources out of the country, and so on. So the apparently 'purely domestic' causes of poverty are sustained by the international system. In so far as an alternative international system would provide less support for the domestic causes of poverty, this may be sufficient to justify the existence of moral duties to help bring about such institutional changes.

Malthusian Objections to Duties to Reduce Global Poverty

It is less common to hear voiced Malthusian objections to duties to relieve global poverty in contemporary discussions. Nonetheless, we will give these views an airing here, as they are sometimes lurking in the background of more congenially stated opposition to anti-poverty programs.

Thomas Malthus was a British economist working in the late 18th and early 19th century. Malthus is famous for his prediction that over time population growth would exceed the growth in food supply, thereby resulting in widespread famine. Malthus opposed the English Poor Laws that provided relief to the poor on several grounds, including that they would lead to overpopulation. For Malthus, the only way to maintain a population at a decent standard of living was to allow severe poverty to provide a check on excessive population growth. Contemporary Malthusians argue that anti-poverty programs should be opposed on the grounds that they keep poor people alive, thus contributing to larger populations, who will have their own families, thus furthering the growth of population and further stretching the already limited resources of the globe.

As an economic matter, Malthus's predictions were wrong. Innovations in the production of food have caused agricultural growth to far outpace growth in population. Malthus's basic mistake was to assume that the available resources are fixed while population growth would continue to increase. There are at least three reasons to reject contemporary Malthusian worries about anti-poverty programs and global population growth. First, the rate of population growth is already rapidly declining, and its decline largely correlates with increased, rather than decreased, living standards. Indeed, the largest contribution to contemporary population growth is not high birth rates but increasing life expectancies. Presumably Malthusians do not think that we should prevent progress in global health to reduce life expectancy and thus global population. Second, while it is correct that there are still occasional famines and many people who are malnourished, these famines are primarily caused by a lack of democratic accountability and the low purchasing power of the poor, rather than by a shortage of aggregate food supply (Sen 1981). Indeed, the problem with hunger and malnutrition is not one of output but of distribution: the world grows more than enough food to feed its 7 billion inhabitants. Third, contemporary Malthusian predictions also appear unlikely to come true, as rising living standards are predicted to continue to rise, leading to further reduction in fertility rates, especially when rising living standards are paired with decreasing levels of gender inequality.

Ought Implies Can

There is one final objection to the existence of duties to support poverty reduction and eradication. It is generally taken as true that ought implies can. This means that one can only have a moral duty if they can reasonably discharge that duty. This final attempt to deny the existence of anti-poverty duties holds that the efforts of the wealthy are often unsuccessful, and indeed can be very harmful. Making an inference from these specific failures to a more general claim about the impossibility of providing successful anti-poverty assistance, this becomes the claim that the wealthy do not have duties to assist with global poverty reduction because they cannot assist in global poverty reduction. International aid is ineffective or worse, and political reform can only be driven by domestic actors, not outsiders. The arguments against foreign aid will be given thorough treatment in the next section. It is sufficient to note here that even if one is persuaded of the normative case for wealthy individuals to support poverty reduction efforts, if there are no available avenues through which one can discharge these duties, then the duties no longer exist. And this is perhaps the strongest form of argument in support of the claim that the wealthy have no moral duty to support poverty eradication, which we will examine in greater depth in the next section.

Self-Interest

In this chapter we have considered arguments that purport to show that wealthy individuals do not hold anti-poverty duties. There is one related position that is worth mentioning. Even if one does not think there is a moral obligation to reduce global poverty, one might still endorse supporting some anti-poverty programs. Why? This support might be justified on the grounds of self-interest rather than concern for others. Spending on public health programs can be justified on the grounds that infectious diseases do not respect national borders and may be a threat everywhere. Supporting international security can be justified on the grounds of limiting the flows of refugees to one's own country. Support for international environmental protection can be justified on the grounds that biodiversity, clean oceans, and reduced greenhouse gas emissions are global public goods from which we all benefit.

But there is a limit to how far arguments of self-interest extend. A great deal of unnecessary suffering and misery presents no direct threat to people in high-income countries. If a husband abuses his wife, or a child needlessly starves to death, or a worker is forced to work long hours without pay, this makes no difference to the life prospects of people in high-income countries. Malaria kills millions but it will not spread to the United States or United Kingdom. Imagine you are a policy maker and a call comes in warning of an impending famine in a far off country, and you are asked to authorize humanitarian support. It is a rather unattractive morality that would suggest your first thought should be, 'Well, that depends. Will those who are suffering and dying end up on my shores? How will these starving people affect my constituents? What is in it for me?'

Chapter Summary

Arguments to deny the anti-poverty duties of wealthy individuals either deny arguments offered in the preceding three chapters, or offer positive arguments against such duties. These positive arguments either rely upon the normative view that individuals just don't have strong moral duties to assist others, or on the empirical views that wealthy individuals are not causally responsible for global poverty, nor are they well positioned to reduce it. It is the latter of these empirical views that we turn to in the next section.

Questions for Discussion

1   Do you think you have a moral obligation to support anti-poverty programs abroad? If not, why not?
2   In the community where you live, what are the major social problems? What do you think the relative priority of these problems is to global poverty?
3   You are just one person among millions represented by your government and served by corporations. Does the fact that you, individually, have very little influence over these institutions mean that you are not responsible for their impact on global poverty?

Notes

1   Left-libertarianism describes a family of positions that are committed to libertarian ideals of individual freedom and market economies while also sharing leftist commitments to social, political, and economic equality.

2   That said, some canonical libertarian thinkers including Milton Friedman defended basic income grants to all citizens and universal health coverage.

3   These figures rely on the tool 'How Rich am I' from Giving What We Can, at www.givingwhatwecan.org/get-involved/how-rich-am-i (accessed December 10, 2015).

Further Reading

Lomasky, L. and Teson, F. *Justice at a Distance: Expanding freedom globally*, Cambridge: Cambridge University Press, 2015.

References

Cohen, J. 'Philosophy, Social Science, and Global Poverty', in *Thomas Pogge and His Critics*, ed. A. Jaggar, Cambridge: Polity, 2010.

Godwin, W. *An Enquiry Concerning Political Justice*, ed. M. Phillip, Oxford: Oxford University Press, 2013 (originally published 1793).

Nagel, T. 'The problem of global justice', *Philosophy and Public Affairs*, 33.2 (2005): 113–147.

Narveson, J. *Moral Matters*, Toronto: Broadview Press, 1999.

Pogge, T. *World Poverty and Human Rights*, 2nd ed., Cambridge: Polity, 2008.

Sen, A. *Poverty and Famines: An essay on entitlement and deprivation*, Oxford: Oxford University Press, 1981.

Part III

Foreign Aid and Its Critics

Presented with the problem of global poverty in the context of vast disparities in wealth and income, a natural response is to redirect some of the world's wealth and income to alleviating the severe deprivations that cause global poverty. Indeed, within countries, redistributive programs are one of the two primary means of poverty eradication, and one of the central tasks of governments. Although public redistributive programs within countries have existed in their modern form since the 19th century, the phenomenon of regular public and private transfers across international borders to alleviate global poverty is largely attributed to the programs that arose following reconstruction efforts in Europe following World War II. The advent of international development as an explicit project of national governments is often traced to President Truman's inaugural speech in January 1949. He famously (and perhaps infamously) argued:

> We must embark on a bold new program for making the benefits of our scientific advances and industrial programs available for the improvement and growth of underdeveloped areas. More than half the people of the world are living in conditions approaching misery. Their food is inadequate. They are the victims of disease. Their economic life is primitive and stagnant. Their poverty is a handicap and a threat both to them and to more prosperous areas. For the first time in history, humanity possesses the knowledge and the skill to relieve the suffering of these people. The United States is pre-eminent among nations in the development of industrial and scientific techniques. The material resources which we can afford to use for the assistance of other peoples are limited. But our imponderable resources in technical knowledge are constantly growing and are inexhaustible. I believe that we should make available to all peace-loving peoples the benefits of our store of technical knowledge in order to help them realize their aspirations for a better life. And, in cooperation with other nations, we should foster capital investment in areas needing development. Our aim should be to help the free peoples of the world, through their own efforts, to produce more food, more clothing, more materials for their housing, and more mechanical power to lighten their burdens.
>
> (Truman, 1999)

So began a major push from western nations to offer financial assistance, in a variety of forms, to attempt to combat global poverty. Many of these efforts were cynical and self-interested—international aid commonly propped up dictators in exchange for political support during the Cold War, or was used to finance military expenditures rather than improvements in livelihoods. Many other efforts were genuine attempts to relieve serious material and social deprivation, with some failures and some phenomenal success in helping people live longer, healthier, and more productive lives. Foreign aid has helped to vaccinate children, decrease child mortality rates, increase enrollment in schools, and increase access to essential medicines.

Today, international aid faces an uncertain future. In some countries, including the United Kingdom, Norway, and Sweden, foreign assistance represents 0.7 percent or more of gross domestic product, and there is support across major political parties for maintaining this assistance. In other countries, such as Australia and the United States, foreign aid as a percentage of GDP is stagnant or in decline, and at least one of the major political parties stands largely opposed to foreign aid.

More generally, various trends are redesigning the landscape of foreign aid. Foreign direct investment (FDI), remittances, and loans far outpace the level of traditional development assistance in most countries. (Some countries, notably China, link their public assistance programs with commercial deals designed to secure access to natural resources.) Remittances and FDI are expected to continue to increase in most low-income countries, while a small portion will remain heavily reliant on international developmental assistance.

Many emerging economies are also changing the landscape of foreign aid, designing their own bilateral aid programs, and creating new multilateral institutions. Brazil, India, China, and South Africa all have their own foreign aid programs (despite being recent, and sometimes current, recipients of foreign aid). At the time of writing, the new Asian Infrastructure Investment Bank aimed to challenge the dominance of North America and Europe in international financial institutions, especially the World Bank and International Monetary Fund.

While the world of aid is changing, it is unlikely to go away. And some of the most debated questions in the philosophy and economics of global development focus on foreign aid. Philosophically, is there a moral requirement for the wealthy to provide foreign aid? Do these moral requirements change in light of the possibility that foreign aid can be ineffective or even harmful? Economically, what is the relationship between aid and growth? Which foreign aid programs work best in reducing global poverty?

In this third part of the book, we will begin to address some of these questions, with a focus on the ethics of foreign assistance. We will examine foreign aid, morally evaluate the benefits and harms that result from foreign aid, and determine whether new initiatives to improve foreign aid might be preferable to current forms of assistance.

Reference

Truman, H. S. (1999). Inaugural Address: Thursday, January 20, 1949. Western Standard Publishing Company.

9 Aid, Critics, and Innovators

Many people lack access to clean drinking water. This lack of access creates significant burdens, especially for women, who must walk long distances to secure small amounts of water for drinking, cooking, and cleaning. Contaminated water causes a range of illnesses, many of which are fatal. Two million people die each year from diarrheal diseases, which are mostly preventable by using simple treatments to ensure water is clean enough to drink. Poor-quality drinking water is one of the largest causes of morbidity and mortality worldwide.

In 2005, a South African entrepreneur named Trevor Field heard of an invention called a PlayPump. The pump was designed as a merry-go-round. When pushed, the pumps would extract fresh water from underground and store it in an above ground tank, creating a source of fresh drinking water. Better yet, the pumps would be a source of amusement and fun for children, whose energy would make the pump go around. And when the pumps carry advertising on the side, their cost can be offset through commercial sponsors, or they can carry public service announcements. Fields founded a company that would manufacture the devices and place them in locations with significant water scarcity. He quickly attracted 15 million USD in financing from the American government and private philanthropic donors.

Three years later, one of the philanthropists involved in supporting the project went to visit PlayPump installations in several African countries. She found pumps idle, many broken down without repair, with local communities complaining that they were not consulted about the change from their old hand pumps. Reports commissioned by the government of Mozambique and UNICEF found widespread failure and dissatisfaction with the devices. Fields claimed the problems were with partner NGOs who had selected bad sites for the pumps, while others claimed Field's company was not providing enough support. With evidence mounting that the pumps were burdensome, prone to failure, tiresome for children, and much less effective than the traditional hand pumps they replaced, many communities had to remove the play pumps and return to their old technology. In short, millions of dollars spent, the daily lives of thousands of people disrupted, and no increase in the supply of clean water (Frontline 2010).

In contrast to Field, who had little experience in the provision of clean water but thought he knew the right way to proceed, a team of researchers knew that clean water was important but had no idea how to increase the consumption of products that make it safe. To the researchers, it was simply not known how to foster behavioral and market changes needed to increase the use of these relatively inexpensive techniques. So they created an experiment to find out which works best.

Water Guard is a relatively inexpensive chlorine solution which, when mixed with unclean water, prevents most water-borne illnesses. But even when the product is available for sale in local communities, it is rarely used. The researchers wanted to figure out how to increase its uptake. They tested various ways of getting the product to consumers, by distributing the solution for free to households, or providing it at half price. They tested community education events using personalized tutoring sessions and community-wide trainings. And they tested providing Water Guard at public water sources, available for free. It turned out that putting free chlorine solution at the public sources was about as effective as distributing it free to people's homes, and much cheaper. Apparently, social norms spread regarding Water Guard because it was in public places, and this was particularly important in increasing usage (Karlan and Appel 2011, pp. 247–252). With this evidence in hand, public health officials now had reason to invest in the provision of chlorine solutions at public water pumps: a proven, cost-effective way to save lives.

These are the two faces of foreign aid. On one hand, it is thought to be paternalistic, imposing the values of outsiders, disrupting local institutions and practices, with no impact (or worse) on poverty reduction. On the other hand, when undertaken with rigor, humility, and respect for the way people actually live and the preferences they actually have, carefully designed foreign assistance can prevent senseless, premature deaths and reduce extreme deprivation.

In this chapter, we consider arguments in favor of and against foreign aid, with special attention to the ethical issues that arise in the provision of foreign aid. And we see how a number of innovators are trying to change traditional aid programs. And in the second chapter of this section, we will examine the ethical issues involved in the allocation of scarce aid resources in a world characterized by widespread deprivation.

The Case for Foreign Aid

Foreign assistance as a means of promoting human and social development has been contested since it entered mainstream foreign policy. Beginning in the middle of the 20th century, macroeconomists argued that the reason that poor countries were poor is that they lacked access to financial capital and modern technology. Possessing other standard macroeconomic inputs of natural resources and a large labor supply, poor countries simply needed the financial backing to raise productivity, industrialize, and move to the prosperity enjoyed by what was then known as the first world. So began the first big push—get investment of capital and technology into low-income countries, and growth will follow.

Beginning in the 1990s and continuing in many circles today, the Big Push approach to economic development and poverty alleviation was reborn among academics and policy makers and led to an increase in the provision of foreign assistance. We've already met Peter Singer, the most influential philosopher promoting massive increases in foreign aid from both individuals and governments. His corollary among economists is Jeffrey Sachs, who has done more than any other public figure to promote the view that increases in foreign aid can eradicate global poverty once and for all. Sachs has had a remarkable career. He has advised senior policy makers in some of the world's most turbulent economic circumstances, including Russia following the collapse of the Soviet Union and Bolivia during a period of hyperinflation. He is the only person to have nominated himself as a candidate for the presidency of the World Bank, and has two books written about his life's work (the better of which is Nina Munk's *The Idealist* [2013]). He is as comfortable on the morning talk shows discussing the latest policy announcement from the US Federal Reserve as he is joining celebrities to advocate with heads of state to reduce poverty, increase health, and increase environmental sustainability.

Sachs believes that many people and societies are stuck in a poverty trap. In his most famous book on the subject, *The End of Poverty: Economic possibilities for our time*, he writes:

> The key problem for the poorest is that poverty itself is a trap. When poverty is very extreme, the poor do not have the ability—by themselves—to get out of the mess. Here is why: Consider the kind of poverty caused by a lack of capital per person. Poor rural villages lack trucks, paved roads, power generators, irrigation channels. Human capital is very low, with hungry, disease ridden, and illiterate villagers struggling for survival. Natural capital is depleted: the trees have been cut down and the soil nutrients exhausted. In these conditions the need is for more capital—physical, human, natural—but that requires more saving. When people are poor, but not utterly destitute, they may be able to save. When they are utterly destitute, they need their entire income, or more, just to survive ... They are too poor to save for the future and thereby accumulate the capital per person that could pull them out of their current misery.
>
> (Sachs 2015, pp. 56–57)

Sachs argues that similar poverty traps exist for countries as a whole. They can be trapped by bad geography, bad finances, bad governance, bad culture, and bad demographics. And if societies are trapped in poverty, then by definition they need external assistance to get out of these traps.

Sachs calls for the lifting of the constraints faced by poor people through a package of carefully targeted investments. These investments are to come from foreign donors and are required to lift people and communities to the first rung of economic development. Sachs focuses on five areas in which investment is needed: human capital, natural capital, public institutional capital, infrastructure, and knowledge capital. By targeting interventions that raise agricultural yields, improve transport to markets, improve the function of markets, increase health, and protect the environment, foreign aid can end poverty in our lifetime.

Partnering with major donors and the United Nations, Sachs established a series of Millennium Villages (see http://millenniumvillages.org). These villages were to receive large sums of financing, to be matched by local governments and NGOs, that would fund investments described above. With a big, targeted push of foreign assistance, villages were going to leave poverty behind and move permanently on to an upward trajectory of growth and development.

The importance of foreign aid is echoed in the rhetoric of the United Nations. In the year 2000, the United Nations General Assembly adopted the Millennium Declaration. Known as the 'world's biggest promise', this document pledged the world's governments to commit to uphold fundamental values of freedom, equality, solidarity, tolerance, respect for nature, and shared responsibility. Following the adoption of the Millennium Declaration, then Secretary-General Kofi Annan sought a way to maintain the momentum behind this global commitment to shared values and goals. He selected a team of experts and advisers to develop what became known as the Millennium Development Goals. The MDGs identified eight goals in which development progress was to occur. Commitments were made to combat extreme poverty and hunger; to achieve universal primary education; to promote gender equality; to reduce child mortality; to improve maternal health; to combat HIV/AIDS, malaria, and other diseases; to ensure environmental sustainability; and to establish a global partnership for development. After a rather meagre start, the MDGs came to dominate the discourse in international development.

The provision of foreign aid was central to the vision of meeting the MDGs. Achieving reductions in maternal mortality, universal primary education, gender equality, and other goals could only be achieved in the allotted time period only with the assistance of developed countries. The MDGs were designed and upheld to maintain political will in donor countries for foreign aid in a post-Cold War era when there were declining budgets for foreign aid.

It is very difficult to disentangle what caused an increase in official development assistance during the MDG period. There is at least some reason to think that the commitment to the MDGs, and the general advocacy behind global poverty eradication, contributed to the rise in foreign assistance (Sumner and Kenny 2011). It is harder to show that the MDGs had any noticeable impact on the policies of developing countries, or on the reduction of deprivations in the many indicators tracked by the MDGs. Much of the success in reducing deprivation occurred before the MDGs were adopted (which were strangely backdated to begin tracking progress in 1990). And, the rate of progress actually slowed after the MDGs were adopted. Furthermore, there is little evidence that the policies of developing country governments were significantly changed as a result of the adoption of the MDGs (Friedman 2013).

The MDGs have now expired, and been replaced by the Sustainable Development Goals. The SDGs are much more ambitious and expansive. The SDGs aim to wed concern for sustainability with concern for economic development. The SDGs now contain 17 goals, and an astonishing 169 targets. Most of the goals are more ambitious than their predecessors, and many appear impossible to reach. For example, the target on economic development calls for 7 percent per annum growth rates in least developed countries, with most of that growth accruing to the poorest people in those countries. This is extremely rare for any country to achieve, let alone those that are currently the worst economic performers. Nonetheless, defenders of the SDGs argue that it represents an important milestone, establishing shared norms surrounding social and economic development with concern for environmental protection. While the SDG framework continues to support the use of foreign aid, there are broader interests in policy reform that animate the newest global development goals. Many stakeholders involved in the development of the SDGs argue we must move beyond aid and focus on more comprehensive development policy.

Underlying all views and frameworks that support the provision of foreign aid is a simple argument. Part of the explanation of why individuals, communities, and countries are poor is that they do not have enough resources. The provision of resources will reduce the deprivation experienced by individuals, communities, and countries. Therefore, foreign aid should be provided to reduce global poverty. As we will see in the next sub-section, this second premise is where critics suggest the argument for foreign aid fails.

Aid's Critics

To the critics of foreign aid, the rhetorical success of the MDGs and the new mobilizations of foreign aid money are no cause for celebration. In their view, these often well-intended efforts are disconnected from the grim reality of why and how societies fail to prosper, and risk making the situation worse by sustaining extractive political institutions.

Aid and Autocrats

One way to morally criticize foreign aid is to note that it can be repurposed to repress fundamental human rights. As discussed in Chapter 3, the Ethiopian government under President Meles Zenawi was characterized by high levels of political repression but also a commitment to economic and social development. Often referred to as a 'darling' of the development community, Zenawi was believed to be at his most comfortable when discussing technical details involved in international development programming. Zenawi got his start as a rebel commander in the revolutionary army that eventually overthrew the Derg, a government which ruled Ethiopia for 13 years and murdered thousands of political opponents.

After serving as president in a transitional government, Zenawi was elected Prime Minister in 1995, a position he held until his death in 2012. Under his reign, Ethiopia was formally a multi-party democracy, and he shared a commitment to social and economic development. During this period, Ethiopia saw rapid progress against childhood mortality and increases in life expectancy. But it also ruthlessly suppressed political dissent, in part with the support of funds provided by western taxpayers. Human Rights Watch released a report in October of 2010 detailing, and condemning, the role of foreign aid in supporting political repression.

Ethiopia is also one of the world's largest recipients of foreign development aid. It receives approximately US$3 billion in funds annually—more than a third of the country's annual budget—from external donors, including the World Bank, the United States, the European Commission, the United Kingdom, Germany, the Netherlands, Canada, and Japan. Indeed, Ethiopia is today the world's second-largest recipient of total external assistance, after Indonesia and excluding wartime Iraq and Afghanistan ... However, Human Rights Watch research shows that development aid flows through, and directly supports, a virtual one-party state with a deplorable human rights record. Ethiopia's practices include jailing and silencing critics and media, enacting laws to undermine human rights activity, and hobbling the political opposition.

Led by the ruling Ethiopian People's Revolutionary Democratic Front (EPRDF), the government has used donor-supported programs, salaries, and training opportunities as political weapons to control the population, punish dissent, and undermine political opponents—both real and perceived. Local officials deny these people access to seeds and fertilizer, agricultural land, credit, food aid, and other resources for development ...

Ethiopia's foreign donors are aware of this discrimination, but have done little to address the problem or tackle their own role in underwriting government repression. As a result, Ethiopia presents a case study of contradiction in aid policy. Donors acknowledge that aid is most effective when defined by accountability and transparency, and when programs are participatory. But development agencies have turned a blind eye to the Ethiopian government's repression of civil and political rights, even though they recognize these rights to be central to sustainable socioeconomic development.

These concerns also mean that donor strategy toward Ethiopia needs fundamental rethinking. In light of the government's human rights violations, direct budget support to the government should not even be considered, and programs supported by international funds should be independently monitored. Credible audit institutions should examine aid to Ethiopia in the context of whether it contributes to political repression. External donors must also demand that Ethiopia does more than pay lip service to respecting fundamental human rights; they must be more vocal about the steps Ethiopia should take to ensure that its citizens enjoy the rights to which they are entitled under the country's constitution and international human rights law.

(Human Rights Watch 2010)

Autocratic governance presents a difficult problem for foreign donors. One natural solution is to direct aid away from repressive governments and through non-governmental organizations that can provide public services. But this raises further challenges. By relieving pressure on the government to provide these resources, this aid may still be freeing up resources that can be directed towards the military and its campaign of repression. The successful provision of public services through NGOs may also reduce the demand for democratic governance by citizens living under autocratic governments. Furthermore, even when resources move through non-governmental organizations, these organizations are often highly constrained by host governments. Autocrats may restrict what they do and how they operate, decreasing the effectiveness of aid.

Aid in War

A distinct set of concerns arises in the context of war. When providing aid in war zones, it is often not possible to avoid the messy reality that armed groups may attempt to interfere with or coopt foreign assistance for their own purposes. Transportation through war zones often involves paying bribes to armed groups. These funds then finance future fighting. Food aid is often diverted from supply lines, and used to manipulate and coerce local populations. Worse, food aid may increase rebel violence in civil wars, as it creates opportunities for looting and may present a threat to rebel authority (Wood and Sullivan 2015).

Despite these challenges, aid in war zones appears to improve well-being considerably. The Human Security Report (2010, p. 110) finds that during wartime, national mortality rates decrease. This is obviously not because war is good for extending life expectancy. Rather, contemporary warfare tends to be geographically concentrated, with a smaller number of combatants, and humanitarian assistance is effective at driving down deaths from disease and malnutrition. It therefore may be that while some foreign aid in war zones contributes to significant harm, in aggregate, aid in war zones is morally good. The moral decision of whether to provide or withhold aid in a war zone then depends on weighing up the benefits that arise from foreign assistance against the harms that it may contribute to.

Aid and Effectiveness

More generally, there are critics who argue that foreign aid does not improve material prosperity. There is a large and contested literature on the relationship between foreign aid and growth. There is considerable outstanding social scientific dispute regarding this relationship. Some studies have found a small positive relationship between foreign aid and growth in the context of good policies (Burnside and Dollar 2000). But others have shown that these findings are not robust (Roodman 2007).

The central problem with aid and poverty reduction, as Nobel Prize winning economist Angus Deaton has noted, is that when the conditions are right for promoting economic growth (that is, political institutions are functioning such that they will promote growth), then aid is not needed. When the conditions are not right for promoting growth (that is, political institutions are functioning poorly, thereby undermining economic activity), aid will not work (Deaton 2013, pp. 273–274).

But perhaps even if aid is not effective at promoting society-wide growth, it can promote human well-being in other ways. Perhaps it can increase life expectancy, improve education, and make people's lives go better, even if they are not more economically productive. Critics allege that even at the micro-level, some foreign aid appears to be ineffective or worse. Consider the Millennium Villages, discussed above, where large infusions of cash were to fund the investments that would help people leave poverty. Evaluation of the Millennium Villages has not been rigorous, providing the evidence needed to learn what might work in promoting development (Clemens and Denombynes 2013). Furthermore, many of the projects in the Millennium Villages were unsuccessful. The infusion of millions of dollars made many villagers better off, but the Millennium Villages certainly have not vindicated the idea that a complex targeted investment can move people out of poverty. For example, in Dertu, an ethnic Somali community in Northeast Kenya, water security is a big problem. The Millennium Villages project purchased a new state-of-the-art system to provide water. But when the pump broke, it took 4 months to find a replacement part, because the technology was foreign to the area. And it was a further struggle to find someone to do the repairs. All this occurred while a drought loomed. The community also used to be a way-station for nomadic herders. But with the infusion of large amounts of foreign money, people migrated, settled, and established shanty towns. There was certainly lots of change, but hardly the kind of economic and social progress Sachs had promised (Munk 2013).

One important response from the development community regarding the effectiveness of foreign aid has been to increase the rigorous measurement of outcomes from development projects (see Chapter 4). The shift to increased monitoring and evaluation, and rigorous randomized control trials, is part of a broader effort to ensure that foreign aid is effective in reducing global poverty.

Aid and Corruption

A further critique of foreign aid involves allegations regarding the presence of corruption in foreign assistance programs. There are three kinds of corruption that concern critics of foreign aid. First, there is corruption in donor countries. The United States, for example, requires food aid to be sourced from domestic farmers. This means that rather than paying for agricultural products made in low-income countries, food aid involves large purchases from major American agribusiness. These 'beltway bandits' are the beneficiaries of taxpayer beneficence rather than the global poor.

Second, recipient governments may have high levels of corruption. Even if donors attempt to 'ring fence' their donations or ensure that they go to particular programs, public finances are fungible, and the payment for new programs in one part of the budget may simply relieve the pressure on other parts of the budget, allowing monies to be siphoned off for private gain rather than public good.

Third, if aid money does not go through governments, there is a (relatively small) risk that non-governmental organizations will be corrupt. While this is a fear often promoted in the public discussion of foreign aid, there are very few confirmed instances of high levels of corruption in non-governmental organizations.

Aid and Institutions

One of the most persuasive arguments against foreign aid is the view that foreign assistance undermines the development of effective political institutions. As we saw in Chapter 3, inclusive, accountable, and capable political institutions are the best explanation for growth and prosperity. Critics of foreign aid argue that foreign aid can undermine the development of domestic political institutions. If foreign aid is provided directly to governments, then government officials will be more accountable to donors than to their own citizens. This weakens the social contract that is at the heart of accountable political institutions. It also fosters opportunities for corruption, and creates incentives for recipient governments to demonstrate continuing need for foreign aid. It is often alleged that, for example, governments permit some terrorist groups to continue to operate so that they can receive western financial and military assistance as partners in counter-terrorism operations, and subsequently use these funds to further violate human rights (DeWaal 2014).

If foreign aid is provided outside of governments, you risk reducing citizen demand for good governance, and you risk hollowing out the public services that ought to guarantee basic rights and livelihood protection in the long term. Skilled employees leave the public service for non-governmental organizations, and state capacity can diminish.

This raises a stark dilemma for the morally reflective donor. On one hand, a donor does not want to undermine domestic institutions, especially government institutions, as they are the only thing that can guarantee human rights in the long term. Nor do they want to be complicit in human rights abuses that may be perpetrated by predatory governments using foreign financial assistance. On the other hand, donors do not want people to needlessly suffer as they wait for high-quality political institutions to develop. This is a process that has taken many centuries in the most successful cases, and even then, often with periods of civil war, strife, political corruption, and autocracy.

Morally Assessing Aid

Much of the debate about foreign aid involves assessing its actual impact in the world. But there is a further philosophical question about how to morally assess aid when we agree on its impact.

One approach is purely utilitarian, to be discussed more in the next chapter on aid allocation. Utilitarians seek to maximize utility (measured by happiness, preference satisfaction, or some other subjective state) and are insensitive to the distribution of utility among a population. From the utilitarian perspective, we should simply maximize overall good. For the utilitarian, foreign aid should be assessed by calculating the aggregate amount of good it does minus the aggregate bad, and comparing this figure to alternative uses that aid money could be put toward. There is no constraint on doing harm with aid and no concern for distributive justice.

Another option is to take a strictly deontological approach. It is common in development circles to hear that the Hippocratic maxim to do no harm should be the first principle governing global development. This is initially plausible— whatever else you are going to do, don't make people worse off. Of course, as you can tell from the discussion above, it is not always readily apparent when one has done harm. The slow corrosion of domestic institutions will be far harder to identify than normal cases of harm. But even with full information, do no harm is too strict a principle to govern foreign aid. Surely it is permissible to do some amount of harm (if unintended) so that many other people benefit? Suppose the free distribution of anti-malarial bed nets does put the local seller of bed nets out of business. Does this make it the case that the free distribution of bed nets should be avoided, even if many people, especially children, will be spared premature death by their provision?

An alternative approach concedes that the provision of aid will result in some harm that would not have otherwise occurred. Therefore, even if one has done large amounts of good through the provision of material aid, they are still complicit in moral harms. On this third view, if one is considering undertaking an action that may foreseeably harm some individuals, one is not morally prohibited from undertaking that action. Rather, that person is required to avoid complicity in so far as possible, and discharge derivative duties that arise as a result of that complicity. For example, if one provides food aid in a war zone, and most of it feeds hungry people, but a small portion feeds rebel groups and increases fighting, the donor then ought to take on derivative duties to compensate (perhaps through further aid) those who have been harmed as a result of their actions. One accepts the messiness of the world, and the possibility of doing harm while doing good as a cost of the aid business. But one does not deny that doing harm while doing good confers obligations of rectification.

A further challenge for the normative assessment of aid in non-ideal circumstances is that one must attempt to weigh the immediate impact of aid delivery versus the longer term, and more uncertain, consequences that may arise. It will often be easier to determine the impact of aid on human welfare, but much more difficult to determine with any precision the impact of foreign assistance on institutional arrangements. For the critics of aid, even if some programs or projects are successful in reducing poverty and promoting longer, healthier, more productive lives, these benefits may be outweighed by the negative impact of aid on institutions in the long term.

Aid Innovators

The normative case for giving support to those who are in need is persuasive. But as we have seen, critics have highlighted significant practical challenges in successfully delivering anti-poverty programs. A number of innovators aim to respond to these criticisms to improve the impact of foreign aid both on human welfare and on poverty reduction. We consider two such innovations here.

Cash Transfers

Paternalist objections to foreign aid hold that most foreign aid programs assume that outside actors know what poor people need better than themselves. They claim that as an epistemological matter, it is poor people who know best what it is that they need. Poor people have better knowledge of their own preferences, and indeed better knowledge of their own economic, environmental, political, and social circumstances. It would be very surprising if an official from a foreign aid agency, such as the United States Agency for International Development or the United Kingdom's Department for International Development, had a better understanding of what the victim of a drought in Malawi needs to meet her basic needs than she does. It is, of course, possible, but unlikely. Following a natural disaster in a high-income country like the United States or Australia, the most common form of governmental support is a subsidy provided to families who need to rebuild their homes or recover from lost wages. Why isn't this also the best response to people who are in need in low-income countries? As a normative matter, it is preferable that people be in charge of, and responsible for, the decisions that affect their own life. When a donor decides whether to spend money on sanitation or shelter, education or health, these decisions are not taken by the people whom they affect directly.

One surprisingly obvious, but until relatively recently little tried, response to this objection is to agree that poor people know what is best for themselves and their families, but are often unable to meet their needs because they face significant financial constraints. And these constraints can be lifted, or at least loosened, through the direct transfer of cash. When a person is given cash, and then free to choose how these funds are invested among possible options of sanitation, shelter, health, and education, she is in charge of the choices that affect her life. For the anti-paternalist, cash transfers represent a vast improvement over development projects that are planned by NGOs, governments, or international institutions.

Cash transfers also help to avoid the problem of coordination. As we saw in the last chapter, when there are many different actors who are involved in the provision of foreign aid, donors can often work at cross-purposes. A great deal of coordination is required. Who should build housing? Who should do sanitation? Who should do schooling? If one schooling project is being undertaken by one donor, might that undermine the effectiveness of another schooling project undertaken in the same location by a different donor? With cash transfers, the only question of coordination is how cash is to be distributed among a population. But in the circumstance where cash transfers are poorly coordinated, the worst thing that happens is some poor people get more money than they had already planned.

A third advantage that can be claimed for cash transfers is that they do not have deleterious impacts on domestic institutions. When provided as an unconditional transfer, very little institutional interference is possible. Governments that would like to use the money for public purposes—such as building roads or schools—must raise revenue through taxation. And this taxation strengthens the social contract between citizens and governments and raises the prospect of improved governance over time.

A different form of cash transfer does involve institutions. Conditional cash transfer programs provide cash transfers in exchange for successfully meeting some pre-arranged target or objective. For example, a conditional cash transfer program may make a payment to a family if they bring all of their children to be vaccinated. Conditional cash transfers do require greater institutional involvement, but these also appear likely to strengthen rather than undermine the quality of institutions. Just as recipients of conditional cash transfers must be prepared to get their children enrolled in school or vaccinated, so too must governments be prepared to provide these public services.

In general, it appears that cash transfers are more likely to enhance local financial and market-based institutions than to undermine them. Shopkeepers stay open, markets thrive, and producers keep producing when demand is increased by the infusion of cash. There is still a great deal of learning to be done about what works best in the world of cash transfers. When should conditional cash transfers be used versus unconditional cash transfers? Should cash transfers be paid in large lump sums, or should they take the form of regular payments over time? Within a household, who should receive the transfer? Should men and women receive equal transfers? Should women receive greater cash transfers given their responsibility for children, or does this wrongly reinforce traditional gender roles? And the answers to these questions require normative input. Figuring out the preferred distribution among genders requires both social scientific and philosophical argumentation. Whatever the future holds, cash transfers appear to be a welcome innovation in the provision of foreign aid, on the grounds that they produce more benefits at lower costs, do not have negative impacts on institutional development, and accord much greater respect to the preferences of people living in deprivation.

A common objection to unconditional cash transfers is that they are likely to be badly spent by poor people, especially poor men, who many people believe will use the money on alcohol, tobacco, gambling, and prostitution. Worse, cash transfers will fuel dependency among recipients, reducing their incentives to find productive work. This surprisingly persistent view of the bad choices of people living in poverty is inconsistent with the available evidence.

Poor people do not mostly waste their cash on non-necessities. Banerjee and Duflo (2007) find that

> The extremely poor in rural areas spent 4.1 percent of their budget on tobacco and alcohol in Papua New Guinea, 5.0 percent in Udaipur, India; 6.0 percent in Indonesia and 8.1 percent in Mexico; though in Guatemala, Nicaragua, and Peru, no more than 1 percent of the budget gets spent on these goods (possibly because they prefer other intoxicants).

While these numbers could be slightly lower, they do not suggest that a major constraint on poverty reduction is the consumption of alcohol and tobacco—the additional five cents per day for other items is unlikely to make the big difference in moving out of poverty. Like everyone else, they could allocate their consumption expenditure more efficiently. But, importantly, this is exactly what happens when offered a cash transfer. Some recent studies find that investments of money and time in agriculture and non-agriculture businesses go up when people are given cash transfers, and consumption of alcohol goes down.[1] In other words, rather than causing dependency, increasing the capital available to people living in poverty causes them to work harder. It is the tool they need to raise their productivity.

Working Politically

A second form of aid innovation involves efforts to focus on institutional change. As we saw in Chapter 3, institutional quality is the primary determinant of the prosperity of societies. A new body of scholarship has emerged that aims to investigate how concern for the quality of political institutions can be integrated into development work. This framework for working politically often falls under different headings—'doing development differently', 'working politically', 'bringing politics back in', 'problem driven and adaptive development', etc.

The politically informed approach to international development eschews the traditional 'log-frame' method of project management, where a project is decided upon, set over a period of years, and then donors stick to the plan and proceed, with disregard to changing local dynamics. Rather, the politically informed approach takes a different starting point. Change is nearly always going to be locally led; it is hard to know ahead of time when opportunities for change will arise; institutional reform is key to improving outcomes for the poor; external intervention can have unintended and unwelcome consequences; donors must adapt to shifting circumstance; and development plans should expect the unexpected, allowing development workers flexibility to modify plans when this would be beneficial.

A 2014 workshop of development professionals committed to doing development differently signed a manifesto that committed to the following principles which are characteristic of successful initiatives.

> They focus on solving local problems that are debated, defined and refined by local people in an ongoing process. They are legitimised at all levels (political, managerial and social), building ownership and momentum throughout the process to be 'locally owned' in reality (not just on paper). They work through local conveners who mobilise all those with a stake in progress (in both formal and informal coalitions and teams) to tackle common problems and introduce relevant change. They blend design and implementation through rapid cycles of planning, action, reflection and revision (drawing on local knowledge, feedback and energy) to foster learning from both success and failure. They manage risks by making 'small bets': pursuing activities with promise and dropping others. They foster real results—real solutions to real problems that have real impact: they build trust, empower people and promote sustainability.
>
> (Building State Capacity 2014)

Efforts to do development differently deserve both praise and healthy skepticism. Praise is deserved as politically informed development is less likely to override the preferences, interests, and efforts of local agents working to enact change. It is also more likely to have good consequences as it takes seriously the possibility of failure and the constraints presented by current domestic political arrangements. But skepticism is warranted in so far as a mere attentiveness to local politics may not be sufficient to overcome the obstacles those domestic political economies present. Furthermore, there is some reason to doubt that donors can become good at working politically. Initial assessments of efforts to take domestic political economies seriously show that donors have largely failed to truly integrate local political concerns into their programs (Fisher and Marquette 2014).

Chapter Summary

The case for foreign aid relies heavily on empirical premises. While some foreign aid is successful in reducing global poverty, it is uncertain what the broader impacts of foreign aid are on institutional quality. Proponents of continued foreign aid must focus on continuing to improve the quality and effectiveness of that aid, rather than simply increasing its aggregate quantity. This will require continued innovation in the way aid is delivered, and attentiveness to the institutional as well as individual impacts of foreign aid.

Questions for Discussion

1   Suppose you were given $5 million to devote to poverty alleviation. Do you think it could be effectively spent on anti-poverty programs, or would it be better spent advocating for institutional reform?
2   Should a food aid program go forward if it is known that 20% of the aid will be captured by rebel soldiers but the remaining 80% will help people in need?
3   Is it morally wrong to deliver foreign aid that is not consistent with the preferences of recipients?
4   Should all foreign aid be given as direct cash transfers to people living in poverty? If not, why not?

Note

1   For a review of several recent pieces of evidence, see Davis, Ben, 'Dependency is dead!', available at http://www.fao.org/world-food-day/blog/dependency-is-dead/en/ (accessed December 7, 2015).

Suggested Reading

Easterly, W. *The Tyranny of Experts: Economists, dictators, and the forgotten rights of the poor*, New York: Basic Books, 2013.
Riddell, R. *Does Foreign Aid Really Work*, Oxford: Oxford University Press, 2005.

References

Banerjee, A. V. and Duflo, E. 'The economic lives of the poor,' *The Journal of Economic Perspectives: A Journal of the American Economic Association* 21.1 (2007): 141.

Building State Capacity. 'The doing development differently manifesto', 2014, available at http://buildingstatecapability.com/the-ddd-manifesto

Burnside, C., and Dollar, D. 'Aid, policies, and growth,' *American Economic Review* 90.4 (2000): 847–868.

Clemens, M. and Denombynes, G. 'The new transparency in development economics: Lessons from the Millennium Villages project', Center for Global Development Working Paper 342, 2013.

Deaton, A. *The Great Escape: Health, wealth, and the origins of inequality*, Princeton: Princeton University Press, 2013.

DeWaal, A. 'Why Obama's $5 billion counterrorism fund will actually support terrorism', *Boston Review Online*, June 11, 2014, available at http://bostonreview.net/blog/alex-de-waal-obamas-5-billion-counterterrorism-fund

Fisher, J. and Marquette, H. 'Donors doing political economy analysis: From process to product and back again?' Birmingham: Development Leadership Program, April 2014.

Friedman, H. 'Causal inference and the millenium development goals: Assessing whether there was an acceleration in MDG development indicators following the MDG declaration', MPRA Working Paper, 2013, available at http://mpra.ub.uni-muenchen.de/48793/1/MPRA_paper_48793.pdf

Frontline. 'Troubled water', PBS, 2010, available at www.pbs.org/frontlineworld/stories/southernafrica904/video_index.html

Human Rights Watch. 'Development without freedom: How aid underwrites repression in Ethiopia', 2010, available at www.hrw.org/print/reports/2010/10/19/development-without-freedom

Human Security Report Project. *Human Security Report 2009/2010: The causes of peace and the shrinking costs of war*, New York: Oxford University Press, 2011.

Karlan, D. and Appel, J. *More Than Good Intentions: How a new economics is helping to solve global poverty*, New York: Penguin Press, 2011.

Munk, N. *The Idealist: Jeffrey Sachs and the quest to end poverty*, New York: Anchor Books, 2013.

Roodman, D. 'The anarchy of numbers: Aid, development, and cross country empirics', *The World Bank Economic Review* 21.2 (2007): 255–277.

Sachs, J. *The End of Poverty: Economic possibilities for our time*, 2nd ed., New York: Penguin Books, 2015.

Sumner, A. and Charles K. 'More money or more development: What have the MDGs achieved?' Center for Global Development Working Paper 278, 2011.

Wood, R. and Sullivan, C. 'Doing Harm by doing good? The negative externalities of humanitarian aid provision during civil conflict', *The Journal of Politics* 77.3 (2015): 736–748.

10 Aid Allocation

Consider the following claims. There is too much money being provided to combat the spread of HIV/AIDS. AIDS victims are being lavished with scarce public resources. This privileged group has claimed too great a share of the world's resources for too long. It is morally obligatory that resources be diverted away from AIDS patients receiving antiretroviral medicines. Failure to direct resources away from these patients amounts to death sentences for the many individuals who suffer from diseases that are far easier to treat but receive far fewer resources. Similarly, the victims of genocide in Sudan and South Sudan are wrongly benefitting from disproportional access to international resources. These refugees, survivors of famine, war, and sexual violence, claim too great a share of the world's anti-poverty resources. Their disproportionate access to these resources is depriving other victims from gaining the help they need.

At first glance these claims appear shocking and deeply immoral. AIDS-related illnesses killed approximately 1.5 million people last year, and 75 million people are infected with HIV (WHO 2015). With a proper course of treatment, they can still live long, meaningful lives. Without it, they will likely face a painful, premature death. Many of the disease's current victims have no access to the antiretroviral treatments that can greatly extend the length and improve the quality of a patient's life. Sudan and South Sudan remain countries in which severe suffering and injustice persist. Few populations have suffered more since independence than the Sudanese. South Sudan, whose creation was intended to leave behind nearly five decades of conflict, descended into civil war within three years of independence. Millions of people in both countries face displacement, disease, famine, sexual violence, and premature death. Surely no one thinks that victims of the AIDS epidemic or the Sudanese civil wars receive too much support?

Well, not exactly. But many people argue that issues which galvanize the attention of aid donors often draw disproportionate resources, thereby reducing the resources available to combat other problems. The argument is not that HIV/AIDS victims receive more money than can be effectively used, but that, as a comparative matter, much more money is allocated to fight HIV/AIDS than to other deadly diseases. There are two possible complaints one might make about the allocation of scarce resources to antiretroviral treatment. The first is that other interventions are more cost-effective. In a review of the cost-effectiveness of health interventions (where cost-effectiveness is measured by disability adjusted life years[1] saved) related to HIV/AIDS, Toby Ord finds that,

> Antiretroviral therapy is estimated to be 50 times as effective as treatment of Kaposi's sarcoma; prevention of transmission during pregnancy is five times as effective as this; condom distribution is about twice as effective as that; and education for high risk groups is about twice as effective again. In total, the best of these interventions is estimated to be 1,400 times as cost-effectiveness as the least good, or more than 1,400 times better than it would need to be to be funded in rich countries.
>
> (Ord 2013)

Not all treatments or interventions against HIV/AIDS are equally cost-effective. A second complaint is that treating other diseases, or other important deprivations, is more important than treating HIV/AIDS. Combatting malaria, or waterborne illnesses, may save many more lives at equivalent costs than HIV/AIDS interventions.

As with HIV/AIDS, one can claim that too much money has been spent on the victims of ethnic cleansing and genocide in Sudan and South Sudan. On this view, their suffering is diverting needed dollars from neighboring countries that have not received the same level of international attention but where much more good could be done. Two of the most destructive wars in terms of human suffering at the start of the twenty-first century were in Sudan (and now South Sudan) and the Democratic Republic of Congo. In the United States, faith-based groups became very active in seeking to end the fighting in Sudan and to provide humanitarian assistance to victims. In 2004, under pressure from advocacy groups in the United States, President Bush declared that genocide was occurring in Darfur, the western region of Sudan. This declaration, in combination with a large mobilization of activist groups, led to huge increases in the provision of humanitarian aid to Sudan. At the same time, fighting, arguably more widespread, was occurring in the DRC. But there were no large advocacy campaigns at the time pushing western governments to address this issue. As a result, Sudan was receiving aid at a higher rate than the Democratic Republic of Congo. This despite the fact that the Sudanese government was actively thwarting the operations of humanitarian organizations. One way of stating this is that too much aid money has gone to Sudanese refugees and not enough has gone to victims in the DRC.

In the preceding chapters, we explored arguments for and against the provision of foreign aid, and looked at some of the innovative efforts to deliver aid in a way that respects the rights of poor people, supports their agency, and improves the institutions that shape their lives. In Part II, we examined the reasons that might be given to justify the existence of moral duties to alleviate global poverty. Those chapters are related to the content of the current chapter, in so far as the moral reasons that are given in favor of providing foreign assistance are also reasons that can inform how aid ought to be allocated.

Allocating Scarce Resources

In this chapter, we examine the ethical issues surrounding the allocation of aid.[2] This is a critical, and often overlooked, issue in international development. International financial institutions and international development agencies rarely give explicit reasons for their preferred allocation of resources. And when they do give guidance on how their resources are allocated, it is difficult to find any plausible moral principles to guide existing practices of allocation.[3]

The starting point for thinking about the allocation of scarce resources is to understand the economic concept of opportunity costs. Opportunity costs refer to the value of the opportunities that one forgoes if one directs a scarce resource (whether time or money) to one purpose when it could have gone to other purposes. Opportunity costs are involved in all decisions we make involving scarce resources, including the provision of foreign aid. Any money expended in one anti-poverty program is money that is not expended somewhere else. In aid allocation, the opportunity cost of any particular aid program is whatever value should be assigned to the next best scheme of aid allocation in comparison to that which is selected. We can use the term moral opportunity cost to refer to the normative value (as opposed to more narrow economic value) that an alternative resource allocation scheme has in comparison to the scheme chosen. The central question for this chapter is whether aid ought to be allocated in the way that does the most good possible. In other words, is it wrong to allocate aid in a way that diverges from a benefit maximizing allocation?

Examining the value of aid allocation is ethically complex territory because it requires considering how to weigh different values that arise from competing schemes of resource allocation, some of which appear initially incommensurable. In Chapter 2, we saw that upward of half the world's population can plausibly count as monetarily or multidimensionally poor. One natural perspective from which to morally evaluate alternative schemes of aid allocation is to examine the potential beneficiaries of aid, and the aggregate poverty reduction that would occur for the beneficiaries under competing schemes of allocation. In a world of scarce aid resources, surely it is the morally relevant facts about the beneficiary's life that should determine whether she should have a justified claim to some of the available resources. But what features of her life are relevant to making this determination? When only focusing on beneficiaries, how should aid be allocated? For the purposes of this section, let's hold fixed the amount of aid dollars available to treat these diseases.

Need

An initial thought is to allocate aid based on the need of the recipient. If the purpose of foreign aid is to help people, shouldn't aid be allocated to those who need the most help? Need might be measured in terms of one of the conceptions of poverty considered in Chapter 2—those with the lowest incomes, most unable to meet basic needs, with the fewest capabilities, least able to secure basic economic and social rights, or the most socially excluded. Alternatively, some other conception of need (such as the least healthy or the most at risk of violence) might be used to determine who is the most badly off.

Benefit

But not all people who are in great need are equally easy to assist. Consider a case in which the metric by which need is to be assessed is health. The cost-effectiveness of treating life-threatening diseases is measured by the degree to which one's life is extended, and the quality of that extension, versus if they were not treated. This is measured by two common metrics: Quality Adjusted Life Years (QALYs) and Disability Adjusted Life Years (DALYs). These measures aim to take account of not just the length of a person's life, but whether it is affected by illness in such a way as to limit the person's ability to live an active and full life. The people with the greatest health needs, however, are not the same as the people who are most likely to benefit from treatment. Some individuals have chronic or terminal diseases that, even if subjected to the most expensive and best available medical treatments, will only see their lives extended a short period of time. Other individuals have equally debilitating diseases that can be treated by relatively inexpensive and easy to administer treatments. In other words, some lives are more costly to save than others.

If you are persuaded that we should treat more of the latter group rather than fewer of the former group, you might endorse a principle that allocates aid according to benefit, also known as cost-effectiveness, where effectiveness is understood in terms of the benefits that accrue to individuals. On this view, we should allocate aid where it will do the most good. This view is often (though not exclusively) endorsed by utilitarians, who think we ought to maximize utility in all of the moral decisions we make, and other non-utilitarians who are nonetheless persuaded that we should maximize the amount of good that can be done with available anti-poverty resources. Where good is understood as the amount of benefit that will accrue to the potential recipients of beneficence.

Priority

While allocating aid to optimize benefit is a plausible principle to guide aid allocation, there are some reasons that might lead us to endorse a divergence away from benefit maximization in foreign aid allocation. One reason we might diverge is that we want to give greater priority to the worse off.

Prioritarianism is the view that there is more marginal moral value in assisting those who are worse off than those who are better off (Parfit 1997). On prioritarian grounds, providing an additional 5 years of life to someone who faces a life expectancy of 45 is more morally valuable than adding those same 5 years of life to someone who faces a life expectancy of 75. In fact, a strong form of prioritarianism might hold that it would be better to add 5 years to a short life than to add some larger number of years, say 10, to a person who has already lived a long and happy life.

Prioritarian considerations need not be exclusive to the health sphere. Suppose that you could add an equal amount of material benefit to a person who is living on 1 USD a day or 10 USD per day. (It is generally thought that there are diminishing returns on the value of money as incomes go up, but let's assume those diminishing returns have not set in.) If you are inclined to think that the person living on a dollar a day has a greater claim to an additional dollar a day, this implies a commitment to prioritarianism. Prioritarianism offers a variant of the principle that aid should be allocated based on benefit, which reflects some consideration for the level of well-being of the potential recipient. Prioritarian aid allocations might be thought of as allocating aid based on how much a person will benefit, with adjustments giving greater weight to benefits accruing to the worse off.

Agency

A different kind of reason that might factor into one's determination of who should receive aid is whether the potential beneficiaries are organizing and actively pursuing a remedy to their deprivations. If civil society has organized against injustice and is calling for support, this generates a *prima facie* reason to provide that support. Respect for the agency of potential beneficiaries is not normally factored into standard cost-effectiveness analyses, but it is a plausible consideration to weigh in the allocation of aid. Suppose, for example, that you know that an oppressive government is cutting access to needed social services in two countries. But in one of those countries, there are widespread protests on the street, where protestors are being jailed and calling for supporters in the international community to lend a hand. In the other country it does not appear that such collective action is underway. Giving consideration to the agency and expressed preferences of those who are fighting against their impoverishment might be an additional consideration in determining where to allocate aid.

Of course, one can resist arguments in favor of allocating aid based on the demonstrated agency of potential beneficiaries. Some victims of oppression and deprivation are unable, due to very high levels of repression, to organize in a way that demonstrates the kind of agency that someone allocating aid dollars might take notice of. And other victims are nearly invisible. People who are victims of sex trafficking, or child laborers, cannot take to the streets to demonstrate that they are organizing against oppression.

That said, many philosophers think there is normative value in political solidarity, including in the transnational sphere (Gould 2007, Gilabert 2006). Among other things, political solidarity requires providing support to social movements when those movements request it (and are otherwise morally deserving). For political solidarity to be meaningful, one must maintain solidarity (through the devotion of time or resources) to organized movements even when some alternative allocation of those resources would bring more benefit.

The Perspective of Donors

To this point, we have only considered features of the potential recipients of aid that might guide a morally justified allocation of aid. However, as discussed in Chapter 7, donors are not impartial observers plopped down into the world with buckets of money to donate. They are people, or institutions, who inhabit particular places and are embedded in relations that shape their interests, motivations, and preferences. This place in the world might also affect the moral reasons that ought to govern their aid allocation. To what extent might donors have agent-relative reasons to diverge from benefit maximization?

Interest

Most governments say something about national interest to explain why they provide foreign aid and to whom they provide it. National interest can be interpreted narrowly or broadly. On a narrow interpretation of national interest, foreign aid should be provided to gain things (power, influence, commercial ties) for the donor country. Few national governments admit to exclusively using aid in this way today, but many do aim to align national interest with charitable efforts. On a broader interpretation of national interest, countries share a set of values that are to be promoted by government policy makers, and in this sense the national interest is served when efforts are made to promote global public health, or respond to natural disasters, or to prevent war and mass atrocities. When a government declares that it is in their interest to fight famine or provide support to refugees in war zones, they may have both of these interpretations in mind. They may think that they will win the hearts and minds of potential enemies, or prevent the spread of infectious diseases that could arrive in their country. Or they might mean that it is in the national interest of the citizens of their country to prevent hunger, or war, or illness simply because the persistence of these problems is at odds with nationally shared values.

Individual donors rarely state that they give charitable donations to achieve personal gain, but this can be a motivation for private donations. When a wealthy donor contributes to a university, for example, she may expect that her family members will be guaranteed admission. Or if she contributes to community organizations or the arts in her city, she may hope for favorable treatment in bidding for government contracts. These narrow interests are not morally important and may be condemned in so far as they may corrupt other institutions. They are only important in so far as they bring about morally good donations. And given that there is a high likelihood that narrow self-interest will not align with beneficiary interest, we ought not give weight to self-interested reasons in determining how aid should be allocated.

Preference

Another factor that might guide aid allocation is the preferences of donors. Consider a wealthy donor who decides to leave a large portion of his wealth to his alma mater. Assume that this university already has a nice endowment and is already able to fund important research and subsidize tuition for students demonstrating financial need. Given that this money could be spent to prevent a mother having to bury her child because it had not received its vaccinations, it certainly appears that allocating money to the university is suboptimal from the perspective of cost-effectiveness. While helping students go to an elite university is good, preventing needless suffering and death is better.

But the donor might reply, 'I earned this money! It is my choice whether to give it away, and if I do give it away, it is my decision on how it should be spent!' Indeed, many foundations argue that their funds should be allocated according to donor intent, especially if the original donor is deceased. The deference to donor interests is common among philanthropic organizations. For example, the Bill and Melinda Gates Foundation, which does a huge amount of good in global public health and global poverty reduction, has one of its five priority areas as promoting college-ready education in the United States. (Their work has, controversially, focused on, among other things, standardized tests and the promotion of charter schools.) While educational inequality in the United States is an important issue, it is hard to imagine that, on cost-effectiveness terms, it can compete with global health and global hunger. The Gates Foundation may simply reply that the foundation's aid allocation reflects the donor's preferences, and no further justification is needed.

Critics of the use of donor preference to allocate aid will again note that there are much better ways to allocate money that would do much more good. And the preferences and interests of donors are not morally weighty, at least not in any way comparable to the moral concerns involved in global poverty reduction.

But donors might respond that it is not implausible to think that their interests and preferences should shape how they give their money away. For example, suppose that you have a family member who is struggling with a difficult-to-treat illness. You might make a donation to an organization that is searching for a cure to that illness, or organize a fundraiser, or participate in an event supporting the organization. Most people think these actions are morally commendable, and certainly morally permissible. Why should we not hold similar views about other large financial donations?

Association

Of course, even if one denies that moral preferences and interests should be given any weight in deciding how to allocate aid, as a matter of practical consideration, advocates for the global poor may strike a balance between providing clear moral guidance on which allocations are morally best, and permitting some donors to pursue those activities that they care about the most, thereby maximizing the net moral benefit. But one does not have to concede to the natural self-interest of donors to make a case for aid allocations that take account of the preferences or interests of donors. As we saw in Chapter 7, associative reasons may provide independent grounds for justifying anti-poverty duties. If we should take associative reasons seriously, then this provides further grounds for diverging from benefit-maximizing aid allocations. Bill and Melinda Gates can justify their investments in American education by saying that they are Americans, educated in the American education system, and they bear the right kinds of associations to that system to justify it as a priority area. So too might they justify their allocation of aid dollars to various programs increasing access to technology, given that their wealth comes from technological innovation, and they may have specific expertise in this area.

Procedural Justice

At this point, we have given a great deal of consideration to the substantive questions regarding the allocation of aid. It is equally important to reflect on the procedures by which decisions regarding aid allocation and planning are made.

Suppose one day you awake to find that the water flowing to your house had been shut off. Upon investigation, you find an official who says he represents an agency that is interested in helping you. Your access has been cut off to divert water to a hydro-power plant that is meant to spur growth in your community. Or perhaps they tell you that you must move off your land, to make room for a planned highway or a new mining project. This person who has come to change how your community functions says his organization has approved the plans with your government, and is committed to getting the best for you and your family. But you hadn't heard anything about the plans, and in any case you wouldn't dare speak your mind to the government, which has a history of throwing dissidents in jail.[4]

What sorts of reasons might you raise in defense of your claim against this treatment? One kind of reason relates to well-being. You are made worse off, and harmed, by the displacement or development projects that alter lives. But there is another feature of what has happened that warrants moral complaint. Even if a proposed project would be in aggregate beneficial for a community, it is arguably wrong to undertake it without proper deliberation and authorization by the relevant stakeholders. In democracies, several layers of representative government are justified not simply on the grounds that they produce the best outcomes for citizens, but that there is independent value in participating in the decisions that affect our lives. As Amartya Sen (1999, p. 9) argues, democracy is valuable in three distinct ways.

> First, political freedom is a part of human freedom in general, and exercising civil and political rights is a crucial part of good lives of individuals as social beings. Political and social participation has intrinsic value for human life and well-being. To be prevented from participation in the political life of the community is a major deprivation. Second ... democracy has an important instrumental value in enhancing the hearing that people get in expressing and supporting their claims to political attention (including claims of economic needs). Third ... the practice of democracy gives citizens an opportunity to learn from one another, and helps society to form its values and priorities.

The value of democratic participation is equally important in the planning of development projects—it is both likely to make those projects more successful, and intrinsically important to take part in the decisions that affect one's life.

A second procedural concern involves the promises or commitments that are made by development organizations. Initiating projects, hopefully undertaken with proper community consultation, raises hopes, changes expectations, affects life plans, and potentially disrupts (for better or worse) existing traditions and institutions. Involving oneself or one's organization in the life chances of people living in deprivation is a form of promise-making, akin to a contractual arrangement in which one undertakes various obligations even if one is merely acting on altruistic grounds and attempting to provide benefits to the community. A distinction must be made between the initial decision of aid allocation, and subsequent project implementation. The decision to undertake anti-poverty projects and programs generally involves making commitments to individuals and communities. Once those commitments are made, this generates a new moral obligation which did not previously exist. The history of development practice involves many unfulfilled commitments by would-be do-gooders. The reason for their unfulfilled commitments certainly vary. But if commitments are made to a particular community, commitments which shape the expectations and opportunities available to members of that community, then one ought not abandon those commitments merely on the grounds that they could do more good elsewhere. To the person who has been uprooted or disrupted by a development project, it is insufficient justification to say that one could not complete the project because they had to go do more good elsewhere.

But does procedural justice have anything to do with aid allocation? Before a scheme for allocating aid is selected, is it even possible to involve potential beneficiaries in a discussion? Should Oxfam host poor people at their executive committee to determine strategic priorities? And if they should, how would they go about initially selecting participants in those discussions? While initial decisions to allocate aid among potential beneficiaries may not be fully participatory, there are ways in which poor people can be included in setting global priorities. In advance of the decision to agree to the Sustainable Development Goals, the UN ran 'My World', a global survey asking people about their development priorities. Over 5.7 million people participated from low- and middle-income countries. While imperfect in many ways, it shows the potential for at least some deliberation with potential beneficiaries about candidate schemes of aid allocation. This may lend legitimacy to decisions made by governments and non-governmental organizations with regard to their aid allocation decisions.

Chapter Summary

The allocation of scarce resources always raises important philosophical questions. In the case of foreign assistance, the allocation of international aid is rarely governed by firm moral principles, but it ought to be. A range of moral reasons must be brought to bear in determining what is permissible and optimal in the allocation of international aid. In this chapter, we have considered the view that aid ought to do the most good possible, as well as plausible alternative moral reasons that might lead one to diverge from a benefit-maximizing approach to foreign aid.

Questions for Discussion

1   Think about the last time you, or someone close to you, made a charitable donation. What moral reasons could be given for that donation? Do you think they are good reasons?
2   Should foreign aid be allocated to maximize overall benefit? If not, why not?
3   Most national governments allocate aid in a way that is highly beneficial to their own self-interest. Is it morally wrong to allocate aid in this way?
4   If you had to choose between a relatively certain investment in anti-malarial bed-nets, or an uncertain investment in the development of an anti-malarial vaccine, what would you choose?
5   Is it possible to compare very different goods, like health and physical security, that can be promoted through international aid?

Notes

1   This is a measure of the number of healthy years of life lost to early death or to living with disease and disability.
2   This section draws on ideas developed in Wisor 2012.
3   On the patterns of aid allocation, see Neumayer 2003.
4   This hypothetical example might be more common than you think. The International Consortium of Investigative Journalists (2015) argues that World Bank funded projects have resulted in the displacement of 3.5 million people over the course of a decade, and that those displaced have found few avenues for holding accountable governments, companies, or the World Bank itself for human rights violations or needed restitutions.

Suggested Reading

DCP3. 'Disease control priorities in developing countries', 3rd ed., available at http:// dcp-3.org (accessed December 10, 2015).
Illingworth, P., Pogge, T., and Wenar, L. *Giving Well: The ethics of philanthropy*, Oxford: Oxford University Press, 2011.
MacAskill, W. *Doing Good Better: How effective altruism can help you make a difference*, New York: Gotham, 2015.
Penz, P., Drydyk, J., and Bose, P. *Displaced by Development: Ethics, rights, and responsibilities*, Cambridge: Cambridge University Press, 2011.
Rubenstein, J. *Between Samaritans and States: The political ethics of humanitarian NGOs*, Oxford: Oxford University Press, 2015.

References

Gilabert, P. 'Global justice, democracy and solidarity', *Res Publica*, 12.4 (2006): 435–443.

Gould, C. 'Transnational solidarities', *Journal of Social Philosophy*, 38.1 (2007): 148–164.

International Consortium of Investigative Journalists. 'Evicted and abandoned: The World Bank's broken promise to the poor', 2015, available at http://www.icij.org/project/world-bank (accessed December 11, 2015).

Neumayer, E. *The Pattern of Aid Giving*, London: Routledge, 2003.

Parfit, D. 'Equality and priority', *Ratio*, 10 (1997): 202–221.

Sen, A. 'Democracy as a universal value', *Journal of Democracy*, 10.3 (1999): 3–17.

WHO, World Health Organization, 'Global health observatory data', available at www.who.int/gho/hiv/en (accessed December 11, 2015).

Wisor, S. 'How should INGOs allocate resources?' *Ethics and Global Politics*, 5.1 (2012): 27–48.

Part IV
Global Institutional Reform

The preceding chapters may have left the reader skeptical as to whether much of what is currently practiced in the name of poverty alleviation is effective, or simply aims to serve the national interests of donor governments and the self-interest of do-gooder philanthropists. For those who doubt the effectiveness of some foreign aid or believe it is paternalistic, global institutional reform offers a more promising normative perspective with a greater potential impact on poverty reduction. Rather than focusing on what can be done in poor countries to improve the lives of people living with deprivation, institutional reformers focus on the way in which legal, economic, and political arrangements currently impede poverty reduction. They argue that systemic reform in global institutions will do far more to reduce global poverty than will foreign aid. Furthermore, as a normative matter, they argue that individuals in high-income countries should focus to a much greater extent on the institutions that they uphold, and the ways in which these institutions produce suboptimal outcomes for people living in poverty, rather than attempting to interfere in communities that they little understand with programming that has at best a mixed record of improving outcomes.

In this section we briefly consider several different reforms that have been proposed to the global institutional order which are argued to have strong anti-poverty potential. We consider some of the ethical issues involved in international migration, international trade, and humanitarian intervention. We do this with particular focus on the poverty-related issues that are raised by each of these topics, and consider some of the normative trade-offs that are involved in alternative institutional arrangements.

Part IV

Global International Relations

11 Immigration

In the summer of 2015, two international migration crises made headlines across the globe. One involved millions of refugees and migrants who had left their countries of birth, fleeing war and oppression, trying to reach the shores of Europe. About two-thirds were fleeing the war in Syria, while others fled conflict in Afghanistan and Iraq, repression in Eritrea, and poverty elsewhere. While the vast majority of Syrian refugees were either internally displaced, or residing in overburdened, underfunded camps in Jordan and Lebanon, as time wore on, the number of people seeking to enter the European Union continued to grow.

The most common response from European countries was to make it more difficult for people to enter: they tightened or closed border crossings, built fences, and increased border patrols. For example, the Italian government, in agreement with the European Union, decided to restrict its search and rescue operations in the Mediterranean Sea, on the grounds that these operations created an incentive for potential migrants to attempt the dangerous crossing to Europe by boat. By suspending search and rescue, they believed they could reduce the number of migrants attempting to enter Europe by sea.

Following this decision, the number of migrants dying at sea while attempting to cross international borders increased considerably. In the first 3.5 months of 2014, 17 people were reported to have died attempting to migrate to Europe by sea. In the first 3.5 months of 2015, 900 migrants died attempting to make the journey. On one day, February 8, 2015, some 300 people died at sea. Amnesty International documented some of the stories of those who perished:

> Some 420 refugees and migrants had left together from the Libyan port town of Garabouli, 40km west of Tripoli, in four inflatable dinghies. Most were young men from West Africa and several were minors. People smugglers had kept them near Tripoli to await the journey after charging them the equivalent of around 650 euros. On the evening of 7 February, the smugglers, armed, made them board the dinghies, which were numbered 1 to 4. The boats were powered by small outboard motors, and the smugglers had not provided enough petrol for the trip. Italian coast guard officials, later interviewed by Amnesty International, stressed that the weather forecast in that part of the Mediterranean was bad for the entire week and that the refugees and migrants were sailing towards certain death.

Early on 8 February, the boats drifted in the Mediterranean Sea north of Libya, in serious danger. High waves were washing people off the dinghies and into the sea. The first dinghy deflated and started taking on water until it was found by the Italian coast guard patrol boats. The second was never found and left no survivors. Merchant vessels assisted two more dinghies. One of these had only seven people alive on board and it went down with many dead bodies while the survivors were climbing the rope thrown to them by the crew of the merchant vessel. The fourth dinghy was found by another merchant vessel in the afternoon of 9 February, deflated and with only the front side afloat, to which two men had managed to hold on.

Survivors believe that more than 330 of their fellow travellers perished, as they estimated that about 105 people were on board each of the four dinghies.

(Amnesty 2015)

Much less publicized, but equally harrowing, was the departure of large numbers of people from Myanmar (Burma). Long suffering from persecution as an ethnic and religious minority, the Rohingya people were fleeing Myanmar in large numbers by boat and land. Persecuted at the hands of government forces and rival ethnic and religious communities, and threatened by the treacherous journey by sea on poorly constructed vessels, one would hope great relief would come to those who escaped violence and repression. But arriving on the shores of neighboring countries, Rohingya found themselves in many cases sent back to sea, by countries eager to see these refugees land on other shores. Indonesia, Thailand, and Malaysia all refused to offer support to the persecuted group. The Deputy Home Minister of Malaysia proclaimed, 'we have to send the right message that they are not welcome here' (Tennery 2015). The difficulty finding refuge was reminiscent of the voyage of the St. Louis, 80 years before. Fleeing Nazi Germany, the St. Louis docked in both Cuba and the United States, only to have both countries say that they could not accept most of the fleeing refugees. The St. Louis returned to Europe, where refugees who made it to Britain largely survived World War II, while about half of those who returned to Western Europe died in the Holocaust (USHMM 2015).

There was no denying the dire circumstances potential migrants were trying to leave behind. And there was little doubt that people would be far better off if they resettled in countries that they were trying to reach. But despite some notable exceptions (including the initial German decision to accept up to 800,000 refugees per year for 5 years and the Swedish decision to accept 100,000 refugees, the highest per capita acceptance rate of any European country), the overwhelming response by most countries was to build fences and other barriers, to target so-called people smugglers, and in some cases to further support military activities in countries from which refugees were fleeing, as if the dropping of a few more bombs might stem the flow of people.

The movement of people across international borders raises some of the most important and contentious questions in contemporary moral and political philosophy. Adequately answering these questions requires giving a philosophical account of the state, of the rights of citizens, of the moral status of residents and foreigners, of the importance of occupancy, and the ways in which the rights of individuals and collectives should be understood, especially when they appear to be in conflict. In the brief space here, we won't have the opportunity to explore many important questions involved in international migration. Rather, we will focus on the ethical questions surrounding migration and its relationship to global poverty. Proponents of international migration and more permissive migration policies argue that it is the greatest anti-poverty mechanism in the world, and freedom of movement is a fundamental human right. Critics allege that international migration violates collective self-determination of recipient countries, and undermines the development prospects of low-income countries.

The Case for Increased Migration

Many philosophers advocate increased levels of international migration on purely philosophical grounds. Some even argue for entirely open borders. They argue that freedom of movement is a basic fundamental right, and moral agents who choose to leave their country of birth ought to be free to do so. This freedom involves not only the right to leave but the right to arrive somewhere else. This basic concern for the freedom of individuals to live where they choose is combined with a rejection of arguments supporting a state's right to exclude would-be residents. Our focus here will be on a narrower set of arguments that support increased levels of migration on the grounds that more migration means more poverty reduction.

Economists have long argued that many barriers to trade reduce global welfare. By erecting barriers that prevent the exchange of goods and services, governments create economic inefficiencies that tend to reduce aggregate economic well-being. During the current phase of globalization, persuaded by economic arguments in favor of trade liberalization and under pressure from business interests who would benefit from increased international trade, governments have considerably reduced the barriers to trade. Today, international trade is such a common feature of daily life that it is unremarkable to note that our T-shirts and televisions involve supply chains that reach across much of the globe. But there is one thing that cannot travel easily across borders in the era of globalization: labor.

Workers seeking to earn higher wages within a country are generally free to move from, for example, rural areas to the city in search of employment in the manufacturing sector. Such urban to rural migration is extremely common and has been characteristic of countries that have made the transition to high-income economies. But when workers attempt to move across international borders in search of better economic opportunities or greater security, they have extremely limited legal options in attempting to find better work.

To get a sense of the mismatch between the extremely high demand from people in low- and middle-income countries to live and work abroad, and the very small amount of legal opportunities for doing so, consider the following. In any given year, about 15 million people apply for the Diversity Immigrant Visa program in the United States, colloquially known as the green card lottery. Of these, only 50,000 will gain a green card, less than half a percent. The huge demand for this program suggests that these people believe their living standards will be much better should they move to a high-income country. In fact, the Gallup World Poll finds that while 13 percent of people globally would like to permanently migrate, as many as 40 percent of people in some low-income countries would like to move to another country (Clemens 2011).

In theory, one would anticipate that migration would have poverty-reducing effects for the migrant. Moving from an economy where people mostly earn low incomes to an economy where people mostly earn high incomes should be expected to raise the standard of living for the person who moves. Furthermore, multidimensional poverty should also fall for the migrating person and her family, as she would have better access to infrastructure like sanitation and clean running water, better schools and higher quality healthcare, and better physical security.

As with other areas of anti-poverty policy, there are significant disputes among social scientists regarding the effects of international migration. Nonetheless, the best available estimates suggest massive economic gains, and subsequent poverty reduction, from international migration. In the words of Michael Clemens (2011), even moderately more permissive regimes of international migration represent 'trillion dollar bills' left on the sidewalk, economic gains orders of magnitude greater than other reforms, such as the elimination of inefficient trade barriers. Where do these poverty-reducing economic gains come from? First, as suggested above, large economic gains go to the person migrating. Consider moving a person who works the same job, say construction, in Peru, to the United States. That person's wages go up dramatically, often several fold. Second, migrants often send large remittances back to their country of origin, providing significant financial support to their families. These economic benefits far outweigh any downward pressure on domestic employment or recipient state fiscal positions (and, in any case, these negative effects do not necessarily materialize).

The Case against Increased Migration

However, a number of ethicists and development scholars argue against more permissive international migration. Many do not do so with explicit reference to global poverty. They simply assert that states have the right to exclude potential migrants: on the grounds that states are associations that are generally free to choose their members, on the grounds that state legitimacy entails territorial rights to exclude, or on the grounds that shared national communities (based on religion or culture or language) may exclude non-members (Fine and Sangiovanni 2015). Pragmatists also emphasize that citizens in recipient states will never accept more liberalized borders, and this should be treated as a fairly firm feasibility constraint in the design of migration policy. However, some arguments against international migration are made explicitly on the grounds that higher levels of international migration will exacerbate rather than help to solve the problem of global poverty.

First, critics claim that international migration reduces the available pool of talented, productive workers who can create positive economic activity, provide needed social services like medical care and education, and improve political institutions in countries that have a net outflow of international migrants. This is often known as the brain drain thesis. For example, Gillian Brock argues that 'developed countries permitting entry to more immigrants can have disastrous effects for the countries they exit' (Brock 2009, p. 198). While Brock concedes that skilled emigrants gain valuable experience and training, and send remittances back home, she argues that,

> When rich countries recruit workers trained in poor countries without compensation, what is effectively happening is that poor countries are subsidizing the health care of citizens of affluent countries, while losing significant resources in the process ... For countries which already have severe shortages of health professionals ... further loss of workers is most likely to result in loss of health services and significant loss of health in the countries' populations.
>
> (Brock 2009, p. 199)

The brain drain thesis faces significant, and in my view decisive, objections. It appears to be based on a mistaken reading of the available evidence on the impacts of skilled emigration and the potential impacts of restricting or taxing skilled emigrants. The departure of highly skilled migrants is much more likely to be a symptom, rather than a cause, of international migration. Consider migrants fleeing political persecution and civil war. For the doctor or lawyer or accountant who leaves Syria or Sudan or Zimbabwe, it is hard to imagine that if they stayed in their home country, they would be able to effectively provide important social services, or generate large amounts of economic activity, or lead political reform. Extractive or broken political institutions make it such that a person cannot easily convert her productive capabilities into good outcomes for herself, her family, or her community. Poor-functioning health care systems, where salaries are low and conditions are bad, are the cause of both poor health outcomes and the out-migration of health care workers.

The financial losses that are thought to accrue to the populations of sending states must be evaluated against the financial gains that accrue to the migrant, her family, and her society more generally. For the migrant, she receives higher wages, often times much higher than she would earn in her home country, by migrating. Most migrants send remittances back to their countries of origin, as cash transfers to families and friends, but also as investments in productive activities in their home countries. In fact, in the world's poorest countries, remittances are often the most important economic lifeline for families who remain in the country. For example, in Somalia remittances can make up to 40 percent of the income of urban households (Maimbo 2006).

Furthermore, the investment by individuals in developing skills and gaining education in sending states may be incentivized by the possibility of international migration. It is precisely the demand for labor from abroad that encourages people to invest their time and resources to gain the skills necessary to work in productive sectors abroad. Critics who ignore this incentive effect treat investments in training as a net loss every time a migrant leaves. But this calculation fails to take account of the fact that the investment would not have taken place if the migrant only had the opportunity of entering the domestic labor market.

Second, critics of more open immigration policies allege that the arrival of new migrants exacerbates the (relative) poverty of low-income individuals in countries that receive migrants. These critics claim that the arrival of new sources of labor has two negative effects on the under-employed, unemployed, and lowly paid workers in recipient countries. New potential employees 'take' the jobs that would have otherwise gone to domestic workers. And, more generally, an increase in the pool of available labor decreases the wages that will be paid to low-income workers.

This raises both economic and philosophical questions. As a philosophical matter, what is owed to citizens in migrant-receiving countries and what is owed to migrants who have arrived in those countries? How should combating the relative poverty in high-income countries be weighed against the moral priority of combating poverty experienced by people in low- and middle-income countries? States generally have much greater duties to their own citizens, especially the worst off, than to non-citizens. But the question is whether these greater duties imply that full restrictions on immigration, even if such migration would have great global poverty-reducing effects, are justified in order to protect domestic workers. These are difficult moral trade-offs, but it is implausible to think that no amount of absolute global poverty reduction would be worth sacrificing any domestic relative poverty reduction. Furthermore, the economics of this domestic egalitarian argument against immigration are implausible. The best available evidence from natural experiments shows that there are no substantial negative impacts on employment or wages for low-income workers as a result of increased immigration (Roodman 2014).

Third, critics allege that these new migrants also place great strains on the social safety nets in recipient countries, to the detriment of the provision of health care, education, and other social services meant for the most needy citizens of migrant-receiving countries. From this view, the services that are most valuable to the economically worst off in recipient countries are over-burdened by the arrival of new migrants who also gain access to these systems. This 'fiscal' version of the domestic egalitarian argument against more immigration suggests that the worst off (and other) citizens are indirectly harmed by the burden imposed by recent immigrants on public resources. As previous, this involves making a normative evaluation of how to weigh concern for the domestic poor in high-income countries against the global poor. But, as seen already, it may be beside the point, as the economics are often misunderstood. Most recent immigrants are actually net contributors to the social system. In general, migrants to high-income countries end up paying considerable taxes which support public services. Even if a person is an undocumented employee, they may have wages withheld for taxes, and also pay consumption and property taxes in their local community. Furthermore, migrants often do not have access to many public benefits in their receiving country. And international migrants are usually young and healthy, thereby placing little strain on health care and social security systems. In the most comprehensive analysis to date, the OECD finds that on average the fiscal impact of migrants is near zero, and rarely goes above or below 0.5 percent GDP in either positive or negative directions (OECD 2013).

Another version of the brain drain thesis involves the emotional and caring relationships that appear to be severed by international migration, especially for women, who do care work abroad. In the colorful language of Eva Feder Kittay, this involves a global heart transplant, whereby women seeking better economic opportunities by working as careworkers abroad must leave behind those with whom they held emotional ties and caring relationships (Feder Kittay 2014). There is no doubt that international migration can involve emotional costs that do not register in estimates of the economic benefits of labor mobility. But it is far from clear that such costs justify restrictions in international migration. If the departing migrant considers the emotional and financial costs and benefits of departing, and still chooses to depart, it would be hard to defend restricting her entrance to a high-income country on the grounds that she should be at home providing care work. Rather, reforms to migration policies which permit one to easily and legally travel back home, remit money without taxation, and reunify families separated by international borders, appear preferable to the restriction of the entrance of care workers.

The most serious and significant argument against increased international migration, and the one that is perhaps least addressed by current proposals for reforms in international migration policy, involves the vulnerability and exploitation of many international migrants. Migrants are often highly vulnerable, and without both legal protections and social support networks, when they arrive in recipient countries. This is true in western liberal democracies but even more so when migrants travel to non-democratic and non-liberal societies. For example, Nicola Jones et al. (2014) examine in detail the case of young women who migrate from Ethiopia, especially its rural areas, to Saudi Arabia and other Middle Eastern countries. They find that facing poor schooling, weak economic opportunities, the looming risk of early and unwanted marriage, and discriminatory gender norms, many young women, sometimes through illegal, informal migration brokers, leave home to become domestic workers in high-income countries. Domestic workers in all countries are among the most vulnerable and exploited workers. In many jurisdictions, these migrants face risks of abuse, confiscation of wages, the burden of debts incurred by migration brokers, and little recourse to legal protection or social support. For example, Zem Zem, an 18-year-old Ethiopian, facing limited opportunities at home, spent 10,000 birr to travel to Saudi Arabia. Immediately upon arrival with her employers at their desert compound, she was forced to work day and night, given limited opportunity to contact her parents, beaten by many of the family members, and violently raped by one of the family's sons. On the return flight to Ethiopia, Zem Zem found many of her peers had similar experiences of violence, exploitation, and confiscated wages. While she would counsel would-be migrants against making the journey, they all viewed the possibility of financial gain as far preferable to remaining at home with limited economic opportunities.

The risks of exploitation and violence faced by potential immigrants raises a different normative challenge than those previously considered. To this point we have been weighing reductions in monetary and multidimensional poverty when considering the poverty-reducing effects of immigration. But the risks of severe exploitation and physical and sexual violence raise distinct, and in some ways incommensurable, concerns. In some circumstances states might be justified in creating barriers to their migrants departing for other states where their rights are likely to be violated, but such a restriction would only be justified if their prospects for securing rights are better at home than in other countries to which they intend to migrate.

Migration Reform in Non-Ideal Circumstances

As a general matter, the full prohibition of international migration is philosophically difficult to defend. From the perspective of global poverty reduction, barriers to migration prevent extremely large improvements in the welfare of migrants and their families, benefits far greater than those that might accrue from reforms to international trade or the provision of foreign aid. That said, international migration can place people in dangerous, violent circumstances with little recourse to legal or social protection, can divide families, and leave children without parents. Furthermore, the politics of international migration are extremely challenging. Politicians who aim to support more permissive migration policies must face the potential backlash of nativist sentiment, and are unlikely to be rewarded at the polls for strong stances in favor of global poverty-reducing international migration schemes.

As with other issues, the important ethical problems to be worked out involve the normative trade-offs between various candidate migration schemes. Public opinion and potentially destabilizing effects on social fabric, combined with the need for effective states to function in order for poverty to be reduced, makes fully open borders unfeasible. But other schemes are available which might reduce the most morally problematic effects of migration, and increase the poverty-reducing effects of immigration.

First, ensuring that refugees can be resettled and, in resettlement, have basic economic rights, would do much more to improve the economies in countries where refugees resettle than does preventing them from working. While this policy may be intended to protect domestic jobs, it decreases the fiscal input of migrants and decreases aggregate economic activity in the recipient country, thereby hurting the prospects for better wages for everyone.

Second, countries that support the sending of their citizens abroad must work, when possible, in concert with the receiving government to ensure that basic security rights are respected and that workers have access to support and options for exit when under threat. Whatever levels of migration there are going to be, those who go as migrants should not be subject to violence or exploitation as a result of their status as non-citizens.

Third, we should promote programs that provide for temporary economic migration which encourage the poverty-reducing effects of international labor migration while reducing the vulnerability of the migrant and allowing for the preservation of social and financial connections to her home country. Allowing temporary workers to legally work in recipient countries will both benefit the migrant, secure needed labor in recipient countries, and allow for workers to maintain strong familial and social ties in the sending country.

Fourth, making international payment of remittances at low tax or tax free, easy, reliable, and protected from political interference will enhance the poverty-reducing effects of international migration (Barry and Overland 2009). When migrants must go through informal channels to finance international money transfers, or pay additional taxes, this raises the costs of making cash transfers, and makes it more, rather than less, likely that illicit financial transfers to terrorists or other nefarious organizations will proceed.

And finally, increasing legal routes of migration to higher-income countries are the best known anti-poverty tool, far outstripping the success of any known development intervention. Migration policy is generally thought of as border control in most countries. But it ought to be properly integrated into global development programming, with resources devoted to maximizing the poverty-reducing impact of international migration.

Some of these policies will have greater poverty-reducing effects than others. But poverty reduction is not the sole value to be considered in immigration policy. Family reunification, for example, may provide important normative benefits even though admitting other potential migrants who are not family members would have greater poverty-reducing effects. For example, admitting larger numbers of nearby migrants, such as Mexicans to the United States, might have very positive impacts for poverty in Mexico, but from a global perspective far more poverty reduction would be created by admitting people from less developed countries. The associative reasons in favor of reuniting Mexican families must be weighed against the greater poverty reduction that would occur from admitting others. Hopefully this chapter helps to highlight the importance of considering the impact of poverty reduction in the design of migration programs. These normative trade-offs must be made explicit, and be subject to democratic deliberation in the design of international migration policy.

Chapter Summary

This chapter does not aim to settle the many difficult normative questions that arise in international migration. More modestly, it aims to introduce the normative issues involved in international migration and explain its relationship to global poverty reduction. In contemporary debates about international migration, we often tend to overlook how a serious emphasis on the anti-poverty potential of international migration might produce public policies that are quite different from those that are promoted both by folks in the 'open borders' camp and those who largely favor immigration restrictions.

Questions for Discussion

1   Do you think it is morally permissible for states to enact policies preventing people, such as highly skilled workers, from entering their countries, and to attempt to force those people to remain in their home countries, where they might provide valuable services for much less pay?
2   Many international migrants are from neighboring countries. But the poorest and wealthiest countries are, for the most part, geographically distant. Do you think migration policy ought to foster more migration from people from lower-income countries, at the expense of people from middle- and higher-income countries who seek to emigrate?
3   Do refugees fleeing conflict or political oppression have a greater claim to residency in foreign countries than economic migrants fleeing hunger, poverty, and deprivation?
4   Does the strength of a migrant's claim to resettlement depend in part on how poor she is?

Suggested Reading

Brock, G. and Blake, M. *Debating Brain Drain: May governments restrict emigration?* Oxford: Oxford University Press, 2015.
Carens, J. *The Ethics of Immigration*, Oxford: Oxford University Press, 2013.
Oberman, K. 'Poverty and immigration policy,' *American Political Science Review* 109.2 (2015): 239–251.
Wellman, C. and Cole, P. *Debating the Ethics of Immigration: Is there a right to exclude?* Oxford: Oxford University Press, 2011.

References

Amnesty International. 'Europe's sinking shame: The failure to save refugees and migrants at sea', London: Amnesty International, 2015.
Barry, C., and Overland, G. 'Why remittances to poor countries should not be taxed', *NYU Journal of International Law & Politics*, 42 (2009): 1181.
Brock, G. (2009). *Global Justice: A cosmopolitan account*. Oxford: Oxford University Press.
Clemens, M. 'Economics and emigration: Trillion-dollar bills on the sidewalk?' *Journal of Economic Perspectives*, 25.3 (2011): 83–106
Feder Kittay, E. 'The Moral Harm of Migrant Carework: Realizing a Global Right to Care', in *Gender and Global Justice*, ed. Alison Jaggar, Cambridge: Polity, 2014.
Fine, S. and Sangiovanni, A. 'Immigration' in *Handbook of Global Ethics*, ed. Heather Widdows and Darrell Moellendorf, New York: Routledge, 2015.
Jones, N., Prester-Marshall, E., and Tefera, B. 'Rethinking the "Maid Trade": Experiences of Ethiopian adolescent domestic workers in the Middle East', London: Overseas Development Institute, 2014.
Maimbo, S. (ed.). Remittances and Economic Development in Somalia, An Overview, Social Development Papers, Working Paper No. 38. Washington, DC: World Bank Publications, 2006.

OECD. *International migration outlook 2013*, Paris: OECD Publishing, 2013.

Roodman, D. 'The domestic economic impacts of migration', September 3, 2014, available at http://davidroodman.com/blog/2014/09/03/the-domestic-economic-impacts-of-immigration.

Tennery, A. 'Why is no one helping Myanmar's Rohingya?' *Reuters,* June 17, 2015, available at http://blogs.reuters.com/great-debate/2015/06/17/why-is-no-one-helping-myanmars-rohingya

USHMM, United States Holocaust Memorial Museum. 'Voyage of the St. Louis', August 18, 2015, available at www.ushmm.org/wlc/en/article.php?ModuleId=10005267 (accessed December 8, 2015).

12 Humanitarian Intervention

In early 1994, Canadian Major General Roméo Dallaire was commanding a small mission of United Nations peacekeepers in Rwanda. Dallaire had received credible information that a plan was being developed to 'exterminate' ethnic Tutsi populations in the country. Dallaire believed that he could use his troops (and more reinforcements) to capture arms caches stored throughout Kigali to prevent the impending genocide, and sought permission from UN headquarters to authorize such a mission. The response from headquarters, including from Kofi Annan, then head of Peacekeeping Operations and later UN Secretary-General, was to dismiss Dallaire's request, saying that there could be unintended consequences from such an operation. In April, months after Dallaire had submitted his request, President Juvenal Habyarimana's plane was shot down. Within hours, previously mobilized militias began attacks against ethnic Tutsis and moderate Hutus. In the next 100 days, over 800,000 Rwandans were killed. Dallaire and his troops stayed on through the violence, but with a small force and limited mandate, they were only able to protect 30,000 Rwandans (Power 2002).

For liberal interventionists, the Rwandan genocide is the paradigmatic case in which outside military intervention could have protected the human rights of those who were threatened. Armed humanitarian intervention involves the forceful intervention of external military forces, without the consent of the host state, for the purposes of civilian protection. Proponents of armed humanitarian intervention argue that outside actors are both morally permitted and sometimes morally obligated to intervene militarily to prevent mass atrocities from occurring and to protect innocent civilians. Some even argue that outside military assistance will be necessary for countries to end cycles of conflict and begin to move their populations away from severe poverty and deprivation (Collier 2007).

They point to various apparent successes in providing security and stability through military intervention. In 2010, Alassane Outtara defeated incumbent Laurent Gbagbo for the presidency in Cote d'Ivoire. The holding of elections fulfilled a commitment made by Gbagbo at the end of hostilities in the early 2000s. Gbagbo refused to cede the office of the president, and Outtara's supporters took up arms against the government. Fighting and abuses by both sides caused several hundred thousand civilians to flee. The international community recognized Outtara as the outright winner of the election, and with the United Nations Security

Council's authorization, French forces intervened, under the auspices of protecting French nationals and other civilians. Within a week of the intervention, Outtara's forces succeeded in capturing Gbagbo. Five years later, Outtara won a second term in a landslide, leading some to predict the solidification of an electoral democracy, while others worry that Outtara may be less of a democrat than he once appeared (Crisis Group 2012). Gbagbo was subsequently taken to the International Criminal Court, where he awaits trial. Time will tell, but some analysts describe this as a model humanitarian intervention that laid the groundwork for peace and prosperity.

Civil Conflict and Poverty

What does humanitarian intervention have to do with the ethics of global poverty? Many of the world's poorest countries are either in the midst of civil war or in a tenuous post-conflict period in which political instability prevents economic progress that might address the severe material and social deprivations citizens face. It is widely predicted that in the coming decades the countries with the highest risk of conflict will continue to fail to produce prosperity for their citizens. Extreme poverty in the future may be largely inseparable from civil conflict and political instability. While stable, secure countries are able to grow, both economically and in the quality and capacity of political institutions, conflict-affected states can make no progress. Even if humanitarian organizations are able to increase vaccination rates, reduce the incidence of malaria, or increase access to minimally adequate nutrition, deeper changes in living standards appear unlikely as long as countries are at war. Furthermore, war can destroy what were previously economically decent lives. In the years before the Syrian civil war, Syrians were by no means excessively wealthy but had reached global middle-income status. Today much of Syria's accumulated income and wealth is gone.

For some scholars, the poverty-creating effects of civil conflict give further justification to use military intervention in the near term to protect civilians and prevent the widespread abuse of human rights, and in the long term guarantee the political stability needed to promote economic development.

Consider the example of the Central African Republic (CAR). At the time of writing, this was the latest dispatch:

> BANGUI, Central African Republic—Hundreds of demonstrators, some armed with machetes and AK-47s, marched in the capital city of the Central African Republic on Monday before clashing with U.N. peacekeepers guarding the presidential palace.
>
> The protesters demanded an end to the 20-month-old transitional government and the exit of French troops, which have struggled to tamp down intercommunal violence alongside a 12,000-strong U.N. peacekeeping force. Protesters said the Central African Armed Forces (FACA) should be reinforced so that they can assume responsibility for the rapidly deteriorating security situation.

The demonstrations come on the heels of 48 hours of bloody sectarian violence in Bangui. Dozens of homes and offices were looted or burned over the weekend, including the offices of several international NGOs. At least 36 people are confirmed dead and nearly 100 wounded, although sources at medical NGOs caution that some casualties may still be unaccounted for, because roadblocks have made it harder to transport patients to hospitals.

Sporadic shooting has continued throughout the day on Monday.

(McCormick and Fouchard 2015)

The CAR has had several years of severe political instability, ever since a rebel coalition known as Seleka toppled the government of Francois Bozize. Clashes between the largely Muslim Seleka and the largely Christian Anti-Balaka have led many analysts to warn that the CAR is at risk of genocide. Several thousand people have been killed in clashes, and several hundred thousand people have been displaced by the fighting.

CAR was formerly a French colony. Like many other former colonies, being colonized by the French did not leave the CAR with the political or economic institutions needed to foster prosperity and growth. Since gaining independence from the French in 1960, the country has suffered coup d'états in 1966, 1979, 1981, and 2001, as well as attempted but unsuccessful coups in 2003 and 2013. Several changes of power have been brought about through widespread fighting and violent overthrow. Unsurprisingly, this political instability and periodic outbreaks of widespread civil conflict is accompanied by very poor performance on most economic and social indicators. Per capita GDP is approximately 480 USD per year, the infant mortality rate is 93 per thousand live births, and life expectancy at birth is 50 years.

The recent history of the Central African Republic is reflective of what some development economists call the conflict trap. Countries which have recently had a civil war are much more likely to return to civil war in the next decade than are countries which have not experienced civil conflict (Walter 2015). Even if countries avoid a full onset of civil war, the political institutions that follow conflict often tend to be autocratic, clientilistic, or politically oppressive, making the country more prone to coups, and fostering a climate of instability that prevents economic and social progress.

Given the link between civil conflict and persistent poverty, some scholars argue for the increased use of external military intervention to provide security and break the cycle of conflict that keeps countries from prospering.

The Case for Humanitarian Intervention

State sovereignty has been a foundational concept in the international system since the Peace of Westphalia in 1648. This series of treaties ended the Thirty Years War and enshrined the basic principle of non-interference into international law. On the Westphalian system, state sovereignty meant, among other things, that states were legally guaranteed non-interference in domestic affairs by other sovereign states.

But state sovereignty, understood as implying robust protection against external interference, is difficult to defend in the face of widespread human rights abuses, especially mass atrocities. Since Nazis committed genocide against Jews and other minority groups, we do not think that a claim to national self-determination and non-interference can be sustained. In these cases of widespread atrocity, the moral rights of potential victims take moral priority over any claims of collective self-determination or rights of non-interference.

This normative view has been broadly endorsed by the international community in the form of the Responsibility to Protect doctrine. The Responsibility to Protect doctrine was developed in response to uncertainty in the international system regarding how to respond to genocide, crimes against humanity, and other widespread human rights abuses. Following uneven NATO intervention in the Balkans, failed American intervention in Somalia, and no intervention to protect civilians in Rwanda, the international community needed a clear set of guidelines to determine when and on what grounds external humanitarian intervention should be justified. The Responsibility to Protect doctrine does not have the status of international law, but is a recognized norm of the international system, and is regularly invoked in UN Security Council resolutions on peace and security that are legally binding.

The Responsibility to Protect doctrine frames sovereignty as responsibility. On this view, states retain the sovereign right of non-interference just in so far as they adequately exercise their responsibility to protect citizens from genocide, crimes against humanity, war crimes, and ethnic cleansing. When states fail to act responsibility toward their citizens, either by being unable or unwilling to protect them from mass atrocities, they cede the right of sovereign non-interference. The doctrine encompasses three related responsibilities that are understood to be jointly held by the international community; the responsibility to prevent atrocities from occurring; the responsibility to protect civilians at risk once conflict has broken out; and the responsibility to rebuild societies after conflict has ended (ICISS 2001).

Some scholars go further, and advocate even greater use of external military interventions to guarantee and secure democratic progress. Most prominent among the advocates for external military intervention to promote economic development is Paul Collier. Collier is famous for his book *The Bottom Billion* (2007), which argued that around a billion people will remain mired in poverty as long as their countries are stuck in one of four traps: being stuck in a cycle of conflict; suffering from the resource curse; being landlocked with bad neighbors; or suffering from bad governance in a small country. In his next book, *War, Guns, and Votes* (2009), Collier advocated several solutions for countries that are plagued by civil war and political instability. His central proposal is that the international community must provide the public good of security in order for societies to make progress. He suggests that when rulers violate democratic standards, the international community should use military force to promote the return to democratic institutions. He cites British intervention in Sierra Leone to put down a coup and Australian intervention in East Timor as examples of successful intervention. Collier suggests that 'over the horizon' security guarantees (meaning that outside militaries commit to turn back coups against democratic leaders, and permit coups against undemocratic leaders with an assurance of a quick return to democracy) could both improve the security situation in countries and improve democratic accountability over time.

Even if one is persuaded that there is a case for military intervention, a number of other difficult questions must be answered. First, if there is a moral justification for humanitarian intervention, who is justified in intervening? One answer is that any morally justified intervention must be authorized by the United Nations Security Council. The UNSC is the multilateral body that is invested in international law with maintenance of international peace and security. If the UNSC does not authorize a humanitarian intervention, it is not morally justified.

However, there are reasons to object that UNSC authorization is a necessary condition for a morally just humanitarian intervention. For one thing, the UNSC itself is not a very legitimate international body. Its permanent members (P5) are the five victors of WWII and the first five countries to possess nuclear weapons. Power, not legitimacy, gave these countries a permanent seat at the UNSC. Furthermore, each P5 state retains veto power over any potential UNSC decision. This means that if any member of the UNSC perceives its national interests to lie with the state against whom intervention is being considered, they will be likely to exercise their veto power. China's commercial interests in Sudan, for example, have long been thought to protect the Sudanese government from stronger UN sanctions. Arguably, the views and perspectives of those who would be the intended beneficiaries of (and those potentially harmed by) an external intervention are highly relevant to whether an intervention is justified. People within countries in which atrocities are occurring or may be about to occur are arguably more likely to understand their circumstances, and have greater legitimacy in authorizing a military intervention that will directly affect them, than outsiders who do not represent them.

In addition to proper authorization, a morally justified humanitarian intervention must meet several other conditions familiar from just war theory.[1] Justified humanitarian military intervention is generally thought to be a matter of last resort, requiring that other diplomatic and non-violent coercive methods be tried first. The intervention must be necessary, in that there are no other options that could equally secure the just cause. The harms to be prevented by the intervention must be severe and widespread, establishing a just cause. And the intervention must be proportional, in that the aggregate relevant moral good of the intervention must outweigh its aggregate relevant moral costs.

Under these constraints, humanitarian intervention is thought to be permissible, and sometimes obligatory. The central argument is simple. Innocent civilians are sometimes at great risk from their governments or other armed groups, and only external military intervention can protect them. Whereas with Nazi concentration camps and Rwandan génocidaires, the outside world let atrocities occur, contemporary liberal interventionists argue that outsiders ought to intervene to avoid repeating the mistakes of the past (Power 2002).

The Case against Humanitarian Intervention

The case in favor of humanitarian intervention initially appears strong. How could one disagree with a responsibility to protect innocent people from the world's worst atrocities? Surely if faced again with the atrocities committed in the gas chambers at Auschwitz or the killing fields of Cambodia, we would have a moral responsibility to respond. And given the overwhelming military power possessed by many western countries, failure to use this power condemns many innocent people to horrific and premature death.

Most critics of humanitarian intervention do not disagree with the basic moral intuition that innocent civilians deserve protection. Rather, they argue that in the real world, characterized by vast inequalities of power, and complex societies in which it is far easier to intervene and initially defeat than it is to protect and rebuild, and in which states generally pursue their own self-interest, humanitarian intervention is both less successful and more harmful than its proponents suggest.

Consider the record on humanitarian intervention in recent years. Since the adoption of the Responsibility to Protect doctrine in 2005, there have been a number of outright military interventions with the stated aim of protecting civilians. While some of these interventions were initially successful, they have in general failed to produce secure, well-governed societies in which, among other things, poverty reduction may proceed.

The military intervention in Libya was as close to meeting all of the criteria for a morally justified humanitarian intervention as any in recent memory. Just cause: the intervention was in support of a citizenry who appeared at great risk from Muammar Qaddafi. Proper authorization: it was endorsed by regional organizations (the African Union), the United Nations Security Council, and many people within Libya were calling for military support. Probability of success: outside interveners needed to provide only a small amount of military force to create the conditions in which Qaddafi's regime would be halted in its attacks on civilians. Necessity: there did not appear to be diplomatic or non-military means of halting Qaddafi's attack on his citizens. This was, *ex-ante*, close to a textbook case of justified humanitarian intervention.

Three years after this intervention, the International Crisis Group (2012) described the situation in Libya as follows:

> Over six months of fighting between two parliaments, their respective governments and allied militias have led to the brink of all-out war. On the current trajectory, the most likely medium-term prospect is not one side's triumph, but that rival local warlords and radical groups will proliferate, what remains of state institutions will collapse, financial reserves (based on oil and gas revenues and spent on food and refined fuel imports) will be depleted, and

hardship for ordinary Libyans will increase exponentially. Radical groups, already on the rise as the beheading of 21 Egyptians and deadly bombings by the Libyan franchise of the Islamic State (IS) attest, will find fertile ground, while regional involvement—evidenced by retaliatory Egyptian airstrikes—will increase.

A defender of the Libyan humanitarian intervention might argue that the problem was not with the intervention itself, but with the lack of plans to rebuild following the intervention. If only a better plan for political transition to functioning democratic institutions had been in place, today things would be much better in the country. But the critic will reply that nation-building will take more than a good plan, and it will always appear in retrospect that if we had done things slightly differently the outcomes would have been better.

Similarly, the defender of humanitarian intervention must give an account of failed nation-building exercises in Afghanistan and Iraq. While neither of the wars in Iraq or Afghanistan can be plausibly identified as pure humanitarian intervention (though both were sometimes justified on humanitarian grounds), they too show the great difficulty in establishing secure political institutions that will promote economic and social development. Whatever the motives for initial interventions in each country, one assumes that the interveners in both would have been happy to see liberal democracy take hold, and the kind of political institutions be in place that, as we saw in Chapter 3, are necessary for economic and social development. But after 15 years in Afghanistan and 13 in Iraq (perhaps more at the time you are reading), with trillions of dollars in direct and indirect economic costs incurred in fighting both wars, neither country appears close to democratic governance or stable political institutions. If anything, this goal appears as far away today as at any point in the past decade. Any poverty reduction that has occurred may evaporate as humanitarian assistance that accompanied these interventions begins to dwindle.

Why haven't better political institutions taken hold? This may be in part due to the continued presence of the interveners, whose military backing of governments with at best autocratic and sectarian tendencies may prevent the needed political reconciliation for democratic political institutions to take hold. But perhaps more important is that deeper structural problems were present in each of these societies before the intervention, making reconciliation, reconstruction, and growth far easier said than done.

Critics of humanitarian intervention also argue on empirical grounds that military intervention is extremely costly in comparison to other alternative methods of promoting human welfare. Benjamin Valentino, one of the leading scholars of mass atrocities, provides a compelling argument against humanitarian intervention on the grounds that much more good could be done by devoting the same resources elsewhere.

> Washington should replace its focus on military intervention with a humanitarian foreign policy centered on saving lives by funding public health programs

in the developing world, aiding victims of natural disasters, and assisting refugees fleeing violent conflict. Abandoning humanitarian intervention in most cases would not mean leaving victims of genocide and repression to their fate. Indeed, such a strategy could actually save far more people, at a far lower price ...

Each of the more than 220 Tomahawk missiles fired by the U.S. military into Libya, for example, cost around $1.4 million. In Somalia, a country of about 8.5 million people, the final bill for the U.S. intervention totaled more than $7 billion. Scholars have estimated that the military mission there probably saved between 10,000 and 25,000 lives. To put it in the crudest possible terms, this meant that Washington spent between $280,000 and $700,000 for each Somali it spared. As for Bosnia, if one assumes that without military action a quarter of the two million Muslims living there would have been killed (a highly unrealistic figure), the intervention cost $120,000 per life saved. Judging the 2003 Iraq war—now a multitrillion-dollar adventure—primarily on humanitarian grounds, the costs would be orders of magnitude higher ...

Even using the exceedingly generous estimates above of the number of lives saved by military intervention, this means that on a per-life basis, measles vaccination would be 3,000 times as cost-effective as the military intervention in Somalia and more than 500 times as cost-effective as the intervention in Bosnia. The provision of antimalarial bed nets may be more efficient still—costing only between $100 and $200 per life saved. The final bill may be even lower, since preventive public health expenditures such as these often more than pay for themselves in averted medical costs and increased productivity.

(Valentino 2011)

Indeed, even within war zones, where the provision of humanitarian assistance is most challenging and costly, vast improvements in health and education are possible (Human Security Report 2012). This is not because warfare is good for welfare—it is obviously not. But when a country becomes a war zone, the entrance of humanitarian organizations like the Red Cross/Red Crescent significantly contributes to improved humanitarian outcomes. From the perspective of global poverty reduction, dollars spent supporting livelihoods in war zones and refugees who have fled are far better than those spent on cruise missiles and attack helicopters.

In addition to these empirical concerns about the comparative cost effectiveness of humanitarian intervention, critics note that there are reasons to be skeptical of humanitarian interventions on normative grounds. First, humanitarian intervention can directly inflict grave harm, including death, upon innocent civilians. In interpersonal ethics, we tend to think that there are moral constraints on actions that inflict harm upon some to benefit others and maintain a general prohibition on the intentional or foreseeable violation of human rights, unless the good consequences that result from such harm are quite large. In fact, it would be very unlikely if any significant humanitarian intervention did not involve the violation of some human rights. Violating these rights may be justified on the grounds that many more human rights would be protected by the intervention. But if another policy option is available that would save as many or more lives, and would not involve inflicting serious harm upon non-liable civilians, this is a reason in favor of choosing non-violent forms of resistance. It therefore appears that proponents of humanitarian interventions face a high justificatory burden to establish that such interventions are both morally permissible and morally preferable to other actions governments could take to reduce global poverty.

Second, even if humanitarian interventions did not directly inflict serious harm, they may indirectly cause other actors to engage in wrongful, violent activity that they would not have otherwise done (Kuperman 2008). There is a difficult philosophical question regarding to what extent one bears moral responsibility for actions one has not undertaken but foreseeably provoked. One plausible position suggests that even if one is not fully responsible for the actions that others undertake in response to their own, one does bear some responsibility for these provoked actions, and must take them into account when morally evaluating candidate courses of action. As John Gardner writes,

> I am responsible for what I do, and you are responsible for what you do. But on any credible view, I need to give attention, in what I do, to what you will do in consequence. And you need to give attention in what you do to what I will do in consequence. In that sense, there are two parts of morality. There is what I should do simpliciter, and there is what I should do by way of contribution to what you should do.
>
> (Gardner 2007)

When a state or international organization intervenes militarily, it may have a number of knock-on effects that involve serious harm. The targets of intervention may increase repression and violence against their opponents. Similarly, rebel groups may be empowered by the prospect of outside military support to keep fighting when otherwise they would be inclined to enter peace talks and cease hostilities.

Furthermore, when outside militaries (usually of powerful states) are authorized to intervene in the affairs of countries in conflict (usually weaker states) it is very likely that those intervening states will abuse that power. In the military intervention that was authorized by the United Nations to protect civilians in Libya, NATO quickly overreached its mandate and used the intervention to ensure regime change, directly attacking the forces of Moammar Qaddafi, then the head of state, who was promptly captured and executed by rebel forces. States who were hesitant to support the Responsibility to Protect doctrine, and the military intervention in Libya, quickly jumped upon this shift to note that, as they had always suspected, so-called 'humanitarian intervention' was really just old-fashioned, self-interested regime change.

In response to these empirical and normative objections to humanitarian intervention, the defender of humanitarian intervention can offer several replies. One might hold that even if specific instances of humanitarian intervention have not been particularly positive for promoting development in the countries that are targets of intervention, the upholding of a general rule which prohibits states from committing (or permitting the commission of) genocide, crimes against humanity, and other mass atrocities has benefits which extend beyond the particular states in which intervention occurs. That is, even if military intervention in Somalia or Libya or Syria has not produced good outcomes in those countries, the establishment of a shared norm of permissible military intervention to prevent mass atrocities may create a general deterrent effect, leading to fewer mass atrocities over time.

A second reply would focus on the practical details of generating support for military interventions versus non-military humanitarian assistance. The cost-benefit calculation which shows that many more lives can be saved through public health programs than through military interventions might be misleading, in so far as resources which are currently dedicated to armed forces are unlikely to be reallocated from defense budgets to aid budgets. If true, the defender of humanitarian intervention can maintain that the question is not whether financial resources should shift from soldiers to aid workers, but simply whether public resources already allocated to militaries should be used to defend innocent civilians abroad.

Third, defenders of humanitarian intervention might reply that regime change is sometimes the appropriate outcome of a humanitarian intervention, just in so far as the current regime creates an existential threat to its citizens and creates an obstacle to peace. There is no reason to preserve regimes that are guilty of committing atrocities. Regime change is just a necessary step for protecting civilians and building peace, and outsiders should not be squeamish about removing oppressive autocrats.

The strongest line of argument in defense of humanitarian intervention involves drawing a clear distinction between external military intervention that attempts to halt atrocities or overthrow regimes while conflict is ongoing, versus peacekeeping missions, which aim to preserve and support a peace process that is already underway. It is very difficult for outside actors to make peace, even if initially militarily successful, as the United States was in Iraq and Afghanistan: if there is no domestic peace to keep, no amount of military might will resolve what are at root political problems. In fact, it may inflame these problems as disputants believe that they have greater bargaining power as a result of external military backing. However, peacekeeping operations, in which a neutral international organization, usually the United Nations, dispatches a peacekeeping force with the (sometimes reluctant) permission of the host state, have a much stronger track record. The peacekeeping force does not claim to be able to force peace where the conditions for it do not exist. Rather, it helps to assist in the process of healing a fractured society, keeping combatants at bay, providing security, and serving as a deterrent to future conflict. Of course, peacekeepers have at times been ineffective, capable of abuse, ill-equipped, governed by unclear or ineffective mandates, guilty of corruption, and have committed acts of physical and sexual violence against local populations. Despite these many flaws, investing in peacekeeping appears to be a very wise investment. One assessment finds that spending 850 million USD annually on peacekeeping over 10 years reduces the chances of armed conflict from 40 percent to 7 percent (Collier et al. 2008). Others find that deploying peacekeeping troops dramatically reduces the killing of civilians (Hultman et al. 2013). And the presence of peacekeepers dramatically reduces the likelihood that conflict will spread to neighboring countries (Beardsley 2011). Peacekeeping appears to be a surprisingly good investment given the astronomic humanitarian and economic costs associated with the outbreak of civil war. From a normative perspective, peacekeepers are far less likely to do harm, and to provoke others to do harm, than is an outright military intervention. More generally, efforts to prevent conflict from breaking out in the first place, from diplomatic efforts to economic incentives to control of the arms trade, all might do far more to prevent civil conflict from impeding progress in global poverty reduction than will armed humanitarian intervention.

Chapter Summary

Civil war, conflict, and attendant political instability will be inextricably linked with persistent global poverty in the coming decades. At the time of writing, the perceived normative consensus surrounding the Responsibility to Protect doctrine was fraying, as some weaker states charged that the doctrine was just a cover for self-interested regime change. States and international institutions will continue to face morally complex questions in the coming years regarding how to respond to civil conflict and mass atrocities. Finding the morally optimal answers to these questions is not easy, but it appears that the case for supporting neutral peacekeeping operations is far stronger than the case for supporting humanitarian interventions.

Questions for Discussion

1   At the time of writing, the conflict in Syria is the world's worst, and is expected to be for many years to come. If you were a government official with 1 billion USD that you had to spend on Syria, how would you use it? Would you support attacks against warring parties guilty of mass atrocities, provide humanitarian assistance in the country, or help refugees fleeing the fighting?

2   In 2011, NATO-led forces intervened in Libya, ostensibly to protect Libyan civilians who were at risk from the counter-insurgency tactics of Moammar Qaddafi. Several years later, the country is in disarray, but it has also not yet experienced widespread atrocities. In hindsight, do you think the intervention was justified?

3   Is there something wrong with enlisting the world's armies in the fight against global poverty? Is this the proper role for the men and women of the armed forces?

Note

1 Here I focus on justice in the decision to go to war. Just war theory traditionally includes also justice in the conduct of war, and justice after war.

Recommended Reading

Bellamy, A. *Responsibility to Protect: A defense*, Oxford: Oxford University Press, 2015.
Frowe, H. *The Ethics of War and Peace: An introduction*, New York: Routledge, 2011.
Welsh, J. 'Civilian protection in Libya: Putting coercion and controversy back into RtoP', *Ethics and International Affairs* 25.3 (2011): 225–262.
World Development Report. 'Conflict, security, and development', Washington, DC: World Bank, 2011.

References

Beardsley, K. 'Peacekeeping and the contagion of armed conflict', *The Journal of Politics* 73 (2011): 1051–1064.
Collier, P. *The Bottom Billion: Why the poorest countries are failing and what can be done about it*, Oxford: Oxford University Press, 2007.
Collier, P. *War, Guns, and Votes: Democracy in dangerous places*, New York: Harper Collins, 2009.
Collier, P., Chauvet, L., and Hegre, H. 'The challenge of conflicts', Copenhagen Consensus 2008 Challenge Paper, available at www.copenhagenconsensus.com/sites/default/files/cp_conflictscc08.pdf (accessed December 8, 2015).
Gardner, J. 'Complicity and causality', *Criminal Law and Philosophy*, 1.2 (2007): 127–141.
Hultman, L., Kathman, J., and Shannon, M. 'United Nations peacekeeping and civilian protection in civil war', *American Journal of Political Science* 57 (2013): 875–891.
Human Security Report Project, *Human Security Report 2012: Sexual violence, education, and war—beyond the mainstream narrative*, Vancouver: Human Security Press, 2012.
ICISS, International Commission on Intervention and State Sovereignty. 'The responsibility to protect: Report of the International Commission on Intervention and State Sovereignty', Ottawa: International Development Research Centre, 2001.
International Crisis Group. 'Côte D'Ivoire: Defusing tensions', Africa Report N°193, 26 November, 2012.
Kuperman, A. J. 'The moral hazard of humanitarian intervention: Lessons from the Balkans', *International Studies Quarterly* 52 (2008): 49–80
McCormick, T., and Fouchard, A. 'Central African Republic: Protests rock capital after overnight clashes', *Foreign Policy*, September 28, 2015, available at http://foreignpolicy.com/2015/09/28/central-african-republic-protests-rock-capital-after-overnight-clashes (accessed December 8, 2015).
Power, Samantha. *A Problem from Hell: America and the age of genocide*, New York: Perseus Books Group, 2002.
Valentino, B. 'The true costs of humanitarian intervention', *Foreign Affairs*, November/December 2011.
Walter, B. F. 'Why bad governance leads to repeat civil war', *Journal of Conflict Resolution* 59.7 (2015): 1242–1272.

13 International Trade

Patients with HIV/AIDS used to face a bleak future, with few prospects for meaningful treatment. Today, that has changed. Thanks to significant innovation in the development of antiretroviral medicines, people living with HIV/AIDS can lead healthy, productive lives. But access to these medicines is essential for successful treatment. And this access can be threatened by international trade agreements.

Atazanavir is at the center of a pharmaceutical patent controversy bubbling in the Andean nation. The Peruvian government paid about $10 USD per pill for atazanavir last year, more than most other countries in Latin America—about twice what Mexico paid and 20 times what neighboring Bolivia paid—according to RedGE, a network of Peruvian organizations that work on human rights and development issues in international relations. Although an estimated 65,000 Peruvians had HIV in 2014, and just more than 1,700 took atazanavir, the country spent $8.4 million USD on the drug, more than half its total spending for antiretrovirals.

Atazanavir is patented by Bristol Myers-Squibb, an international pharmaceutical company, which has exclusive rights to sell the drug in Peru through 2018. So the drug costs whatever the company decides to charge. RedGE wants the government to override the patent, through a legal provision written into international trade agreements, so that generic versions of the drug can be sold in Peru. So far the government has been largely silent on the request, with ministers reportedly disagreeing on whether to go forward.

Although it eats up the antiretroviral budget, atazanavir is hardly the most expensive drug Peru buys. The country faces a growing problem with high-cost brand-name drugs, and RedGE and other patient advocates say that problem [*sic*] could soon get a lot worse, after Peru recently agreed to further limit competition on pharmaceuticals as part of the country's biggest trade deal in decades, the Trans-Pacific Partnership (TPP). Organizations around the world say that provisions included in the deal's chapter on intellectual property will further restrict Peru's and the other member nations' ability to buy cheaper versions of some of the costliest medicines—and limit their access to new types of drugs.

(Barry-Jester 2015)

Large portions of international development work focus on improving global public health. But the success of these efforts is partly determined by the way in which patents on needed medicines are governed in international trade agreements. International trade—the market-based exchange of goods and services crossing national boundaries—is another area in which ethicists have sought to diagnose flaws in international institutions and identify global institutional reforms which would accelerate global poverty reduction and rectify existing injustices. However, moral and political theorists, as well as economists and political scientists, are in considerable disagreement regarding how international trade is to be assessed, and which reforms to the policies and institutions that govern international trade would be morally optimal.

International trade has important implications for global poverty. No country in the history of the world has done more to reduce the number of people living in extreme poverty than China in the past three decades. While many Chinese people still live modest lives by the living standards of European and North American countries, they are undoubtedly better off than they were 30 years ago thanks to export-led growth. The infusion of international capital to finance a booming manufacturing sector, and access to international consumer markets, has led to huge gains in productivity in China, and a rise in the demand for labor, raising wages over time. There have certainly been significant costs—especially environmental, and also in the violation of labor rights and civil and political rights—but there is no denying that China's massive reduction in extreme poverty is tied to its strategy of export-led growth.

The full range of philosophical issues raised by international trade are beyond the scope of this book. We will focus more narrowly on the moral complaints that are made against current features of the international trading system which are most relevant to the reduction of global poverty. On the one hand, international trade is capable of promoting widespread poverty reduction, while on the other hand international trade agreements can threaten the basic rights of already deprived people. We will then consider proposed reforms to the international trading system that are thought to offer morally preferable terms of trade which would accelerate poverty reduction.

The Moral Case for Free Trade

Proponents of free trade, defined as the liberalization of international trading rules such that the tariff and non-tariff barriers to trade are reduced or eliminated, argue that free trade is a requirement of justice (Teson 2012). Restricting international trade or closing markets to foreign competitors hurts poor consumers by increasing the cost of goods, hurts poor producers by decreasing their access to valuable international markets, and is a form of wrongful government interference in consensual commercial relationships. On their view, there are both consequentialist and libertarian reasons that weigh in favor of liberalizing trade.

From a consequentialist perspective, barriers to trade create economic inefficiencies. These inefficiencies reduce both global and national economic output. Furthermore, trade barriers do very little to protect the wages of employees in protected sectors, and do so at very high costs to consumers. For example, the United States was in a trade dispute with China. In an effort to protect US jobs in tire manufacturing, the US imposed tariffs on imported tires beginning in 2009. The increase in the price of tires saved at most 1,200 American jobs in tire manufacturing, at a cost of $1.1 billion to consumers, or approximately $900,000 per job per year (Huffbauer and Lowry 2012). Furthermore, these elevated costs likely resulted in lost jobs in other sectors where the additional money that went to tires would have otherwise been spent. Protectionist trade measures can serve to benefit a small number of producers in a protected sector, but at significant cost to consumers and other (unprotected) producers. Furthermore, the possibility of preserving these benefits leads to political corruption whereby protected sectors attempt to exert undue influence over political institutions to preserve their economically privileged status.

From a libertarian perspective, free traders argue that there should be a general presumption against restricting the exchange of goods and services. In societies where such restrictions have been seriously enforced, we generally view these restrictions as unjustified infringements on personal freedom. If you have a good that I would like, and I have something of value I would like to exchange with you, preventing us from making such an exchange appears to be a violation of economic freedom, absent some other morally compelling reason to prevent the exchange. International barriers to the exchange of goods and services represent just such an infringement on economic liberties. And, as with national borders that restrict the free movement of people, the restrictions on economic liberty make people much worse off.

There is a further argument that can be offered in defense of trade liberalization. In Chapter 3, we noted the importance of the quality of political institutions in fostering prosperity and protecting rights. Recent scholarship in political science suggests that free-trade agreements have a positive effect on civil and political rights and help to protect emerging democracies from anti-democratic threats. Emily Hafner-Burton (2009) argues that the inclusion of human rights standards in preferential trade agreements creates incentives for would-be oppressors to respect human rights. Furthermore, special interest groups who would previously have backed a coup d'état to protect or promote their economic interests would now be constrained by international agreements which tie the hands of any future governments regarding market access and trade subsidies. Should the government attempt to violate the trade agreement, they would face arbitration at an international court that would permit other countries to take retaliatory economic measures. In these circumstances, potential coup leaders face uncertain economic benefits. In other words, free trade agreements lock in certain economic arrangements, thereby reducing incentives for corruption (in which private sector actors pay bribes for economic protection) and undermine incentives for coups, since a successful coup cannot lead to a change in the trade agreement (Liu and Ornelas 2014).

Critiques of Trade Liberalization

Despite the initially plausible case for free trade, critics have raised a number of moral concerns about the unfettered trade in goods and services.

Infant Industry Protection

One argument regarding restrictions in international trade is known as the 'infant industry' argument. This position holds that while companies in mature economies can compete on international markets, those mature economies initially grew by protecting key industries or sectors from international competition until they reached a stage at which they were strong enough to compete internationally. In the memorable words of University of Cambridge economist Ha-Joon Chang, a leading critic of free-trade orthodoxy, policies that force market liberalization on low-income countries are a form of kicking away the economic ladder that high-income economies want up. Whereas the United States, United Kingdom, and other countries imposed trade tariffs to protect key industries while they grew, these same countries now prescribe eliminating trade tariffs before industrialization can take hold (Chang 2008).

From the perspective of poverty reduction, the protection of infant industries is thought to be important for the employees who work in these industries, but also for the broader societies in which institutional learning is taking place that should foster economic progress in the long term. Dani Rodrik (2004), one of the most important analysts of the global political economy, argues that the key to infant industry protection is the design of institutions that are responsible for determining which industries to protect. It is difficult to know in advance which companies and sectors are likely to succeed. The key is designing institutions that are able to learn when to let companies fail. So trade tariffs or subsidies that are meant to support certain sectors of the economy must be removed if it becomes clear that a particular sector or company is not going to succeed, and institutions responsible for making these decisions must be able to do so free from undue political interference.

This presents a challenge for the defender of the infant industry argument. Protecting infant industries to spur broader economic growth requires political institutions that are capable of removing support for targeted industries when they are likely to fail. But political institutions in low-income countries are often easily influenced, or captured, by elites in the country. If a sector or company becomes reliant on support from government, and that sector fears government support will be withdrawn, they will have reason to exert undue influence on government institutions. In low-quality institutional environments where corruption of political officials is rife, commercial actors will be likely to buy rather than earn government protection. As with foreign aid, it may be that the institutional environments where infant industry protection is most needed will be the same environments where it is least likely to succeed. A further challenge then emerges—could international trade agreements be structured that permit infant industry protection in some jurisdictions and restrict them in other jurisdictions? While these questions remain outstanding, there is now significant support among many economists for some forms of infant industry protection and state-led economic development.

Race to the Bottom

A related criticism of an international free trade regime is that it incentivizes a downward race in wages and labor and environmental standards. On this view, countries seeking to attract foreign investment and to pursue export-led growth weaken labor and environmental standards so that companies looking to locate factories, or extract natural resources, will invest in their countries (Stiglitz 2007). Strict protections of labor rights or the environment are thought to lead investors to search for other potential locations, where costs of compliance with these standards will be lower, thereby raising the financial profitability and competitiveness of their operations.

Defenders of trade liberalization regimes reply that countries should set labor and environmental standards that are appropriate for their own levels of development and consistent with national preferences, and these may be very different than the preferred standards in high-income countries. Environmental protection may be of greater value when living on 30,000 USD per year than when living on 500 USD per year. Similarly, the protection of labor rights, such as restrictions on the number of hours worked per week or the safety standards in a workplace, may be less important to a laborer who is desperate to feed her family (Bhagwati 2004). Other critics note that there is little evidence that the race to the bottom actually occurs: if anything, labor and environmental standards tend to increase with a rise in international trade (Drezner 2009). This may be because international trade increases demand for labor, thereby increasing the bargaining power of laborers.

Opponents reply that reducing environmental harms and protecting minimal labor standards are a matter of basic human rights that ought not be traded off in exchange for access to paid employment. Being beaten by one's supervisor, or killed in a mine accident, or exposed to toxic chemicals, represents a basic rights violation, and this conduct is morally impermissible regardless of the prevailing level of economic development in a country. Furthermore, compliance with basic labor and environmental protections would represent a small fraction of the overall cost of production, therefore having minimal impact on both aggregate employment levels and corporate profits.

Losers in Trade Liberalization

Relatedly, critics of fully liberalized trade arrangements argue that trade liberalization creates winners and losers within countries. While aggregate economic output may generally increase as a result of trade liberalization, some people will lose out as a result of reduced trade tariffs or subsidies. In perhaps the most famous case, following the adoption of the North American Free Trade Agreement (NAFTA), many Mexican farmers were hurt by an immediate flood of cheap agricultural produce from the United States, while Mexican manufacturers benefitted from increased access to American markets.

Aaron James argues that liberalization ought not proceed unless the countries that enter trade liberalization agreements are able to compensate the losers, through job retraining, unemployment insurance, or other policies that may protect displaced workers and their families. He defends the principle of Collective Due Care: trading nations are to protect people against the harms of trade (either by temporary trade barriers or 'safeguards,' etc., or, under free trade, by direct compensation or social insurance schemes). Specifically, 'no person's life prospects are to be worse than they would have been had his or her society been a closed society' (James 2012, p. 203). For James, and other critics, international trade agreements which proceed without concern for the possible uneven distribution of benefits and burdens from liberalized trade ought to be rejected.

Resource Curse

The resource curse is a phenomenon whereby countries that become dependent on the export of natural resources, especially oil and minerals, are disproportionately prone to autocratic governance, civil war, economic mismanagement, and gender inequality (Ross 2012). In countries where strong, accountable institutions are not yet in place, access to revenue from natural resources allows autocrats to fund repression and resist demands for democratic governance. Resource revenue creates incentives for opposition groups to take power by force. Once you control the resources, you control the rents. Economies which become dependent upon natural resources often underperform: they are highly sensitive to volatile commodity prices, and make export-led growth more difficult due to the increased costs of exports, also known as Dutch disease. Because export-led growth is more difficult, there are fewer employment opportunities for women. In modern economies, increased female labor force participation is correlated with increased political empowerment, as incomes create opportunities for independence and workplaces create spaces for feminist organizing.

The resource curse is made possible by international markets in natural resources, which grant authority to sell natural resources to whomever takes and holds power. Except in rare circumstances, those who come to control the territory are treated as the owners of the resource, and permitted to sell that resource on international markets. Internaitonal sale is possible even when the owners are known to be illegitimate owners of the resource, as with rebel groups in the Democratic Republic of Congo who control mines or the Islamic State controlling oil fields and refineries, groups are often able to sell natural resources on international markets despite international condemnation of the groups and refusal to recognize their right of ownership.

Critics of free trade in natural resources argue that trading in resources which have been extracted and sold to the benefit of dictators and warlords is tantamount to theft. Just as you would be acting wrongfully if you bought a watch that was stolen from your neighbor, so too are you acting wrongfully when you consume natural resources that are rightfully owned by the people in their country (Wenar 2008). They argue that restrictions on the international trade in natural resources from authoritarian or conflict-affected countries will improve prospects for development in those countries.

Intellectual Property

A further concern about international trade and international trade agreements involves the protection of intellectual property. Trade agreements often extend intellectual property protections from the jurisdiction from one signatory state to other signatory states. The result is that violations of intellectual property that were previously illegal in only one country are now extended to trading partners. In some cases, this may be somewhat benign. For example, pirated copies of movies or music in trading partner countries may be harder to come by after the signing of a free trade agreement. While this may represent minimal inconvenience for consumers in low- and middle-income countries, it is unlikely to make a lasting impact on global poverty. But in the case with which we began this chapter, the consequences of intellectual property protection can be the difference between life and death for patients in countries where monopoly patents on needed medicines are extended. The prohibitive cost of atazanavir in Peru is one among many instances in which access to essential medicines is blocked by the extension of intellectual property rights abroad. For the critics of free trade, the extension of monopoly patents into international trade agreements represents a grave threat to the health of the poor, and offers a prima facie reason to reject such agreements.

A number of weak arguments can be given in defense of the extension of intellectual property rights over needed medicines in poor countries: that innovators have a right to patents over what they invent, or that the use of generic versions of medicines represents wrongful theft. While these concerns may carry some small moral weight, they cannot outweigh the importance of access to lifesaving medicines that is denied by the extension of intellectual property rights. But the strongest defense of the extension and protection of intellectual property rights proceeds from the shared premise that the best institutional arrangement is that arrangement which is most likely to improve public health. The protection and extension of intellectual property rights may be justified on the grounds that it is very expensive to develop and test new drugs to treat diseases. Pharmaceutical companies simply will not make expensive investments unless they anticipate financial reward. If financial gain is abandoned by permitting generic versions of new medicines to be sold at highly discounted prices, at no financial gain to the innovating company, they will stop developing new medicines. On this view, innovation requires profits, and any effort to restrict profits will also restrict innovation, meaning needed medicines will not be developed.

Proposed Reforms

While defenders of liberalized trade may argue that the problems noted above are not sufficient reason to abandon the many benefits of liberalized international trade, nearly everyone agrees that current trade arrangements are not optimal. Below we examine three reforms in international trade that are focused on creating greater benefits for the global poor.

Linking Trade and Labor Rights

Christian Barry and Sanjay Reddy (2008) argue for the linkage of market access to the protection of labor rights in international trade. They propose that an international institution be created which would grant increased access to international markets conditional upon the exporting state meeting certain standards of labor protection that are appropriate to their particular level of development. Increasingly, labor rights and environmental protections are included in the text of international trade agreements. These agreements are often pursued by high-income countries because unions in those countries believe their jobs are threatened in part by the weak regulations abroad that make the cost of labor so cheap. But they can also be motivated by a genuine concern for people abroad: it is directly harmful to employees in global supply chains when their rights to organize are not recognized, when they are forced to work long hours in dangerous conditions, and when they are exposed to serious environmental harms. By institutionalizing rules that aim to protect labor and the environment in many or all trading partners, there is no race to the bottom, at least in terms of labor and the environment, because all parties to the agreement must abide by equivalent standards.

Restricting the International Sale in Natural Resources

As noted above, the unfettered sale of natural resources perpetuates autocracy, civil war, political instability, economic mismanagement, and gender inequality in countries that have large reserves of natural resources. Several thinkers have proposed reforms to the international trade in natural resources that aim to break the resource curse. Most prominently, Leif Wenar (2015) has proposed a system whereby resource-importing countries make access to their markets conditional upon the status of human rights in the resource-exporting country. Those countries that better protect human rights should be granted greater access to resource-importing markets and greater support for international trade. Those countries that perform worse on human rights should see their access to international markets restricted. Prohibitions on the purchase of natural resources from the extractive sectors in resource-exporting countries with the worst human rights regimes, on Wenar's view, should be complemented by sanctions against third party countries that continue to trade with these regimes. The funds collected from these sanctions should be put in an international fund that will be returned to the citizens of the resource-exporting state once they have returned to decent levels of governance and human rights protection. This approach aims to incentivize good governance in resource-exporting states by imposing punitive measures against resource exporters that do not protect human rights and conferring benefits upon resource exporters that do protect human rights.

Critics of these proposals argue that there are many reasons that countries fail to respect human rights, and external incentives created by the natural resource trade may not be the primary driver of human rights violations. Furthermore, economic sanctions can be more likely to force a regime to rally citizens around the flag and increase repression, while hurting the livelihoods of innocent people. And even if restrictions on the international sale of natural resources would be likely to improve human rights, it would be politically difficult to secure agreement to this regime in resource-importing countries

Prize Funds for Needed Medicines

While some critics of the extension of the global intellectual property regime argue that it should simply be eliminated, and national governments should be able to develop their own IP regime that would best serve national interests (James 2012), others worry that the weakening of the international intellectual property system will reduce the incentives for developing new, needed medicines. Weakening intellectual property protection might increase the ability of low-income countries to produce and sell generic versions of patented drugs, but it will not incentivize the creation of new drugs that are needed to treat previously neglected diseases.

This has led to several proposals to create prize funds that incentivize the development of needed medicines to treat diseases, especially those that create significant health burdens for people living in poverty. The Health Impact Fund, developed by Aidan Hollis and Thomas Pogge (2008), is a proposal whereby governments would contribute to an international fund that would award prize money to pharmaceutical companies based on the degree to which the new medicines that they develop reduce the global burden of disease. In exchange for selling the drugs at the cost of production, pharmaceutical companies receive the prize funds. In this way, an international prize fund is meant to create a profit incentive to develop needed medicines where none existed before. Whereas the Health Impact Fund would allocate prize funds based on the measured health impact of a new innovation (which may be very difficult to measure in particular contexts), Advanced Market Commitments specify an agreement between a funder and a set of innovators. Michael Kremer and Rachel Glennerster (2004) suggest the following mechanism. A legally binding contract is signed between donors and drug manufacturers. This contract specifies that the donors will 'create' a market for a specific drug, such as a needed vaccine against malaria, by topping up the price of the drug sold in a low-income country. So, if Bristol Myers Squib invents a vaccine for malaria, Malawi may pay 1 USD per pill, while donor governments may add 15 USD per pill. This commitment creates a publicly funded market where none existed before, giving the companies reason to innovate, while creating access to medicines where there previously were none. Rather than rewarding any medicine which is developed that has benefits for global health, Advanced Market Commitments pre-specify which medicines should be newly created and subsequently sold at low cost.

This is not exhaustive of the many proposals that have been made to reform the current international trade regime to better promote poverty reduction. But it gives a sense of how reformers aim to harness the power of international trade to reduce deprivation while solving those market failures that are most harmful to the global poor.

Chapter Summary

International trade is a defining feature of the current era of globalization. It raises deep moral and political questions over the role of sovereignty, the nature of global governance, the importance of national self-determination, and the nature of moral duties in international commercial relationships. In this chapter we have examined the arguments for and against fully liberalized international trade, and considered three reforms to international trade agreements that might ameliorate some of the worst harms of contemporary international trade while avoiding the poverty-causing impacts of protectionist trade agreements.

Questions for Discussion

1   At the time of writing, negotiations over the Trans-Pacific Partnership had recently concluded, but had not yet been ratified by the parties of the agreement. Find several opinion pieces regarding the TPP. Do you think, from the perspective of global poverty reduction, that the agreement should be ratified?
2   If a developing country chooses to have weak protections for workers and the environment, is a high-income country obliged to still attempt to create protections for workers and the environment when trading with that country?
3   Should low- and middle-income countries abandon intellectual property protections and allow the sale of generic drugs to treat urgent diseases?
4   Would you support a boycott of natural resources exported from states ruled by dictators? Or would you fear this boycott might harm civilians in those states?

Suggested Reading

Stiglitz, J. and Charlton, A. *Fair Trade for All*, Oxford: Oxford University Press, 2005.
Wenar, L. *Blood Oil: Tyrants, violence, and the rules that run the world*, Oxford: Oxford University Press, 2015.

References

Barry, C. and Reddy, S. *International Trade and Labor Standards: A proposal for linkage*, New York: Columbia University Press, 2008.

Barry-Jester, A. 'The problem with tying health care to trade', FiveThirtyEight.com, October 19, 2015, available at http://fivethirtyeight.com/features/the-problem-with-tying-health-care-to-trade (accessed December 8, 2015).

Bhagwati, J. *In Defense of Globalization*, Oxford: Oxford University Press, 2004.

Chang, H. *Bad Samaritans: The myth of free trade and the secret history of capitalism*, New York: Bloomsbury, 2008.

Drezner, D. 'Bottom feeder', *Foreign Policy*, November 19, 2009.

Hafner-Burton, E. *Forced to Be Good: Why trade agreements boost human rights*, Ithaca: Cornell University Press, 2009.

Hollis, A. and Pogge, T. 'The health impact fund: Making new medicines accessible for all', Incentives for Global Health, 2008.

Huffbauer, G. and Lowry, S. 'U.S. tire tariffs: Saving few jobs at high cost', Peterson Institute for International Economics, Policy Brief, April 2012, available at www.iie.com/publications/pb/pb12-9.pdf

James, A. *Fairness in Practice: A social contract for a global economy*, Oxford: Oxford University Press, 2012.

Kremer, M. and Glennerster, R. *Strong Medicine: Creating incentives for pharmaceutical research on neglected diseases*, Princeton: Princeton University Press, 2004.

Liu, X. and Ornelas, E. 'Free trade agreements and the consolidation of democracy', *American Economic Journal: Macroeconomics* 6.2 (2014): 29–70.

Rodrik, D. 'Industrial policy for the twenty-first century', 2004, available at www.sss.ias.edu/files/pdfs/Rodrik/Research/industrial-policy-twenty-first-century.pdf (accessed December 8, 2015).

Ross, M. *The Oil Curse: How petroleum wealth shapes the development of nations*, Princeton, Princeton University Press, 2012.

Stiglitz, J. *Making Globalization Work*, New York: W.W. Norton and Co., 2007.

Teson, F. 'Why free trade is required by justice', *Social Philosophy and Policy* 29 (2012): 126–153.

Wenar, Leif. 'Property rights and the resource curse', *Philosophy & Public Affairs* 36.1 (2008): 2–32.

Part V

Practical Issues

Thus far, we have examined the nature of global poverty, the possible moral duties to reduce global poverty, the debates surrounding foreign aid, and several proposals for global institutional reform. In the final section, we will investigate a series of applied and practical questions related to the practice of international development.

Anti-poverty work encompasses a wide range of activities that are intended to reduce deprivation and improve well-being. These efforts, while generally well-intended, may nonetheless create new ethical problems that would not exist if such efforts were not undertaken. In particular, we are interested in the moral questions that arise from efforts that are undertaken largely (but not exclusively) by individuals in wealthy countries to alleviate or eradicate global poverty.

14 Advocacy

On February 20, 2012, a little known California-based organization called Invisible Children uploaded a 30-minute video entitled *Kony 2012*.[1] The video contrasted images of former child soldiers and victims of brutal violence in Northern Uganda with scenes of comfortable western lifestyles and the images of increasing international connection. *Kony 2012* aimed to 'make famous' Joseph Kony, the head of the Lord's Resistance Army (LRA). The film (correctly) depicted the LRA as a vicious armed group that has conscripted children, committed widespread abuses against civilians, and had a destabilizing effect in Northern Uganda and other regions in Central Africa. Invisible Children (wrongly) argued that by making Joseph Kony famous, the world would be pressured to finally capture the rebel leader, leading to safety and security for the people of Northern Uganda.

The film's clever marketing strategy, using the power of social media and celebrity promotion, caused a meteoric spread across the world. Justin Bieber, Oprah Winfrey, Rihanna, and Ryan Gosling all implored their fans to support the cause of *Kony 2012*. Thanks in no small part to this celebrity support, the video quickly became one of the most watched viral videos in the history of the world. The film received over one hundred million views in the first month of its release. And Invisible Children raised millions of dollars from donations that poured in after they briefly became a household name.

But shortly after the release, and the undeniable success of the social media campaign, an enormous backlash occurred against the video, the organization, and its strategy to make Joseph Kony 'famous'. At the end of a viewing of the film in Northern Uganda, moviegoers began throwing rocks at the screen displaying *Kony 2012*. Nigerian novelist Teju Cole wrote that *Kony 2012* was an instance of the vast "white savior industrial complex" (Cole 2012). Analysts of conflicts in Central and East Africa highlighted the many inaccuracies of the *Kony 2012* video, and the problems involved in raising Kony's international profile without understanding the political context in which his group is able to survive.

Perhaps the most important strategic mistake was the film's ignorance of the possible role of the Ugandan government in preventing the capture of Kony. The Ugandan government was able to maintain the good will of donors by positioning themselves as partner in the war on terror and an opponent of Kony. If Kony were arrested, the government would not be able to curry as much international support and military assistance. Furthermore, the international spotlight might shift to the authoritarian conduct of the government of Uganda and its role in various human rights abuses. Critics alleged that from the perspective of the autocratic Ugandan government, the *Kony 2012* video was very welcome. Due in part to public pressure, the United States dispatched about 100 military personnel to Uganda to help with the effort to capture Kony, much to the dismay of critics who doubted the viability of an exclusively military solution to the challenges in Northern Uganda. At the time of writing, Kony's whereabouts remain unknown, and there has been no further demonstrable progress in ending the threat presented by the LRA. In 2014, Invisible Children announced it would be closing its doors in the coming year, transferring their remaining work to partner organizations.

While the *Kony 2012* video was remarkable in its meteoric spread, the general phenomenon whereby organizations in wealthy countries have the power to speak about the lives of people living in deprivation in order to change the policies that affect them, is a common feature of contemporary human rights and anti-poverty campaigns.[2] And it is a problem that preceded the era of viral videos. A decade before *Kony 2012*, a letter-writing campaign had spread around the internet to free Amina Lawal, a Nigerian woman who had been sentenced to death by stoning for the alleged crime of adultery and having a child out of wedlock (Jaggar 2005). The case grabbed international attention, and human rights organizations organized large campaigns to pressure the Nigerian government to put a halt to the sentence. Lawal's lawyers subsequently shared a public letter calling for a halt to the campaign. Trained in both Sharia and secular law, the lawyers argued that the public attention was undermining their case. They believed a successful defense of Lawal could be given on grounds recognized by the existing Sharia law, but excessive western attention risked turning the judges against Lawal in a show of anti-colonial nationalism. Eventually Lawal's lawyers succeeded in winning a not guilty verdict.

These are two instances of the more general moral problem of speaking for others. Speaking for others is a necessary feature of at least some anti-poverty and human rights work. It is precisely because the policies of wealthy countries directly affect the worst off that advocates in those countries can prove useful in the struggle to secure human rights and combat global poverty. But the act of speaking on behalf of others, especially people who are particularly vulnerable and in need of protection, raises important moral questions. Often times, people act in morally wrong ways when they attempt to speak for others. In this chapter, we will consider several moral complaints that can be made against advocacy organizations.

Agency

One moral complaint that can arise in the context of advocacy regarding human rights abuses and poverty alleviation efforts is related to individual and group agency. Agency is a central concept in moral and political philosophy, and a full conceptual analysis of agency is beyond the scope of this book. A plausible working definition of agency is 'what a person is free to do and achieve in pursuit of whatever goals or values he or she regards as important' (Sen 1985). Agency is a fundamental component of human well-being and protecting our agency is a basic human interest. Promoting individual agency is also the focus of much anti-poverty work.

Agency is valuable beyond its instrumental role in helping us to secure important goods. It is not just that we need agency so that things work out for us. Independent of the instrumental role that agency plays in our lives, we want to have some degree of control over how things go and we want to play a central role in determining the course of events. Even many basic needs theorists (Chapter 2) identify agency as a central human need in its own right.

Just as individuals have agency and it is centrally important for their flourishing, so too can collectives of individuals be viewed as group or corporate agents for whom agency is an important value. Social groups and community organizations can value their collective agency as much as their individual agency, and these group agents can equally see their collective agency undermined by outside interference.

When advocacy organizations undertake a public campaign that aims to shape policy, or create a narrative, they run the risk of overriding the decisions and actions of local organizations and individuals who are directly affected by the decisions they make. In other words, international activists can threaten local agency.

For example, ENOUGH, a Washington, D.C. based organization working to end mass atrocities, undertook a campaign to address the role of mining in fueling conflict in the eastern regions of the Democratic Republic of Congo. ENOUGH built a very successful advocacy campaign targeting electronics companies (who are very susceptible to consumer pressure and eager to protect their brands), and enlisted college students across the country to support a provision in the Dodd-Frank Act which required reporting from companies that have supply chains which reach the DRC, and asking that these companies undertake due diligence reporting on whether the source of their materials was 'conflict-free'.

The campaign was a plausible effort to address the problem of conflict minerals. There is a non-trivial link between mining and funding for armed groups in the country, and a number of UN and independent reports have documented the way in which armed groups financed their activities through exploitation of mining in the eastern DRC. The relevant provision of Dodd-Frank did not require a boycott—it simply required that companies report on their operations in the country. But associated public appeals suggested that electronics companies were complicit in fueling violence in the DRC, and critics of the campaigned argue a *de facto* ban on purchases followed ENOUGH's advocacy.

Critics also alleged the law risked undermining a number of other initiatives that were already underway to address the role of mining in fueling conflict in the DRC. Specifically, the Congolese government and World Bank had been working with private sector actors on an initiative called PROMINES to improve transparency and accountability in the sector. This and other efforts, which had much greater involvement from local activists, could not proceed if regulatory efforts from the United States led private sector actors to leave the market. According to critics, Congolese civil society did not have sufficient input into the design of Dodd-Frank legislation, and they should have been given greater voice in future efforts to regulate the mining sector and improve security and governance (Seay 2012). Defenders of the ENOUGH campaign note that the only real action from the private sector came after ENOUGH began campaigning. Furthermore, their aims were publicly supported by many segments of Congolese civil society.

Regardless of whether the provision of Dodd-Frank will in the long run turn out to be good for the DRC, the case demonstrates the moral importance of taking seriously the agency of those groups affected by advocacy campaigns. Their own best efforts may be undermined by outside actors attempting to act in their best interests. In general, outside actors ought to prioritize rather than undermine the agency of people who live with material deprivation and are struggling to improve their lot.[3]

Representation

A second, and related, moral issue that arises in international advocacy involves the formal representation of poor people. Even if an organization respects the agency of other individuals and organizations working on a particular problem, it may be the case that the organization or campaign is not representative of the individuals on behalf of whom it purports to work.

There are several ways in which an organization can fail to be representative. First, in the procedures that it uses to allocate resources and set advocacy strategy, an organization can exclude the voices of those who are directly affected by the decisions. In deciding, for example, whether to support a boycott of a particular company for its labor practices, an organization could fail to represent the voices of the workers on whose behalf the boycott would be taken. This failure of representation is rhetorical or discursive. It is a failure to properly represent expressed views and preferences as part of broader decision-making efforts.

Second, an organization's formal staff and leadership may fail to include any members of the community on whose behalf their decisions are taken. On this view, human rights organizations are not merely required to ensure that considerations raised by relevant stakeholders are heard in debates about policies and programs, but they are further required to create formal positions within decision-making bodies for representatives of or members of relevant groups. So, for example, an organization working on human rights in East Africa ought to include staff or board members from East African countries.

This is entirely plausible and many organizations would benefit from increased formal representation. But it is more challenging than it appears. All communities are internally diverse, filled with their own political conflicts, and no single person or group of people will represent the divergent perspectives from that community. And within these diverse communities, most policies would create winners and losers. It is therefore possible that representatives from a given community may seek to represent their own interests and not those of others. There is also a risk of tokenism: that the person who is to 'represent' the interests of people from a particular location or suffering from a particular problem must somehow embody the full set of diverse voices from their community. Furthermore, many human rights and anti-poverty organizations will work on issues that are transnational or global in scope. It is not clear who would be representative of tax laundering, or narcotics policy, or environmental degradation. In the face of these challenges, an organization seeking to ensure meaningful representation may simply aim for internal diversity of backgrounds, interests, and experience while providing discursive or narrative representation to relevant stakeholders.

Depicting People

A different but equally important consideration arises in the context of anti-poverty work. Representing the lives and voices of people is central to the work of many anti-poverty organizations. When CARE International raises an appeal for disaster relief funds in Pakistan, or Oxfam seeks financial support for drought in the Horn of Africa, it is standard practice to use visual images of the victims of these disasters. These strategies are carefully calculated—people feel much greater empathy when they can identify with particular victims than when they are simply presented with general narratives of impersonal statistics, however troubling the scenario is that is being described. Recent work in experimental philosophy and psychology (Small et al. 2007) indicates that individuals are much more willing to make charitable donations when they imagine a single recipient of a donation and are presented with a narrative of her potential to ascend out of poverty than when they are presented with information about large numbers of people who could be assisted by donations. This is true even when the benefit is described as accruing to much larger numbers of people. For example, over the summer months of 2015, news of the refugee crisis was widespread. Four million Syrians had fled the country, but it was not a pressing news story. But when a photograph appeared of a three-year-old Syrian boy, Alan Kurdi, who drowned at sea and washed up on the shores of Turkey, lying face down, in a position reminiscent of how many young children sleep, the world's conscience was shocked, and his image was carried on the front page of newspapers, shaming the international community over its tepid response to the crisis that had let him die a preventable death. It is therefore not surprising that many NGOs use representations of individual people who are deprived and suffering to support campaigns for action and financial donations.

There are a number of moral problems that can arise in depicting the lives of individual poor people. One central complaint is that poor people are often represented as passive recipients who are suffering rather than as active agents who are working hard to get by under extremely difficult circumstances.

Second, visual portrayals of people living in poverty can reinforce a simplistic narrative about aid and development to the detriment of more sophisticated and complex analyses of what causes poverty and how it may be addressed.

Third, individuals visually depicted in anti-poverty campaigns may be harmed by this representation and may not be able to meaningfully consent to their depiction. *New York Times* columnist Nicholas Kristof, perhaps the most widely read reporter and columnist covering human rights and global development, is a major proponent of using individual stories of suffering to prompt action on issues ranging from poverty to war to human trafficking. In January 2010, Kristof wrote a column about rape in the context of war in the Democratic Republic of Congo. In that piece, and an accompanying video, Kristof provided the full name and image of a nine-year-old girl who had been raped by government soldiers. While the *New York Times* has a strict policy of not providing real names of minors who are victims of sexual assault in the United States, Kristof did not believe this policy applied in the case of the child in the DRC. He asked the girl's aunt for permission to use her real name and her image, and also asked the child to consent.[4]

Consent often plays an important role in moral and political philosophy. There are many things that one cannot permissibly do to another without their consent. Sexual contact without consent is sexual assault or rape. Entering someone's property without their consent is breaking and entering. Using someone's car without their consent is automobile theft. And so on. For consent to be genuine, it must be free, in the sense that it is not coerced, and it must be informed, in that the person has full information about what they are consenting to, and is in a state of mind (and has the mental capacity) to give full consent.

In the case of Kristof's reporting, it is difficult to imagine that the child's consent could have been fully informed. For people who have never heard of the *New York Times*, or perhaps even seen the internet, it is not clear that they will fully comprehend what it means to have their name and image broadcast by the world's most prominent media outlet. For this reason, one might think it is permissible to use the child's name and image—her life is too distant from the reaches of the paper of record to be harmed by her depiction in this story. But the world changes, and so do people's lives. Today she is a survivor in a village without access to the internet. But in 10 years she might be living in the capital, attending university. And it may be that when a friend does a quick search to look up her contact details, he comes across an old video by a reporter from the United States detailing her suffering as a child. This may be information she is willing to share, but it should be information that she chooses to share on her own terms. Worse, even if the victim and her aunt do not have access to the *New York Times*, government soldiers and rebels may read online media. There is a non-trivial chance that the child and her family will face retaliation for sharing their story with Kristof. Regardless, it is not possible for the child to meaningfully consent to the use of her image in this way given the significant informational constraints.

Similarly, many of the people who are displayed in the various public relations materials of anti-poverty organizations may be unable to provide genuine consent to their images being used in the way that they are. As many of the images represent potential beneficiaries of anti-poverty NGOs operations, it may be that pressure to receive benefits from NGOs leads people living in poverty to begrudgingly consent to the use of their images. Even if the person is not forcibly coerced, she may be exploited in so far as she accepts the use of her image only because she is vulnerable and in need of assistance. It may therefore be morally wrong to use these images even if consent has been provided.

This is nicely depicted in the novel *We Need New Names*, by NoViolet Bulawayo:

> The man starts taking pictures with his big camera. They just like taking pictures, these NGO people, like maybe we are their real friends and relatives. … They don't care that we are embarrassed by our dirt and torn clothing, that we would prefer they didn't do it. They just take the pictures anyway. Take and take. We don't complain because we know after the picture taking comes the gifts.
>
> (Bulawayo 2014, p. 54)

Since photographs and videos will often contain images of people who have not meaningfully consented to the use of their image; this makes the way in which those people are portrayed much more important. A person who is shown to be desperate, or pathetic, or helpless might rightly object to being portrayed in this way. In contrast, a person shown studying in school, or being well treated by a medical professional, may not find anything to object to in the use of her image and name by an anti-poverty organizations. We therefore have several axes along which to evaluate the depiction of people living in poverty—the degree to which they have meaningfully consented to the use of their image, the degree to which they might find their portrayal acceptable, and the degree to which the image rightly portrays a situation about which other people should be concerned.

This brings an interesting tension to questions about what advocacy and fundraising strategies are morally permissible, and which are morally best. On the one hand, many representations may be misleading or reinforce harmful or counterproductive stereotypes about people living in global poverty, be taken without the consent of the people represented, and portray them in a bad light. On the other hand, it is precisely the simplified stories about basic human need that increase involvement in advocacy campaigns and generate fundraising possibilities for organizations. Many children are actually starving, and the portrayal of their starvation actually does prompt bystanders to act, making donations and joining organizations involved in famine relief. Once people become supporters of Oxfam or Human Rights Watch, perhaps they can then become more informed about the issues on which the organizations are working, and perhaps future donations will not be determined solely by a person's emotive response to the picture of a malnourished child in some far-flung village.

However, this line of reasoning, which justifies some simplistic and paternalistic visual representations on the basis that they generate more support for anti-poverty work, may be overly focused on the short-term costs and benefits. In the long term, it is arguably harmful to perpetuate stereotypes about people living in poverty. Persistent failures to properly understand the context in which deprivation arises leads to misdirected and potentially damaging anti-poverty programming. Even if certain simplistic narratives initially contribute to higher fundraising efforts in the short term, they may corrode long-term efforts to develop an informed, context-sensitive approach to poverty eradication.

Chapter Summary

People who are deprived in the material and social spheres are often deprived of power to control their lives. This lack of power creates reasons for people who have more power to speak on their behalf. This is often a good thing. At its best, informed by a sense of transnational solidarity, advocacy organizations can partner with social movements abroad to create needed change. But with the power to speak for others comes moral responsibility. Too often, this responsibility is overlooked due to the perceived urgency of the cause or the ignorance of the speakers. Advocacy organizations must take great care to represent the preferences and interests of people living in poverty, when possible to include them in decisions that affect their lives, and to portray them as active moral agents with inherent dignity who are working hard to make a better life.

Questions for Discussion

1   Find the materials of a major anti-poverty organization, such as Save the Children or Oxfam, and look at their promotional materials. Do you find the images used to be respectful, or is there something that is morally objectionable about how people are portrayed?

2   Examine a recent call to action from an anti-poverty organization like ONE, or search the site change.org. Does it appear that these calls are representative of the interests of people who will be affected? Can you see any possibility of them infringing on the interests or rights of those affected?

3   Social movements are now often coordinated online. Do you think wealthy individuals should join these online movements? Or does their detachment from global poverty make it unlikely that they will be effective advocates?

Notes

1   That is, little known to the mainstream public. Many people concerned with affairs about Uganda and Central Africa were already familiar with the group based on their previous films.

2   I have certainly been actively involved in a few of these organizations and supported many more.

3   This, of course, is a consideration that could be overridden. If it is shown that local preferences are adaptive in some way, or there is some other, overriding reason to act against the stated preferences of people living in poverty, then there may be occasions on which this should be done. But this should be the exception rather than the rule.

4 For Kristof's account of why this was a morally acceptable approach, see his blog post 'Is It Ever O.K. to Name Rape Victims?', available at http://kristof.blogs.nytimes.com/2010/02/04/is-it-ever-ok-to-name-rape-victims/#preview (accessed March 30, 2016).

Suggested Reading

Alcoff, L. 'The problem of speaking for others', *Cultural Critique* 20 (1991): 5–32.

De Waal, A. (Ed.) *Advocacy in Conflict: Critical perspectives on transnational activism*, London: Zed Books, 2015.

Hamilton, R. *Fighting for Darfur: Public action and the struggle to stop genocide*, New York: Palgrave Macmillan, 2011.

Mamdani, M. *Saviors and Survivors: Darfur, politics, and the war on terror*, New York: Doubleday, 2009.

References

Bulawayo, N. *We Need New Names*, New York: Random House, 2013.

Cole, T. 'The white savior industrial complex,' *The Atlantic*, March 21, 2012, available at www.theatlantic.com/international/archive/2012/03/the-white-savior-industrial-complex/254843/

Jaggar, A. '"Saving Amina": Global justice for women and intercultural dialogue', *Ethics & International Affairs* 19.03 (2005): 55–75.

Seay, L. 'What's wrong with Dodd-Frank 1502? Conflict minerals, civilian livelihoods, and the unintended consequences of western advocacy', Center for Global Development Working Paper 284, January 2012.

Sen, A. K. 'Well-being agency and freedom: The Dewey Lectures 1984', *Journal of Philosophy* 82.4 (1985): 169–221.

Small, D., Loewenstein, G., and Slovic, P. 'Sympathy and callousness: The impact of deliberative thought on donations to identifiable and statistical victims', *Organizational Behavior and Human Decision Processes* 102 (2007): 143–153.

15 Consumption

On April 23, 2013, several thousand Bangladeshi employees went to work at the eight-story Rana Plaza in Dhaka, the capital of Bangladesh, to start their shifts making clothing that would be sold by many of the world's most prominent retailers. The workers were making approximately 37 USD per month—wages very low by international standards but higher than the prevailing wages for low-skilled workers in Bangladesh. Due to poor construction, poor regulatory oversight, and corruption during and after construction, the building was structurally vulnerable. One day earlier, a government regulator ordered the factories closed when he noticed an emerging crack in the walls. But the factory owners, given their influence over workers' livelihoods, were able to persuade (or coerce) employees to return to the factory. On the 23rd, these structural risks turned into catastrophe for the over 1,100 employees who were killed when the building collapsed, the more than 2,000 who were injured, and the many more who lost friends and loved ones.

The employees at Rana Plaza who made clothing for export into the world's garment retailers had few if any protected labor rights. As Human Rights Watch reported two years after the collapse,

> If workers at Rana Plaza had more of a voice, it is entirely possible that the circumstances that led to the thousands of deaths and injuries could have been prevented. None of the five factories operating in Rana Plaza had a trade union, and so workers were powerless to resist their managers who ordered, threatened, and cajoled them to enter the doomed building a day after large cracks had appeared in it.
>
> Similarly, workers at the Tazreen Fashions factory were prevented from leaving their workstations by managers, even after the ground floor of the building caught fire and alarms went off. If the workers at Tazreen had been members of an effective union it is much more likely that staff would have had fire safety training and could have pointed out safety violations like blocked stairwells, lack of fire escapes, and barred windows, all of which contributed to worker deaths.
>
> (Human Rights Watch 2015)

There is nothing particularly unique, except the scale, between what happened in the Rana Plaza on that day and the routine violation of labor rights that takes place every day in the rest of the global economy. Every day consumers purchase goods and services whose supply chains reach across the globe. The clothing you wear may have been manufactured in sweatshops in Bangladesh or Vietnam. Your mobile phone may have been assembled in large factories in China that expose workers to environmental toxins. And the natural resources, both minerals and fossil fuels, on which the modern economy runs are largely found outside your country of residence, often times in countries plagued by civil war such as South Sudan, the Democratic Republic of Congo, and Burma, where miners are at risk of death and oil revenues fund autocrats and rebels. If you take a careful look down the supply chain that produces the modern conveniences high-income consumers take for granted, you will find many workers who are prevented from organizing into labor unions, people fired for becoming pregnant, rampant sexual harassment, people working excessively long hours without extra pay, confiscated wages, exposure to a range of environmental harms, and more.

But you also find people who are better off than they otherwise would have been. Employees are able to secure a better livelihood by working for multinational corporations, women can find formal employment opportunities that were not previously available, freeing them from often oppressive social relations in the home, and industries are developing, helping countries transition from subsistence economies to advanced economic activity.

Given the connection between consumer goods and people who are living in poverty, many anti-poverty campaigners have worked to connect the ethically conscious consumer to poverty eradication programs. These campaigns raise central moral issues about the responsibility of consumers, the role of consumption in reducing or producing global poverty, and the limits of consumer activism. In this chapter, we focus on two ethical questions facing consumers regarding global poverty. The first is whether, and if so to what extent, consumers bear responsibility for the impacts of their consumption on others. The second is whether various contemporary campaigns that attempt to leverage the power of consumers to enact change are morally justified.

Conceptions of Consumer Responsibility

Why might consumers bear moral responsibility for the impact of their purchases on the living standards of workers who produce the products that they consume? Arguments for the responsibility for the impact of their purchases on global poverty mirror the more general arguments encountered in Part II regarding duties of the wealthy to reduce global poverty. We briefly review them here.

Liability

One reason that consumers might bear some moral responsibility for what happens to the employees who make the goods that they purchase is that they are in some way liable for labor violations. This liability conception of consumer responsibility relies on the claim that consumers are part of a causal chain that brings about this harm. Here the term 'harm' involves both the bad treatment of workers and their low pay. On this conception, if the company should be held liable for its bad treatment of workers, then this liability is shared by the consumers (and shareholders) who support the company.

Association

In Part II, we saw that one way to establish that there are duties for the affluent to reduce global poverty is through the claim that affluent people stand in a certain kind of association or structured relationship to the people who are harmed through commercial interactions. This is particularly clear in the case of consumer responsibility. If I purchase a pair of shoes that was made in a factory where people are exposed to hazardous chemicals, I may bear some responsibility for the people who fall ill as a result of those working conditions. This reason does not rely on the claim that I have harmed anyone, but merely that I am engaged in ongoing commercial relations with them that create structured vulnerabilities.[1]

Benefitting

A slightly different way of establishing the moral responsibility of consumers is to show that even if a consumer does not have any power to influence corporations, suppliers, or governments, the consumer benefits from the labor violations that do occur. The low payment of wages, the skimping on safety regulations, the excessive overtime without pay, and other injustices result in lower aggregate costs of supplying the products that we use and enjoy. Arguably, there is more money in consumers' pockets than there otherwise would be because global supply chains pay low wages, offer few benefits, and do not protect basic worker's rights. For this reason, we might think that benefitting from injustice generates obligations to rectify that injustice or prevent it in the future.

Capacity

A final way of conceiving of consumer responsibility is simply to note that consumers have the power, through their purchases, to make a difference in the lives of people living in poverty. They have sufficient incomes to spend on consumer items that can be directed toward improving livelihoods abroad, and they have influence over the activities of the companies that serve them. In these two ways, consumers may be said to bear responsibility for addressing material and social deprivation through their consumption.

Objections to Consumer Responsibility

Critics who reject the idea that consumers bear responsibility for the status of employees across the globe note that there are several features of the global economy that appear to significantly reduce, if not eliminate, the individual consumer's responsibility. First, one might object that an individual consumer has diminishingly small impact on both global demand for products and on the conduct of particular companies. If you drastically shift your consumption patterns today, it will make no difference in the operations of large multinational companies.

It is true that any one consumer has little influence over large multinational companies. But the group of all consumers has very significant leverage over multinational companies. This may simply mean that the responsibility is shared collectively among consumers, and each individual consumer is therefore required to do their part in changing corporate behavior.

Second, because corporations are often not directly overseeing what happens in their supply chains (because they purchase from other suppliers or own subsidiary companies), they are constrained in their ability to protect worker's rights and raise their wages. On this view, Apple and Intel have no control over how miners are treated in the Democratic Republic of Congo, so they cannot be held responsible for their treatment. This responsibility lies with the local company that is employing the miners.

It is also true that retailers in high-income countries are sometimes several steps removed from rights violations in their supply chain. But this should be thought of as a feasibility constraint on what can be required of companies, and thus pushed for by consumers, rather than a reason to deny consumer responsibility altogether. In so far as possible, companies should ensure their suppliers maintain the same standards the company would support. Consumers have a responsibility to ensure that their purchasing power is directed to companies which attempt to improve conduct in the supply chain, and to use their voice, or the possibility of exiting a commercial relationship, to push the laggards to improve their conduct. While responsibility may diminish the weaker the links are in the supply chain where labor rights violations are found, it does not disappear.

Third, one might object that governments, not companies, bear the primary duty for upholding human rights. This kind of objection follows more general criticisms of corporate social responsibility. When operating in countries that have lower labor standards and lower wages, some critics argue that corporations have no special duties to elevate wages above the prevailing legal minimum or to respect labor rights that are not enshrined in domestic law. If this is something employees in that country want, they can lobby their government to change the minimum wage or the national labor laws.

Milton Friedman, one of the most influential free-market economists of the 20th century (still invoked though often misunderstood today), argued against any ethical duties bearing on business corporations beyond their fiduciary duties to shareholders. Friedman opposed corporate social responsibility on several grounds. Friedman argued that labor standards or environmental protections, for example, are issues to be decided by democratic governments rather than individual corporations. The appropriate number of working hours, for example, or the best way to balance increases in living standards versus environmental protection, is through democratically elected legislatures. Corporations are required to follow the laws that representative governments establish for them. But when one encourages corporations to establish the right minimum wage levels, or appropriate levels of philanthropic giving, one takes the right to decide these matters away from democratic publics and places them in the hands of corporate entities. One can extend Friedman's argument to the consumer responsibility for the goods that are purchased. Consumers are not well-placed to determine the right level of environmental protection or labor standards in countries that produce the goods they consume, and even if they were in such a position, it is not clear that consumer movements will successfully be able to determine how best to improve labor and the environment through corporate activity. Furthermore, when consumers make these decisions, they take that right away from democratic governments (Friedman 1970).

Against Friedman, one can argue that it is not clear why, even if human rights are best protected by governments, businesses should be off the hook when governments fail to protect those rights. Many employees work in countries that have autocratic or dysfunctional political systems. In these contexts, it is not possible to have democratic deliberation about optimal levels of wages and protection of workers' rights. Furthermore, it is often the case that companies are violating domestic law, especially in countries where the government has limited capacity to enforce the law. Consumer pressure for corporations to behave responsibly is thus not a call to establish standards where none existed but to comply with standards that are not enforced by host governments. However, critics of corporate social responsibility are right to note that corporations are often not going to be very good at providing public services, and so any philanthropic work they support is best channeled through other providers.

Reform

Many people are persuaded that consumers do bear moral responsibility for helping to protect the labor rights and improve the livelihoods of people involved in supplying consumer goods and services. Since at least the 1990s, activists have worked hard to pressure companies to improve working conditions in the wages and factories that make the products we enjoy. Indeed, Iris Marion Young, who we've encountered elsewhere in this book, dedicated much of her academic work to identifying the structural injustices involved in sweatshops, but also spent some of her spare time working with activist groups campaigning to improve working conditions at home and abroad. If you have spent much time on university campuses over the years, especially in the United States, it is likely you have come across protestors who object to sweatshops that produce university apparel. The protestors aim to force universities to ensure that the workers who produce the clothing that carries their school's name be paid a decent wage and have their labor rights protected.[2]

But even if one is persuaded that she ought to devote her time and resources to make her consumption more ethical, enacting meaningful reform through consumer activity is more difficult than it first appears.

Boycott

One might aim to simply avoid causal connections with international supply chains. This is exceedingly difficult to do in a globalized economy. Even if the most proximate entity involved in the creation of the goods and services you consume is based within your home country, it is extremely unlikely that the entity can avoid using supplies from abroad. If you drink coffee or wear cotton, use electronics or travel by modern transportation, you are involved in the global economy, and people who live with significant economic and social deprivation help to make the products you use. One could choose to live off the grid, the life of a hermit. Most people will not find this option feasible or appealing. But even if you could prevent your consumption from being connected to international economic activities, it is very clear, from the perspective of poverty alleviation, that eliminating commercial relationships with people living in poverty will not help the global poor, and in fact will do them great harm. If you sever your economic ties to laborers abroad, one immediate implication will be a decrease in the amount of paid work available to those laborers. So while one might think that they are no longer morally responsible for harm in the global economy if they cease buying and consuming goods and resources, this will be of little comfort to the poor people who are made worse off by the severing of commercial ties. If an outright boycott of international goods is likely to exacerbate rather than reduce global poverty, what options are available to ethically conscious consumers?

Fairtrade

One of the largest movements to use ethical consumption to improve welfare abroad is the fair trade movement. Here I use Fairtrade with an initial capital letter and as one word to refer specifically to the certification scheme that aims to ensure that products sold under the 'Fairtrade' label help to protect the environment, ensure labor rights, and pay a living wage to low-income workers. The scheme is one of a proliferating set of transnational governance institutions that is independent of state regulations. Whereas environmental protection or labor rights are often enforced and promoted through state action, Fairtrade assumes that either there is a lack of capacity or willingness to protect these rights, or that the prevailing labor and environmental standards in a country are inadequate for protecting these rights. It offers consumers a market-based mechanism to promote employee welfare and protect the environment. Fairtrade products are now commonly found on supermarket shelves throughout OECD countries, and in some communities, such as progressive college campuses, it is common to find campaigns calling for further increases in the purchasing of Fairtrade products. There are approximately 1.5 million workers and farmers in fair trade certified organizations (Fairtrade.org.uk 2015).

But is Fairtrade successful in protecting the environment, guaranteeing labor rights, and raising wages? As we noted in Chapter 3, it is difficult to disentangle cause from effect in various anti-poverty programs. It is reasonable to state that the empirical evidence is not yet strong enough to make very firm conclusions regarding Fairtrade. But there are reasons to be suspicious that Fairtrade has the strong poverty-reducing, rights-protecting consequences that many consumers believe they are supporting when purchasing Fairtrade products.

There are several basic theoretical reasons to be skeptical of the role of Fairtrade in reducing global poverty. First, directing one's consumption toward Fairtrade producers and away from non-certified producers means that while employment, income, or wages may go up for the Fairtrade producer, they go down for whoever used to be making sales and is now losing out as a result of your shifting to Fairtrade purchases. When the average consumer thinks about Fairtrade, they likely think they are supporting environmentally responsible livelihoods abroad when they purchase Fairtrade. But they often fail to recognize that this is at the expense of supporting livelihoods of uncertified producers somewhere else. So for Fairtrade to be morally preferable, it has to be the case that livelihood gains which accrue to Fairtrade producers exceed the costs of diverting resources away from non-Fairtrade producers.

Second, there are limits to the degree to which ethically conscious consumer-driven purchases can reduce poverty in exporting countries. The story of how South Korea or Botswana escaped poverty is not one of reliance upon the generosity of consumers. It is one of learning how to raise the productivity in society, driven by political institutions that foster growth—not the marginal gains accruing to small producers who appeal to the ethical consumer.

Third, it is possible that the promise of being Fairtrade certified attracts producers away from more productive activities. For example, Paul Collier argues that because Fairtrade producers are only certified for a special range of products, they are not able to diversify and pursue comparative advantage because they get locked in to Fairtrade certification, which, in his terms, means 'they get charity as long as they stay producing the crops that have locked them into poverty' (Collier 2009, p. 163).

There is relatively little rigorous empirical evidence on the impact of Fairtrade certification on producers. One study finds living standards are raised by 30 percent from Fairtrade certification, while nearby producers also benefit (Chiputwa et al. 2013). But other studies find little evidence of the purported benefits of Fairtrade certification for employees in low-income countries. A four-year study by researchers at the University of London (Cramner et al. 2014) found that seasonal wage workers, people hired by the owners of small, Fairtrade-certified farms, were actually paid less on sites producing Fairtrade products than at other comparable farms. They were also excluded from many of the public services that are supposed to be part of Fairtrade community development, including health and education projects. Furthermore, as noted above, even if Fairtrade did produce benefits for the producers, it may be at the expense of producers elsewhere in the global economy who lose market share due to their lack of Fairtrade certification. Given the implausible economic theory upon which Fairtrade is based and the at best inconclusive empirical evidence, it is difficult to conclude that consumers are under a strict moral responsibility to purchase Fairtrade.

Buy Local

Many ethically minded consumers in high-income countries aim to buy local. Grocery stores in Colorado proudly advertise cantaloupe and corn grown in Colorado, while British grocery stores tout berries and meat grown and raised in the United Kingdom. Many new restaurants aim to produce a farm to plate meal, which (among other things) intends to eliminate extensive international supply chains. The buy local movement, often involving food and agriculture but in many cases also involving other consumer products, has grown considerably in recent years.

Local food movements are often supported by individuals that are adopting explicitly ethical aims. They believe that large-scale agricultural production, which must transport produce great distances to reach their plates, is bad for the planet and for people. In their view, small, local farms will better protect the environment, will reduce greenhouse gas emissions, will be more likely to reduce or eliminate pesticides and to produce organic food, and will require fewer resources to transport food to consumers' plates. Furthermore, consumers will not be complicit in the bad treatment and low pay of workers abroad if they avoid international supply chains.

The local food movement appears to be directly in conflict with the interests of food producers in low-income countries. In so far as consumption shifts from food produced and exported from countries like Brazil, Paraguay, and Ghana to farms in upstate New York or rural Oregon, this raises incomes for people in New York and Oregon while reducing incomes for people with much lower living standards. It is possible that one could offer a moral justification for this shift. A strong nationalist might argue that a consumer has much greater obligations to direct her purchases to support co-nationals than to support those abroad. But for this argument to succeed it must be the case that these duties are extremely strong—and this seems unlikely. Even the strong nationalist is likely to consume many products that are manufactured abroad and probably does not believe himself to be obliged to direct all consumption toward co-nationals. (Furthermore, it is unlikely that most proponents of eating local are strong nationalists of this type.)

A second way to justify the habits of so-called 'locavores' is to argue that the importance of environmental protection outweighs the values of raising incomes for producers abroad. This argument might be persuasive if environmental benefits were also to accrue to people in low-income countries from the local food movement. One might argue, for example, that climate change threatens to eradicate many recent gains in poverty reduction and to impose great harms on the planet's poorest populations. Environmental protection that arises through locally sourced consumption is thereby consistent with an interest in reducing global poverty.

But are there significant environmental benefits from eating locally? It turns out the environmental benefits are quite small, and in some cases it is actually environmentally worse to consume locally grown products. One reason to think that local purchases have lower environmental impact is that they require less transportation. But for agricultural products, transportation only makes up around

11 percent of the total greenhouse gas emissions associated with the life cycle of agriculture production, and only 4 percent comes from the transportation from the grower to the seller (Weber and Matthew 2008). Most greenhouse gas emissions come from agricultural practices themselves. More importantly, depending on the location in which a particular product is grown, it may be more environmentally friendly to purchase food produced far away in an environment that requires fewer resources for production than close to home where more resources are required.

If this is correct, then it is not clear that the locavore can justify her purchases. As noted above, increasing locally sourced consumption reduces demand for products from low-income countries. It therefore would have to be the case that very significant environmental benefits outweigh the potential poverty reduction that comes from directing purchasing power abroad. Given significant doubts about the environmental benefits of local purchasing, it appears that the movement to purchase goods locally is not worth the potentially negative impact on poverty reduction abroad.

Regulate Prices

In a breathless exposé for *The Guardian*, Jose Blythman's article, titled 'Can Vegans Stomach the Truth about Quinoa?', claimed that consumer demand for the grain was raising food prices, harming local populations in Peru and Bolivia.

> The appetite of countries such as ours for this grain has pushed up prices to such an extent that poorer people in Peru and Bolivia, for whom it was once a nourishing staple food, can no longer afford to eat it. Imported junk food is cheaper. In Lima, quinoa now costs more than chicken. Outside the cities, and fueled by overseas demand, the pressure is on to turn land that once produced a portfolio of diverse crops into quinoa monoculture. In fact, the quinoa trade is yet another troubling example of a damaging north-south exchange, with well-intentioned health and ethics-led consumers here unwittingly driving poverty there. It's beginning to look like a cautionary tale of how a focus on exporting premium foods can damage the producer country's food security.
>
> (Blythman 2013)

This is one of many popular media stories proclaiming that the consumption trends of wealthy individuals threaten poor people.

For many years, activists complained that subsidies for agriculture and farming in developed countries and the dumping of excess produce in developing countries led to artificially low food prices, to the detriment of poor farmers. These practices were thought to hurt local food producers who could not compete with the highly industrialized, and highly subsidized, system of agricultural production in high-income countries.

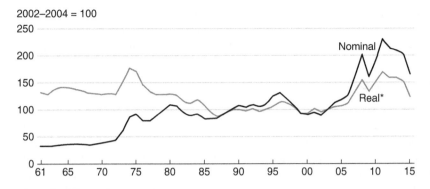

Figure 15.1 FAO Food Price Index in Nominal and Real Terms.

* The real price index is the nominal price index deflated by the World Bank Manufactures Unit Value Index (MUV).

But then things began to change. Food prices, which had been alleged to be artificially low for many years, began to rise rapidly. Now activists argued that food prices can become too high, and food was unaffordable for people living in the Global South (see Figure 15.1).

There are three important points to consider about the role of food prices. First, changes in food prices create winners and losers—price increases are good for net producers but may be bad for net consumers. This means, for example, that rural populations may benefit when the price of a crop they produce goes up, but this will be harmful for urban consumers who are not involved in small-scale agriculture (assuming there is no trickle-down effect from the economic gains accruing to producers). Second, some gains that are attributable to producers may not always reach those individuals who are worst off. A small-scale farmer may have, at the beginning of the season, agreed to a set price for his produce with an intermediary who will get the product to market, and therefore be unlikely to benefit if the international price rises over the course of the growing season. The third is that market volatility, especially in the absence of strong systems of social protection and well-regulated agricultural markets (including, for example, crop insurance) can be harmful for everyone involved if they are not able to hedge against price fluctuations.

For the ethically minded consumer, these complications make it far from clear, from the perspective of poverty alleviation, that they ought to avoid the consumption of products that are produced by poor people to try to regulate prices. Doing so risks lowering the incomes of poor people. Excluding poor people from global supply chains by shifting consumption to producers that are closer to home is not a promising strategy for poverty reduction.

If these views are right, the task for the ethically minded consumer may be less about attempting to direct their purchases away from high-priced food and toward low-priced foods, and more about using their role as consumers to influence the overarching system of food production and consumption, and the systems of social protection that lie behind that system, which create significant vulnerabilities for both food producers and food consumers in low- and medium-income countries.

Spend and Donate

One way that activist organizations have tried to leverage the power of consumption to reduce global poverty is to simply use individual purchases to fund projects or programs directed at reducing global poverty. For example, the Product RED campaign allows companies to sell certain products (such as an iPhone) under the RED brand. A portion of the profits from the sale of the product is then donated to the Global Fund to Fight AIDS, Tuberculosis, and Malaria. A second and very famous case is that of TOMS shoes. TOMS sells a range of shoes to high-income consumers, but promises that for each shoe purchased, a second shoe will be donated to a child in need. They proclaim, "With every product you purchase, TOMS will help a person in need. One for One". TOMS also sells eyewear, and uses profits from those purchases to fund programs that help to restore sight to children. In these and other cases, the power of consumers is leveraged to generate financial or material donations for people living in poverty. Consumers will be purchasing these products anyways, so why not leverage their consumer power to help people in need?

Despite these efforts to make consumption in high-income countries contribute to anti-poverty efforts, many scholars believe that these efforts will have at best a negligible impact on global poverty, and at worst clean the conscience of high-income consumers without making poor people better off. The RED campaign is accused of using global poverty as a marketing tool to sell more products while making comparatively small donations to the Global Fund. One study found that while the RED campaign donated 18 million USD to the Global Fund, companies spent $100 million advertising their association with the RED campaign (Frazier 2007).

There are three ways to run this argument. The first would simply be to point out that an ethically minded consumer can simply forego the purchase of the product, which in nearly all cases will not be a necessity of life, and therefore make a donation directly to the Global Fund. Instead of buying a 30 USD shirt, of which perhaps $.05 will be donated to the Global Fund, why not by a pre-worn shirt for $5 and donate $25 to poverty relief? But the defender of RED may argue that the relevant counterfactual is not whether more resources should be directed to the Global Fund, but whether existing consumption can be leveraged to generate more money for anti-poverty programs.

A second version of the argument would accept that some amount of marketing will go on, but argue that the proportion of charitable donations given to the Global Fund is not high enough. This critique doesn't require that aggregate welfare be maximized, but simply that a higher proportion of aggregate revenue go to public health efforts than currently does if the campaign is to be ethically justified. In other words, when RED starts making larger donations than they are now, RED purchases will become morally commendable.

Third, one might run a deeper critique against the RED model. On this view, it is the very system of production and consumption involved in RED products that helps to create poverty in the first place. When companies extract natural resources in countries beset by civil war, making payments to armed groups or oppressive governments, to make cellphones or laptops, and a miniscule portion of the profits from that product is sent back to combat a disease in the country of origin of the resources, it is hard to see how this is a recipe for global progress. This critic believes that only deep structural change can combat global poverty, and the companies involved in the RED campaign oppose that change. The defender of RED can note, as we have elsewhere, that international exchange is generally good for people in low-income countries, and adding charitable donations to this exchange which promote global public health is only to the good.

The TOMS model is different. Rather than donating a small portion of profits, it dedicates a 50 percent share of product to people in need. Yet here too there are arguments against TOMS' approach to global poverty alleviation. First, it is not clear that new footwear is a priority for the recipients of these shoes. In some markets, donated TOMS shoes are resold by gift recipients back to local vendors. Apparently people who had received free shoes wanted something else more than new shoes. One way to think about this is to think about cash transfers—if the recipients of these shoes, or their parents, were given money instead of shoes, would they use the cash to go out and buy a new pair? Or would they dedicate the money to some other priority—school uniforms, or food, or home improvements. If shoes aren't really what people need right now, is it wise to build an entire business model around delivering them to people? The history of development is littered with projects aimed at improving human welfare that failed because they were ignorant of the priorities of beneficiaries. TOMS used to claim that receiving their shoes considerably improves health for recipients, but this claim has never been established in a rigorous and independent evaluation. In fact, in a rigorous evaluation of the donation of TOMS shoes in El Salvador, while children wore and liked the shoes they were given, they did not have any other positive impact on the children's lives. Children with the newly donated shoes spent about 15 minutes more a week playing outside rather than doing homework. Otherwise, there were no significant impacts from the donation program (Wydick et al. 2015).

There may be a second, deeper problem with freely distributing a company's product. Any time a product is given away in a market where someone currently produces and sells that product, the local producer is likely to lose out. If people can get for free what they used to buy, then the producer will not be able to sell her product. There is a worry that the giving away of free shoes undermines small-scale producers of footwear in areas in which TOMS shoes are distributed. In a rigorous evaluation, researchers found a very small negative impact on local shoe sales when donations occur (Wydick et al. 2014). This criticism has been made of the company's operations for some time. The good news, however, is that the company seems to be responding. TOMS now aims to produce the shoes in countries in which their programs exist. So even if donated footwear does not make a big difference for children, their parents being employed in a factory will make a big difference. And by shifting production to countries where donations may undermine employment among local producers, TOMS may offset any harmful effects of their model. This may be a sign that constructive criticism of consumer campaigns has the potential to improve them over time.

Pressure Corporations

The preceding cases demonstrate that many efforts to leverage consumer pressure in the service of poverty reduction can fail if they are not well intended or are not based on a plausible theory of change. But we should not infer from these difficulties that there is no way for consumers to meaningfully support efforts to protect rights and reduce global poverty. Many consumer campaigns have usefully pressured manufacturers to improve labor standards and raise pay, extractive companies to improve the human rights standards of their security forces, make transparent their payments to governments, and improve their environmental protection, and technology companies to protect the privacy of their customers. These campaigns are successful precisely because companies seek to protect their brands and fear losing consumer and investor support. It is therefore plausible that consumers have a moral responsibility to contribute to these campaigns when they are carefully designed, ideally in collaboration with intended beneficiaries, to best serve the interests of people living in poverty while taking account of potential unintended side effects.

One promising campaign still under way is Oxfam's Behind the Brands campaign.[3] This campaign focuses on the ten largest food and beverage companies and examines their practices and policies regarding land rights, women's empowerment, the treatment of farmers, the rights of workers, climate change, transparency, and water usage. In each of these areas, Oxfam scores companies from 1–10 on their total performance. The scorecard is then publicized and used to encourage consumers to put pressure on their favorite brands to reform their policies and improve their scores. Three years in, hundreds of thousands of consumers have taken action, and companies are beginning to change their policies.

Chapter Summary

As we have seen in this chapter, there is a strong case that consumers bear some moral responsibility for the impact of their purchases on individuals abroad. But this responsibility arises in a complex system in which goods and services are exchanged. Using one's power as a consumer to improve the social and environmental conditions in distant economies requires a hard-nosed look at the possibilities for reform and the potential for unforeseen or unexpected side effects. Simplistic campaigns that either attempt to disassociate consumers from moral harm or attempt to create social benefit merely through the act of consumption may be much more morally problematic than campaigners recognize.

Questions for Discussion

1 Think about the goods and services you have purchased or used in the last 24 hours. What connection, if any, do these have to people living in poverty?

2 If an individual consumer is unlikely to change the practices of multinational corporations, are there any moral obligations for her to take account of social and environmental problems that might be caused by her purchases?

3 Are there moral reasons for you to intentionally direct some of your purchasing power toward anti-poverty relief?

4 Do you think that consumer pressure on multinational corporations can have an impact on improving working conditions and wages for people in low-income countries?

5 Should morally responsible consumers take account of global food prices when making purchases? If so, what should they do?

6 From this chapter, it appears that determining the morally optimal way to allocate one's purchasing is an extremely complex undertaking. Is this a reason to abandon the idea of ethical consumption altogether?

Notes

1 On the associative account, consumers share special obligations to employees who produce their goods and services, but so too might producers owe obligations to consumers.

2 See Worker Rights Consortium to learn more about these activities, available at www.workersrights.org

3 To learn more about the campaign visit www.behindthebrands.org

Suggested Reading

Crocker, D. and Linden, T. *Ethics of Consumption: The good life, justice, and global stewardship*, Lanham: Rowan and Littlefield, 1998.

Dragusanu, R., Giovannuci, D., and Nunn, N. 'The economics of Fair Trade', *Journal of Economic Perspectives* 28.3 (2014): 217–236.

Lawford Smith, H. 'Unethical consumption and obligations to signal', *Ethics and International Affairs* 29 (2015): 315–330.

Schwartz, D. *Consuming Choices: Ethics in a global consumer age*, Lanham: Rowan and Littlefield, 2010.

References

Blythman, J. 'Can vegans stomach the unpalatable truth about quinoa?' *The Guardian*, January 26, 2013, available at www.theguardian.com/commentisfree/2013/jan/16/vegans-stomach-unpalatable-truth-quinoa accessed December 7, 2015).

Chiputwa, B., Qaim, M., and Speilman, D. 'Food standards, certification, and poverty among coffee farmers in Uganda', Global Food Discussion Papers, No. 27, 2013, available at http://ageconsearch.umn.edu/bitstream/161565/2/GlobalFood_DP27.pdf (accessed December 7, 2015).

Collier, P. *The Bottom Billion: Why the poorest countries are failing and what can be done about it*, Oxford: Oxford University Press, 2009.

Cramer, C., Johnston, D., Oya, C., and Sender, J. 'Fairtrade, employment and poverty reduction in Ethiopia and Uganda', 2014, available at http://ftepr.org/wp-content/uploads/FTEPR-Final-Report-19-May-2014-FINAL.pdf (accessed December 7, 2015).

FairTrade.org.uk. 'Facts and figures', www.fairtrade.org.uk/en/what-is-fairtrade/facts-and-figures (accessed December 7, 2015).

FAO, 2016. FAO Food Price Index, available at www.fao.org/worldfoodsituation/food-pricesindex/en (accessed June 9, 2016).

Frazier, M. 'Costly Red campaign reaps meagre $18 million', AdvertisingAge.com, March 5, 2007, available at http://adage.com/article/news/costly-red-campaign-reaps-meager-18-million/115287 (accessed December 7, 2015).

Friedman, M. 'The social responsibility of business is to increase its profits,' *The New York Time Magazine*, September 13, 1970.

Human Rights Watch, 'Whoever raises their head suffers the most: Workers' rights in Bangladesh's garment factories', April 22, 2015, available at http://features.hrw.org/features/HRW_2015_reports/Bangladesh_Garment_Factories/index.html   (accessed December 7, 2015).

Weber, C. and Matthews, H. 'Food-Miles and the relative climate impact of food choices in the United States,' *Environmental Science and Technology*, 42.10 (2008): 3508–3513.

Wydick, B., Katz, E., and Brendan, J. 'Do in-kind transfers damage local markets? The case of TOMS shoe donations in El Salvador', *The Journal of Development Effectiveness* 6.3 (2014): 249–267.

Wydick, B., Katz, E., Calvo, F., Guitierrez, F., and Brendan, J. 'Shoeing the horn: The impact of the TOMS show donation program in rural El Salvador', May 15, 2015, available at www.acrosstwoworlds.net/?p=292 (accessed December 7, 2015).

16 Micro-Finance

In 1976 Muhammed Yunus, a Bangladeshi professor of economics, made a small loan of 27 USD to 42 families. These loans provided them with the opportunity to borrow money for investing in small businesses without the burdens of predatory lending and the very high repayment rates that they often faced. Yunus was inspired by the Bangladeshi famine of 1972 (which also featured in Peter Singer's initial article on poverty relief that we examined in detail in Chapter 4). Yunus learned that small loans allowed these individuals to avoid predatory lenders, invest in their businesses or families, and smooth consumption during times when income was scare. He went on to found Grameen Bank in 1983, and became the 'banker to the world's poor'. Grameen Bank is largely owned by the people it serves, and today employs over 20,000 people and has nearly 200 million USD in annual revenue. Most of the borrowers and employees are women. For a time, micro-finance was heralded as a silver-bullet solution to eradicate poverty, and Yunus was the lead spokesperson for the micro-finance movement. 2005 was declared the year of micro-finance at the United Nations. Muhammad Yunus was awarded the Nobel Peace Prize in 2006.[1]

Micro-finance refers to small financial products that are meant to meet the financial needs of individuals and businesses on low incomes. They operate at the level of tens or hundreds of dollars, as opposed to standard financial products in high-income countries which generally operate in the tens or hundreds of thousands of dollars. While the early emphasis in micro-finance has been on borrowing (micro-credit), the term micro-finance refers to three types of financial products—those for credit, savings, and insurance. Micro-credit allows a client to borrow a small sum of money to be repaid at a later date, with interest. (Interest is generally higher than what a high-income individual would pay on a standard loan, given the shorter repayment period and potentially higher risk of lending to someone on a low income.) Micro-savings allows clients to save small sums of money, accumulating assets for a future big ticket purchase or investment, or for support in the event of an emergency. Micro-insurance allows clients to purchase insurance—for their health, their homes, their crops, or their livestock—at levels that are appropriate to the small value of the total assets that will be insured. Much of the early emphasis in micro-finance was on micro-credit, and this is the most ethically contested kind of micro-finance, and thus will be the focus of this chapter.

In addition to the alleged poverty-reducing effects of micro-finance that made Yunus a star of international development, it has often been claimed that providing micro-finance to women will result in women gaining financial self-sufficiency, improved educational and health outcomes for their children, and more wide-spread social progress through increases in gender equality and women's empowerment. Consider the portrayal of Rose Athieno, from Uganda, on the website of Kiva, an organization that connects lenders to micro-finance organizations. Kiva quotes Rose as saying,

> Today I'm a very respected woman in the community. I have come out of the crowd of women who are looked down upon. Due to the loan that I received … you have made me to be a champion out of nobody.[2]

There has been a massive proliferation of the number of micro-finance institutions since Grameen's first loan. Today, micro-finance products continue to be widely used, with tens of thousands of micro-finance institutions and several hundred million clients across the globe. Yet following this wave of enthusiasm many critics have charged that micro-finance is not worthy of the hype. Worse, critics charge, it may be downright harmful for poor people and a way to exploit vulnerable individuals to make a tidy profit. If 2006 was the height of public support for micro-finance, 2010 represented a low point. The micro-credit industry had experienced strong growth in much of rural India. For-profit lenders increasingly pushed vulnerable borrowers into coercive loans to meet growth targets for their companies. This aggressive marketing created a bubble that eventually burst. Borrowers collectively decided to halt repayment to several micro-finance institutions. The loss of confidence from borrowers coincided with a loss of confidence from investors in those micro-finance institutions that were publicly traded. The government of Andra Pradesh went so far as to pass legislation aiming to protect vulnerable borrowers and arrested several micro-finance employees who were charged with harassing a borrower who was late on his payments. Newspaper headlines declared that predatory lenders were responsible for indebtedness, impoverishment, and a spate of suicides from borrowers who could not repay their loans (Roodman 2010).

As with foreign aid, we have two faces of micro-finance. Proponents claim it offers the critical step needed on the route out of poverty, while critics claim that coercive, predatory lenders are responsible for impoverishment and even death. In this chapter, we will try to sort the truth from fiction, looking at the strongest claims in favor of and against micro-finance. Specifically, we will investigate ethical complaints that might be made against micro-finance institutions, to determine whether micro-finance is ethically defensible, and suggest what a morally optimal future for micro-finance might look like.

Moral Critiques of Micro-Finance

What sorts of moral criticisms might one make about the practice of micro-finance? What might be wrong with making loans to individuals living on low incomes?

Profiting from Poverty?

Some philosophers argue that there is something morally wrong with benefitting from injustice even if one has not contributed to that injustice. Some micro-finance institutions are not for profit. They raise capital from donors who are not primarily interested in financial return but rather seek to serve the common good. But other micro-finance institutions are for-profit, seeking to earn financial returns while combatting global poverty. One complaint that might be made about for-profit micro-finance institutions is that they aim to earn healthy financial returns which depend upon the fact that people are poor. Perhaps it is morally wrong to make money off of the fact that an individual is living in poverty. Ole Koksvik and Gerhard Øverland (2015) argue that if profits counterfactually depend on the fact that a person is living in poverty, this is a prima facie reason to believe that there is something morally wrong with the profit-making activity. That is, if the profit-making enterprise could not exist without the persistence of widespread poverty, it is morally wrong to be involved in the enterprise.

For example, consider a company that is profitable only because it pays its workers extremely low wages. These workers would not accept these wages but for the existence of widespread poverty—without such widespread poverty, wages in their society would be higher and they would not need to take such low paying work. One might think that the company is under a strict moral obligation to reduce their profitability in order to pay at least minimally acceptable wages that lift their employees out of poverty. If they are unable to do so, then they should simply go out of business.

One way to approach this problem is to start by thinking about the limit case. Suppose that a company is unable to be profitable if they pay their employees anything at all—so they withhold all wages from the employees. This would clearly be wrong, akin to a form of slavery. (It would be additionally wrong to force the employees to continue working in the absence of payment.) If your business model depends on forced labor, it is wrong to be in that business in the first place. If the company began paying the employees, but only one penny per day, this would continue to be morally wrong. Employees would still have a moral complaint. While it may be difficult to determine the wage level at which a profit-making enterprise would be able to avoid the complaint that the company is wrongly profiting from the poverty of others, it is clear that, at some level of low wages, they would face this moral complaint.

An analogous argument may be made regarding micro-finance. The moral question that must be answered by for-profit micro-finance institutions is whether they are wrongly benefitting from lending to people who earn low (and highly variable) wages. But even if one thinks it is immoral to pay low wages, it is difficult to argue that profit-making from the mere provision of financial services to people who happen to live on very low incomes is morally wrong in itself. There are several reasons to think that it is not outright morally wrong to profit from the provision of micro-finance.

First, there is a very high demand for micro-finance services. These institutions provide a service that people genuinely want. One might object that this desire is an adaptive or mistaken preference, but that argument is difficult to sustain in the face of the phenomenal growth of micro-finance in extremely diverse social and economic contexts.

Second, absent formal micro-finance institutions, individuals borrow and save in a range of informal ways. In the excellent book *Portfolios of the Poor*, Daryl Collins, Jonathan Morduch, Stuart Rutherford, and Orlanda Ruthven document how people living on less than 2 USD per day manage household finances. They find that the amount of money that is put into and pulled out of various financial instruments far exceeds the net value of a household's assets. And the ratio of cash flow to income is higher the less money a family has. Lower incomes require more active financial management (Collins et al. 2009, p. 33). The provision of micro-finance through formal commercial arrangements merely brings transactions that were already occurring into a formalized, and arguably more efficient and accountable, organization. That is, instead of borrowing from neighbors, friends, family members, and the local loan shark, people on low incomes can now do their borrowing from an institution explicitly set up for this purpose. Many of the most innovative organizations are also able to provide a wider range of financial products than would otherwise be available to clients, tailored to their unique needs.

Third, people consent to participate in micro-finance institutions. Absent misleading marketing or some form of coercion, people choose to enter these borrowing arrangements. We generally think that there should be a presumption in favor of the moral permissibility of commercial transactions that people freely enter, even if one party is poor and another profits.

And finally, it is not clear what would be morally wrong with micro-finance institutions that is not also wrong with finance more generally. Assuming one thinks it is morally permissible for your local community bank to take deposits, offer home and car loans, and to insure against unforeseen losses (and to turn a profit while doing so), it is not clear why these services would be morally objectionable when provided on a smaller scale that makes similar services available to people living on very low incomes, even if doing so returns a profit.

Exploitation

Even if it is morally permissible to turn a profit from an enterprise that depends in some way on the existence of poverty, there is a different way to morally criticize micro-finance institutions. Perhaps the moral problem with micro-finance is not that it generates financial profits from people living in poverty, but that it exploits people who are vulnerable.

Consider a standard case of exploitation. A person's car breaks down in the desert and they are in desperate need of support. They are running out of water and have no way to access help. A tow truck driver happens to pass by and notes that the driver of the vehicle is in great distress and needs immediate assistance.

The tow truck driver normally would charge 100 USD for a tow. But seeing that the person's life is on the line, they raise the price to 5,000 USD. The driver in distress complains that this price is rather high, to which the tow truck driver replies, 'if you don't want to pay it, then I will drive off'. The broken down driver begrudgingly must accept the 50-fold increase in the price of a tow, given his dire circumstances. This form of price gouging, generated by the significant vulnerability of the person in need, is often thought to be morally wrong (Sandel 2009, pp. 1–10). This is true even though the transaction is both mutually beneficial and consensual.

What makes the tow truck driver's conduct exploitative and morally objectionable? Philosophers have debated the best definition of exploitation (Wertheimer and Zwolinski 2015) and there are competing accounts of what makes exploitation wrongful. But one promising option is that there is a general moral constraint on playing for advantage in situations where it is inappropriate to do so (Goodin 1988, p. 144). This may be because such actions harm the person, or coerce them, or reduce aggregate utility, but more generally it may be that there simply is a moral constraint on making the most for yourself out of the bad misfortune or vulnerability of another.

Might micro-finance be exploitative in this way? In the micro-insurance and micro-savings industries, it is unlikely that exploitative arrangements arise in the normal course of good-faith transactions. Individuals will deposit small amounts for savings when doing so is good for them, and be able to withdraw the deposits at a later date. Similarly, they will insure against potential losses, and receive payment should some unforeseen mishap arise against which they were insured. As long as the terms of the agreement are transparent and followed, and the returns offered are at reasonable market rates, it is unlikely that much exploitation arises in micro-insurance or micro-savings.

But in the case of micro-credit, there is more room for exploitation. Individuals who need to borrow small sums of money may need to do so to meet very basic needs—to feed the family during hard economic times, to pay unexpected medical expenses, to repair a leaking roof, or to cover school fees. Facing the desperate prospect of losing a loved one to a preventable illness, or failing to put food on the table for dinner, a borrower may accept loans at exorbitant rates—especially if their desperate circumstances make them a risky borrower from the perspective of market lenders. Furthermore, as we saw in Chapter 3, living in poverty brings mental burdens that may impair cognitive performance, creating additional opportunity for exploitative lending arrangements.

Determining the level at which repayment rates move from being non-exploitative to exploitative is a difficult task. It is important to remember that many borrowers will only hold the money for a short period of time. If you are only taking it for a short distance, the higher cost of taxi transport per mile does not become exorbitant. Similarly, if you borrow money for a short period, a high repayment rate is not as costly as it appears if annualized. That said, there are certainly terms on which a repayment rate will be usurious and wrongfully exploitative of the borrower.

Interestingly, to avoid exploitative lending relationships, micro-finance institutions need to rigorously exclude those borrowers who are the most vulnerable and the least likely to make successful repayments. Micro-lending is therefore unlikely to be something that is permissibly offered to the poorest of the poor, as they in many cases will be unable to make repayments, and be further burdened by outstanding debts.

Harming Some to Benefit Others?

Thus far, it appears that it is morally permissible to engage in micro-finance, including for-profit micro-finance, as long as the terms are not coercive or exploitative. But even if micro-finance is generally morally permissible, and in some cases morally commendable, there is a different question about what may permissibly be done in the conduct of the day-to-day activities of a lender.

In order for commercial lending to work, it has to be the case that borrowers are given incentives to repay their loans plus interest accrued over the borrowing period. Given that micro-finance clients will not generally have significant assets that can serve as collateral for the loans they take out, micro-finance lenders use three common methods for ensuring repayment: careful screening of new borrowers who develop habits of repayment; peer pressure arising from joint liability for group loans; and access to new loans is made contingent on the successful repayment of old loans. One implication of this model is that some people will be excluded from borrowing, and others will face significant pressure from their peer borrowers, or from their lenders, to make successful repayments.

On these grounds, micro-finance may be morally criticized for harming some people (those who are pressured into making repayments) to make others better off (those who successfully use micro-finance). That is, the overall system of micro-finance may be beneficial for many of its users. But for those people who take out loans but become burdened by debt and struggle to make payments, and face social pressure or threats to meet their financial obligations, they might object that they are being harmed in order to make other people better off. In standard interpersonal morality, we are often prohibited from inflicting harm on some people in order to benefit others—perhaps this is a reason to be morally critical of micro-finance.

But it isn't clear that this is a decisive moral reason to oppose micro-finance. Micro-finance, or any other anti-poverty program or policy, need not work for every person who is a potential participant in the program to be morally justified. In fact, many successful anti-poverty programs will come at the expense of some poverty reduction elsewhere. The phenomenal growth of industrialized manufacturing in countries like China and Vietnam has made it harder for sub-Saharan African countries to enter manufacturing sectors. But we do not tend to think China's rapid poverty reduction impermissible on the grounds that it has made poverty reduction more difficult elsewhere. So too with micro-finance—the important question is whether the aggregate benefits of the provision of micro-finance justify the harms that befall some who will be burdened by debt, and whether those people are given reasonable options when facing difficult and burdensome repayments. In so far as they are, micro-finance remains morally permissible.

Micro-Finance Does Not Reduce Poverty

A deeper issue for the ethics of micro-finance is whether it succeeds in its aims of reducing poverty. Here is a standard claim for the benefits of micro-finance from CARE International: 'Affordable financial services are central to addressing poverty. Micro-finance services help the poorest earn a living, grow their businesses and create new jobs, pulling whole communities out of poverty'.[3]

As we saw in Chapter 4, rigorous evaluation of anti-poverty programs is difficult, complex, and often not built into the design of the programs. Many of the early impact evaluations of micro-credit simply looked at how individuals and households did before and after receiving small loans. Many of these evaluations claimed great success for the impact of micro-credit on poverty reduction. But the individuals who pursued small loans and were interested in gaining access to credit may have been a self-selecting group. That is, people who think they can successfully repay loans and will benefit from borrowing are more likely to take out loans than those who cannot. So if they have higher living standards after taking out the loan, this may just be evidence that they were otherwise making progress in income and consumption, rather than getting a boost from the loan itself.

Creating randomized control trials of micro-finance is a difficult task. It would neither be ethical nor informative to simply randomly select individuals otherwise showing no interest in micro-credit to receive a loan. But innovative designs in randomized trials finally did allow for rigorous evaluation of the impact of the spread of micro-finance. In one example, a micro-finance institution planned to open new branches in half of 104 slums in Hyderabad, India. Researchers randomly selected the communities into which new branches opened. This allowed for evaluating not just the impact on individual borrowers but on the community more generally. Fifteen to eighteen months after the branches opened, people were 8.8 percent more likely to have taken out a micro-loan. But there were no improvements in consumption-expenditure, health, education, or women's empowerment (Banerjee et al. 2013) (http://papers.ssrn.com/sol3/papers.cfm?abstract_id=2250500).

In another study in Uganda, a rigorous evaluation actually found that getting access to a small loan and business training hurt female income, while male entrepreneurs were able to grow their businesses when getting access to loans and training. The reason appears to be that pressure within families on women to allocate their resources to the improvement of the welfare of the household, rather than to the growth of their businesses, hurt their prospects for success, whereas no such pressure was placed on male households (Fiala 2013).

It should not be surprising that empowerment of women does not happen in 18 months or two years after receiving a small loan. Empowerment is a process that requires widespread social change. Deep social structures perpetuate gender inequality, and changing those structures requires long-term and widespread social reform. Previous movements that improved women's empowerment—such as gaining the right to vote, gaining access to contraception and abortion, increasing girls' enrollment in education, outlawing various forms of sexual and domestic violence—required coordinated joint action, establishing power together with like-minded individuals and overcoming obstacles presented by opponents of progress over the course of decades.

It is now increasingly clear that micro-credit does not achieve many of the more lofty goals that it was once promised to deliver. Muhammad Yunus will not cure poverty in Bangladesh through micro-loans alone, and women will not have equal power to their male counterparts simply by being able to take on small debts. In the most comprehensive review to date of six randomized control trials in various settings, Abhijit Banerjee et al. (2015) find that

> there is little evidence of transformative effects. The studies do not find clear evidence, or even much in the way of suggestive evidence, of reductions in poverty or substantial improvements in living standards. Nor is there robust evidence of improvements in social indicators.

A Defense of Micro-Finance

But this still does not mean that it is unethical to provide micro-finance. There are several things to be said in favor of the moral permissibility of providing micro-finance.

First, while micro-credit may not have large poverty-reducing effects, micro-savings and micro-insurance may do a great deal more to help people resist the poverty dynamics we learned about in Chapter 2. Being able to save for a rainy day, and to insure against potential hazards, can allow people to weather the potential catastrophic financial risks they face. In fact, micro-savings programs and micro-insurance may prove much more effective than micro-finance in improving outcomes for individuals (Karlan and Appel 2011, pp. 143–167). So the large financial infrastructure which has been put in place during the micro-credit boom might over time evolve to provide financial products that are needed by people living in deprivation that do help to protect them from shocks and accumulate assets over time.

Second, even if micro-loans do not have large impacts on poverty reduction, this does not mean that it is not good for people to have access to these products. The rapid proliferation of micro-finance institutions is demand driven—people certainly seem to desire access to these financial products, which are in many ways safer and more reliable than previous alternatives, including storing cash under the mattress, or borrowing from local predatory lenders. While the occasional bad actor in the micro-finance industry may dupe consumers into using their products, it is much more likely that most people get micro-finance because they prefer to have it. The important ethical consideration is to distinguish from genuine demand for the products, and free and informed consent to enter into borrowing agreements, from coerced or manipulated consumers, who cannot be said to be giving genuinely free and informed consent, and enter into exploitative and overly burdensome borrowing arrangements.

Third, micro-finance is like finance more generally. Access to finance is no guarantee of growth or prosperity, but well-regulated financial institutions are useful for individual consumers and necessary for growth in productivity. Badly regulated finance is also capable of creating unnecessary risks and vulnerabilities. It can make individual consumers vulnerable to exploitation, and entire economies vulnerable to financial crises. Just as badly regulated large financial institutions in the United States and Europe caused a global financial crisis, so too did badly regulated micro-finance institutions cause a crisis in rural India. For micro-finance to succeed, in the modest but worthwhile endeavor of giving people access to financial products that allow them to save, borrow, and be insured at reasonable rates, it must be properly regulated so as to protect consumers from predatory lenders and to ensure that the market is not prone to volatile swings.

And finally, the degree to which international aid should be directed into micro-finance institutions should be determined based on the degree to which micro-finance tools contribute to poverty reduction. If the best available evidence does not suggest that micro-finance has the intended poverty-alleviating effects, then morality requires that the money be dedicated to more effective efforts, should they be available. If innovations in the provision of micro-finance increase its poverty-reducing effects, or it is found to be uniquely effective at reducing poverty in specific social and economic circumstances, then this is a reason for anti-poverty resources to be devoted to micro-finance.

Of course, like other forms of lending, there are many ways in which it can be done that are unethical, as we have seen. A lack of transparency or honesty about the rates of repayment and the burdens this imposes upon the borrower; coercing or manipulating a person into taking a loan; managing the industry in a way that creates broader market risks; or overselling the potential benefits of a micro-loan to would-be borrowers all deserve moral condemnation, and should be regulated by the relevant authorities. That said, having access to financial instruments can be beneficial even if it does nothing to change one's living standards; being able to avoid the local loan shark is very valuable, and innovations in micro-savings and insurance may prove better at protecting the poor than micro-loans have to date.

Chapter Summary

The provision of micro-finance, whether commercialized or not for profit, raises important ethical questions. This chapter suggests that while some conduct is unethical in micro-finance, such as high repayment rates or excessive coercion in aiming to secure repayment, the general provision of micro-finance is not unethical, and indeed is morally preferable to having to borrow from the local money lender. The micro-finance industry is here to stay, thanks to the large demand for financial inclusion from people living on low incomes, and so morally informed regulation of that sector, and the increased provision of savings and insurance products, offers the most promising route forward.

Questions for Discussion

1   Think about people who live in poverty in your community. Do you think that providing them with access to credit—say, a credit card with a 2,000 USD limit and a repayment rate of 25 percent—would help them escape poverty?
2   Is it morally permissible to lend money to someone who the lender thinks will have difficulty making repayments?
3   What, if anything, is a lender morally permitted to do to recover the value of a loan that has not been repaid?
4   Many organizations, such as Kiva, now allow individuals to invest directly in micro-finance institutions, that will then lend the money to individuals in poor countries. What information would you need from these lenders to know that your investment will not contribute to morally impermissible conduct?

Notes

1   For Yunus's own account of the rise of Grameen Bank, see Yunus 2007.
2   This quote was acquired from: www.kiva.org/about/micro-finance#IV-II (accessed December 7, 2015).
3   This quote was acquired from: www.careinternational.org.uk/what-we-do/micro-finance (accessed December 7, 2015).

Suggested Reading

Bateman, M. and Chang, H. 'Micro-finance and the illusion of development: From hubris to nemesis in thirty years', *World Economic Review* 1 (2012): 13–36.
Khader, S. 'Empowerment Through Subordination? Micro-credit and Women's Agency', in *Poverty, Agency, and Human Rights*, ed. D. Meyers, Oxford: Oxford University Press, 2014.
Roodman, D. *Due Diligence: An impertinent inquiry into micro-finance*, Washington, DC: Center for Global Development Books, 2012.
Sorrell, T. and Cabrera, L., eds. *Micro-finance, Rights, and Global Justice*, Cambridge: Cambridge University Press, 2015.

References

Banerjee, A., Duflo, E., Glennerster, R., and Kinnan, C. 'The miracle of micro-finance? Evidence from a randomized evaluation', April 10, 2013, MIT Department of Economics Working Paper No. 13-09, available at SSRN, http://ssrn.com/abstract=2250500 or http://dx.doi.org/10.2139/ssrn.2250500 (accessed December 7, 2015).
Banerjee, A., Karlan, D., and Zinman, J. 'Six randomized evaluations of micro-credit: Introduction and further steps', *American Economic Journal: Applied Economics* 7.1 (2015): 1–21.

Collins, D., Morduch, J., Rutherford, S., and Ruthven, O. *Portfolios of the Poor: How the world's poor live on $2 a day*, Princeton: Princeton University Press, 2009.

Fiala, N. 'Stimulating microenterprise growth: Results from a loans, grants and training experiment in Uganda', December 4, 2013, available at http://ssrn.com/abstract=2358086 or http://dx.doi.org/10.2139/ssrn.2358086

Goodin, R. *Reasons for Welfare: The political theory of the welfare state*, Princeton: Princeton University Press, 1988.

Karlan, D. and Appel, J. *More Than Good Intentions: How a new economics is helping to solve global poverty*, New York: Penguin Press, 2011.

Koksvik, O. and Øverland, G. 'Illicit profit', 2015, manuscript on file with the first author at www.koksvik.net/files/koksvik_overland_illicit_profit.pdf (accessed December 7, 2015).

Roodman, D. 'Backgrounder on India's micro-finance crisis', Center for Global Development Blog, 2010, available at http://www.cgdev.org/blog/backgrounder-indias-micro-finance-crisis (accessed December 7, 2015).

Sandel, M. (2009). *Justice: What's the Right Thing to Do?* New York: Farrar, Straus, Giroux.

Wertheimer, A. and Zwolinski, M. 'Exploitation', *The Stanford Encyclopedia of Philosophy*, ed. Edward N. Zalta, available at http://plato.stanford.edu/archives/sum2015/entries/exploitation (accessed summer 2015).

Yunus, M. *Banker to the Poor: Micro-lending and the battle against world poverty*, New York: Public Affairs, 2007.

Glossary

Associative duties: Those moral duties that arise from the special relationships we inhabit, such as between parents and children or consumers and producers.

Brain drain: The theory that international migration depletes low-income countries of needed human capital, such as well-trained doctors, nurses, and teachers.

Consequentialism: The moral theory which holds that moral agents ought to produce the best overall consequences.

Deontology: The moral theory which holds that individuals are required to abide by certain moral rules, such as to not harm others.

Development: The economic, political, and social process of expanding opportunities and improving living standards.

Donor: An individual, group, or country that provides foreign aid.

Duty: A requirement of morality that one act in a certain way.

Duty of humanity: Also known as duties of beneficence or duties of assistance, a moral duty to provide help to those in need.

Duty of justice: A moral duty to give people what they are owed, often interpreted as a duty to not harm others and a duty to provide rectification when one has harmed others.

Foreign aid: The provision of economic or technical resources intended to reduce poverty and promote development.

Humanitarian intervention: Armed military intervention in the affairs of another state without the consent of that state with the intention of preventing suffering and protecting civilians.

International institutions: Those supranational organizations, such as the United Nations, the World Bank, and the World Trade Organization, that govern various aspects of economic, political, and military relations between states.

International trade: The exchange of goods, services, and capital across national borders.

Libertarianism: The moral theory that individuals have limited moral duties to others and the political theory that only a minimal state is justified.

Material deprivation: Shortfalls in the material resources needed for a decent life, such as adequate shelter, sanitation, water, and food.

Micro-finance: The provision of small-scale financial services, including credit, savings, and insurance, to low-income clients.

Monetary poverty: A state in which an individual or household lacks the financial resources to maintain a standard of living above a certain threshold.

Multidimensional poverty: A state in which an individual or household is deprived of non-monetary goods, such as education, health care, basic sanitation, or freedom from violence.

NGO: A non-governmental organization dedicated to pursuing some form of social change public service.

Paternalism: When an individual or institution takes an action that interferes with the actions of another person or group on the grounds that it will be in that person or group's best interest.

Qualitative method: Research methods that study poverty primarily through in-depth, semi-structured interactions between researchers and community members.

Quantitative method: Research methods that study poverty primarily through statistical analysis of quantitative data.

Randomized control trial: An experimental method where participants are sorted into treatment and control groups to study the effects of anti-poverty programs.

Resource curse: The phenomenon where natural resource-exporting countries are disproportionately likely to be plagued by civil war, autocratic governance, bad economic performance, and high levels of gender inequality.

Social deprivation: Shortfalls in the social resources need for a decent life, such as basic respect in one's community, freedom from violence, access to political opportunities, and freedom of mobility.

Utilitarianism: The moral theory which holds that individuals ought to maximize utility, often defined as happiness or preference-satisfaction.

Index